Contesting the Constitution

Contesting the Constitution

Congress Debates the Missouri Crisis

1819–1821

Edited by

William S. Belko

University of Missouri Press

Columbia

Publication of this volume is made possible with the generous support of the Kinder Institute on Constitutional Democracy

University of Missouri Press, Columbia, Missouri 65211
Printed and bound in the United States of America
 First printing, 2021.

Library of Congress Cataloging-in-Publication Data

Names: Belko, W. Stephen, 1967- editor.
Title: Contesting the Constitution : Congress debates the Missouri Crisis, 1819-1821 / edited by William S. Belko.
Description: Columbia : University of Missouri Press, 2021. | Series: Studies in constitutional democracy | Includes index.
Identifiers: LCCN 2020046406 (print) | LCCN 2020046407 (ebook) | ISBN 9780826222282 (hardcover) | ISBN 9780826274557 (ebook)
Subjects: LCSH: Missouri compromise. | Slavery--Law and legislation--United States--History. | United States. Congress--History--19th century. | Slavery--United States--Extension to the territories. | Slavery--United States--Legal status of slaves in free states. | Slavery--Political aspects--United States--History--19th century. | Missouri--Politics and government--To 1865. | United States--Politics and government--1817-1825.
Classification: LCC KF4545.S5 C66 2021 (print) | LCC KF4545.S5 (ebook) | DDC 342.73/042--dc23
LC record available at https://lccn.loc.gov/2020046406
LC ebook record available at https://lccn.loc.gov/2020046407

∞™ This paper meets the requirements of the American National Standard for Permanence of Paper for Printed Library Materials, Z39.48, 1984.

Typefaces: Celestia Antiqua, American Scribe, and Adobe Jenson Pro

STUDIES IN CONSTITUTIONAL DEMOCRACY

Justin B. Dyer and Jeffrey L. Pasley, Series Editors

The Studies in Constitutional Democracy Series explores the origins and development of American constitutional and democratic traditions, as well as their applications and interpretations throughout the world. The often subtle interaction between constitutionalism's commitment to the rule of law and democracy's emphasis on the rule of the many lies at the heart of this enterprise. Bringing together insights from history and political theory, the series showcases interdisciplinary scholarship that traces constitutional and democratic themes in American politics, law, society, and culture, with an eye to both the practical and theoretical implications.

TITLES IN STUDIES IN CONSTITUTIONAL DEMOCRACY

A Fire Bell in the Past: The Missouri Crisis at 200, Volume 1: Western Slavery, National Impasse
Edited by Jeffrey L. Pasley and John Craig Hammond

The Federalist Frontier: Settler Politics in the Old Northwest, 1783-1840
Kristopher Maulden

Disestablishment and Religious Dissent: Church-State Relations in the New American States, 1776-1833
Edited by Carl H. Esbeck and Jonathan J. Den Hartog

The Pursuit of Happiness in the Founding Era: An Intellectual History
Carli N. Conklin

The Panic of 1819: The First Great Depression
Andrew H. Browning

The Myth of Coequal Branches: Restoring the Constitution's Separation of Functions
David J. Siemers

Aristocracy in America: From the Sketch-Book of a German Nobleman
Francis J. Grund
Edited and with an Introduction by Armin Mattes

From Oligarchy to Republicanism: The Great Task of Reconstruction
Forrest Nabors

Bureaucracy in America: The Administrative State's Challenge to Constitutional Government
Joseph Postell

John Henry Wigmore and the Rules of Evidence: The Hidden Origins of Modern Law
Andrew Porwancher

Lloyd Gaines and the Fight to End Segregation
James W. Endersby and William T. Horner

Contents

Contributors

William S. Belko is the Executive Director of the Missouri Humanities Council. He was Associate Professor of History and Director of the Graduate Program in Early American Studies at the University of West Florida from 2005 to 2014, and is the author of *Philip Pendleton Barbour in Jacksonian America: An Old Republican in King Andrew's Court* (2016), *The Triumph of the Antebellum Free Trade Movement* (2012), *The Invincible Duff Green: Whig of the West* (2006), and editor of *America's Hundred Years' War: U.S. Expansion to the Gulf Coast and the Fate of the Seminole, 1763–1858* (2011). He received his Ph.D. from Mississippi State University.

Christopher Childers is Assistant Professor of U.S. Political History at Pittsburgh State University. He is the author of *The Webster-Hayne Debate: Defining Nationhood in the Early American Republic* (2018), *The Failure of Popular Sovereignty: Slavery, Manifest Destiny, and the Radicalization of Southern Politics* (2012), and co-author of *The American South: A History* (2016). He received his Ph.D. from Louisiana State University.

John Eastman is Senior Fellow at the Claremont Institute and formerly the Henry Salvatori Professor and Dean at Chapman University's Fowler School of Law. He is the author of numerous articles on constitutional law and American jurisprudence. [See https://papers.ssrn.com/sol3/cf_dev/AbsByAuth.cfm?per_id=394734].

Brook Poston is Associate Professor of History at Stephen F. Austin State University. He is the author of *James Monroe: A Republican Champion* (2019). He received his Ph.D. from Texas Christian University.

JOHN R. VAN ATTA is Master Teacher and Oaklawn Chair in American History at the Brunswick School. He is the author of *Charging Up San Juan Hill: Theodore Roosevelt and the Making of Imperial America* (2018), *Wolf by the Ears: The Missouri Crisis, 1819–1821* (2015), *Securing the West: Politics, Public Lands, and the Fate of the Old Republic, 1785–1850* (2014), and *A Place for Boys: Brunswick School and the Building of Young Men* (2001).

Contesting the Constitution

CHAPTER ONE

Introduction: Reinterpreting the Constitution, 1819–1821

William S. Belko

"BUT, THOUGH MY feelings are strong for the abolition of slavery, they are yet stronger for the Constitution of my country," declared Massachusetts congressman John Holmes, representing the Maine District on the verge of joining the Union with her considerably more besieged partner, the Missouri Territory. "And, if I am reduced to the sad alternative to tolerate the holding of slaves in Missouri, or violate the Constitution of my country, I will not admit a doubt to cloud my choice. Sir, of what benefit would be abolition, if at a sacrifice of your Constitution?" Holmes's overriding concern for the sanctity and preservation of the Constitution echoed throughout the halls of Congress during the debates over whether to admit Missouri as a state in the Union. Few congressmen could deny that the prospect of Missouri's admission raised a plethora of constitutional questions of the highest order, ultimately exciting intensive and extensive reexamination of the U.S. Constitution. Not since the ratification debates of 1787–1788 had Americans so intensely scoured the Constitution and reconsidered numerous sections therein. The crux of the issue of admitting Missouri into the Union was, at its very foundation, a constitutional question. Fellow New Englander, New Hampshire congressman Clifton Claggett, recognized, as had so many of his colleagues in the House, that the "subject under consideration involves a Constitutional question of the first magnitude, in which the whole Union is deeply interested." Simply put, the question ultimately to be resolved by Congress was whether that body possessed the authority to place conditions—in this instance, a restriction on the expansion of slavery in Missouri—on a territory before it would be admitted into the Union. To prove the point, for or against slavery restriction, nearly every article and section of the Constitution came under scrutiny, with little if any agreement from opposing sides. "One takes one part of the Constitution, another disclaims that and selects another part; and no two seem to agree throughout," observed Kentucky congressman Benjamin Hardin. "They have hunted through every section of the Constitution; one fixes on one clause, another on another," Virginia's John Tyler concurred. From January of 1819 through the spring of 1821, restrictionists and anti-restrictionists in Congress assumed the garb of Federalists and Antifederalists of the ratification debates, and, as in 1787 and 1788, the fate of a union of states—and a constitution which defined it—initiated intense inspection.[1]

Congress was not the only governmental entity feeling the weight of the immense constitutional character of the subject before them. The president of the United States, James Monroe, likewise understood the constitutional import of the question under consideration. "As to the part which I may act, in all circumstances in which I may be placed, I have not made up my mind, nor shall I until the period arrives when it will be my duty to act, and then I shall weigh well the injunctions of the Constitution; which, according to my understanding of them, will be conclusive with me," he wrote to fellow Virginian Spencer Roane in February of 1820. The president considered loyalty to the Constitution (albeit his interpretation of it) of the utmost importance, even ranking higher than his next consideration, that of "the preservation of the Union." Decades later, in 1848, a U.S. senator from Florida, James Westcott, reflected on Monroe's draft of a veto message on the 1820 Missouri Bill, declaring that the president had sacrificed his own opinions in order to preserve the Union. Still, the Constitution reigned as the president's supreme consideration. "If he violated the Constitution," declared Westcott, "it was to save the Constitution." Congressmen representing every state in the Union, delegates to every state legislature, newspaper editors across the country, and citizens from free states and slave, all understood the constitutional crisis before them.[2]

The following chapters address the most consistently contested parts of the Constitution during the debates that formed the political heart of what came to be called the "Missouri Crisis." Congressmen dissected Article IV above all other sections. The power of Congress to admit new states (Article IV, Section 3, Clause 1), the power of Congress to govern and regulate the nation's territories (Article IV, Section 3, Clause, 2), the Privileges and Immunities Clause (Article IV, Section 2, Clause 1), and the Guarantee Clause (Article IV, Section 4) all came under close and intense scrutiny as the friends and foes of slavery restriction in Missouri attempted to justify their respective arguments in order to deny or to legitimate congressional power to implement the Tallmadge Amendment. New York congressman James Tallmadge, Jr. proposed this amendment very early on in the Missouri debates in an attempt to modify the Missouri Bill to restrict slavery there as a stipulation to its admission into the Union. Three other sections of the Constitution followed closely on the heels of Article IV—the infamous Three-Fifths Clause (Article I, Section 2, Clause 3), the misunderstood Migration and Importation Clause (Article I, Section 9, Clause 1), and the provocative Treaty-Making Power (Article II, Section 2, Clause 2). These sections combined to consume a considerable portion of the 1819–1821 congressional debates over Missouri's admission into the Union. Of course, the specter of slavery lurked always behind these constitutional explorations, most definitely coloring the various interpretations and reinterpretations. In the end, few, if any, congressmen ever came to agreement on how to interpret these clauses. In the absence of a resolution to these disagreements, they left to the next generation sectional discord and bloody conflict.

The authors of each chapter herein focused overwhelmingly on the numerous speeches delivered in Congress, from the second session of the 15th Congress through the second session of the 16th Congress, treating the congressional debates in the exact manner as one would the ratification debates of 1787 to 1788. One must note, however, that this can be an imperfect approach, as the editors of the *Annals of Congress*, Joseph Gales and William Seaton, proved rather sloppy in their reporting. Reporters failed at times to attend a session of Congress, or they arrived too late to record some of the speeches in full. Often speeches were inaudible or background noise prevented the speaker from being fully heard. "The first observations of Mr. L. were lost to the reporter, from the confusion arising from members changing their seats, &c.," recorded one reporter, and another admitted that "Mr. S. made a few remarks which the reporter did not hear with sufficient distinctness to report them." As for a two-hour speech by a Pennsylvania congressman, another reporter apologized that "the following must be considered as a free but not very full report." At one point in the debates a congressman complained to Gales and Seaton that his remarks had been inaccurately recorded, to which the editors had to publish a correction: "We were so cramped for room in our report, that we were obliged to generalize the incidental remarks, and, in doing so, perhaps a wrong impression may have been given to Mr. L.'s observations." In other instances, reporters referred to the fact that a speech was given, simply stating that a congressman advocated or opposed restriction "in a two-hour speech," "in a speech of more than three hours," or "spoke for some time," and spoke "at considerable length." Congressmen often handed copies of their speeches to Gales and Seaton for publication in the *Annals,* thus providing to the public an extended or amended version not always accurately representing what was said on the floor of the House or Senate. Still, the speeches provide the best source for defining the sundry approaches to the monumental constitutional issues being debated.[3]

The Missouri admission crisis coincided with another, equally intense and divisive, political debate consuming Congress in the decade following the end of the War of 1812, one that at its core was also constitutional and, like the debates concerning Missouri's admission, greatly strained the unity of the reigning Republican party. The introduction of the American System—a national bank incorporated by Congress, federally sponsored internal improvements, and a protective tariff—preoccupied Congress throughout the Age of Jackson, stimulating divisive and heated arguments. Combined with the controversial decisions of the U.S. Supreme Court under the aegis of Chief Justice John Marshall, penetrating and passionate deliberation about the nature of the Union and the interpretation of its Constitution defined congressional deliberations in the first decade of the Jacksonian Era. At the heart of this ongoing debate stood the age-old struggle between power and liberty, manifested most generally in the struggle between the reserved and delegated powers, a contest that had defined the entire constitutional development of the United States from its colonial inception through independence, from confederation to the creation and ratification of the Constitution, and throughout its first half century.

The Missouri admission crisis became a central feature of this ideological, political, constitutional struggle, that is, over the proper allocation of power. Although the constitutional war over the implementation of the American System lasted well into the last decade of the Age of Jackson, the constitutional considerations inherent in admitting Missouri rivalled, and arguably surpassed, at least in emotional intensity, those of a national bank, internal improvements, and a protective tariff. The Missouri question involved the issue of slavery, which merely fueled and fanned the flames of political and constitutional contention, further intensifying that traditional contest of the reserved versus the delegated powers. The ideological lines in the Missouri debates followed closely, although never exactly, those defining the American System. Opponents of slavery restriction in Missouri defiantly defended the reserved powers, adhering to a strict construction of the powers of Congress, while the proponents of restricting slavery in Missouri tended to defend a broader definition of congressional powers, thus adopting a more liberal interpretation of the Constitution.

These positions regarding the distribution of power in a federal system were not, moreover, mere rhetorical tools for one side to expand slavery and for the other to prevent its spread. The positions taken throughout the Missouri debates (as with those covering the American System) regarding the reserved and delegated powers were not simply means to justify an end, whether it be proslavery or antislavery. They were not arguments made to advance self-interest, but sincere manifestations of how the individuals involved directly defined the constitutional system and the nature of the Union. The Missouri crisis must be viewed, therefore, in this larger constitutional struggle between the reserved and the delegated powers, of strict construction versus a liberal interpretation of the Constitution, for the episode cannot be dissected from the other prevailing constitutional debates of the day.

During the ratification debates of 1787–1788, Antifederalists constantly harangued their opponents with charges of corruption, conspiracy, and consolidation. This latter evil they felt confident would quickly become a certain consequence of adopting the proposed Constitution. The powers delegated in the Constitution, its opponents consistently claimed, could be open to abuse by way of a broad construction. Two clauses, both in Section 8 of Article I, concerned them above all—the Necessary and Proper Clause and the General Welfare Clause. These two passages in the Constitution had given the founding generation pause, since they empowered Congress with specified powers but might entail an expansion of such powers through a more liberal interpretation; the issue resurfaced in the Missouri debates. In fact, congressmen deliberating the fate of Missouri statehood turned to these two bugaboos in nearly every public address. Both the guardians of strict construction—overwhelmingly anti-restrictionist—and the friends of congressional supremacy—vastly restrictionist—employed these clauses in the attempt to address the legality of the expansion of slavery.

Friends of the Tallmadge Amendment argued that the Necessary and Proper and the General Welfare clauses clearly provided Congress the requisite power to prevent the spread of slavery. The proponents of restriction, nearly to a man, delivered lengthy enquiries "to prove that the Constitution, according to a fair and liberal construction of that instrument," as Illinois's Daniel Pope Cook confidently contended, "does vest the power in Congress to legislate upon this subject." Pennsylvania's John Sergeant praised the latest "fashion to insist upon a liberal construction of the Constitution," which its "most extensive efficacy has been found in the implied powers it is supposed to confer." All powers, he asserted, "are implied that are necessary for the execution of the enumerated powers," a necessity that "need not be absolute," as a "modified necessity or high degree of expediency is sufficient." According to the accepted position of those seeking an emancipated Missouri, "an original power having been granted, every other power is implied which is necessary or useful for carrying that power into execution," and this proved to be an "inherent, essential principle of the Constitution, altogether independent of its express words." Vermont congressman Charles Rich went so far to claim that the Necessary and Proper Clause provided Congress the power to regulate slavery simply because of the express power to protect states from domestic violence. "If, then, it be true, that there is a danger of domestic violence from the existence of slavery, which I am confident none will deny, I should apprehend that a law, the object and certain tendency of which is to diminish the relative number of slaves in our country, and spread a free white population over the fairest portions of it," he pondered, "must not only be proper, but indispensably necessary, to guard against the occurrence of violence, and preserve the United States in a condition to discharge its duties." This assumption proved popular among many Northern congressmen.[4]

Opponents of implied congressional authority, however, greatly feared such assertions of constitutional interpretation by their opponents. They no more believed Congress had the power to incorporate a bank, levy a protective tariff, or fund internal improvements than it could place conditions on a state's admission or interfere with a domestic institution.

Anti-restrictionists repetitively reproached restrictionists for making "the most extravagant of all claims," that of espousing a construction of Article I, Section 8 that "swallows up all the rest" of the enumerated powers. Their interpretation of the General Welfare Clause and the Necessary and Proper Clause, asserted Maine's Holmes, "will not only absorb all other powers," but will also "break down, destroy and overwhelm all prohibitions and restraints." Give Congress such broad powers, he predicted, and it would not be enough. "Their powers are greater than those of any despot in the world." Such assertions were widely accepted within anti-restrictionst circles in Congress.[5]

First, opponents of restriction fought the interpretation of the General Welfare Clause. "With a view to put an end to this claim on the part of Congress, of power to pass whatever law they please," Virginia congressman Alexander Smyth turned to the Constitutional Convention to "prove the falsehood" of those who attempted to interpret the first clause under Section 8 into separate clauses, thereby providing Congress, under the general welfare reference, the authority to pass any legislation deemed beneficial for the general welfare. This clause, he maintained, was "a limitation of the power of taxation" only, which the framers of the Constitution intended "should not be carried further than was necessary to pay the debts and provide for the general welfare." The General Welfare Clause, therefore, merely conferred a power to raise funds as a means of executing the other powers of Congress. "How the clause came to be divided into clauses," he wondered, "cannot perhaps be now ascertained." Hardin of Kentucky rebuked congressmen who argued that the General Welfare clause gave Congress the power to "enact and pass any law that may tend to the permanence, durability, and glory of the General Government." According to such a construction of this clause, if Congress should ever feel that the state governments "retarded the advance and progress of the nation in its rapid and brilliant career of national prosperity," then it could simply "extinguish and annihilate them." Hardin considered this a "great departure from the good old democratic doctrine of 1788," for the clause in question clearly contained no delegation of power other than to lay and collect taxes, duties, imposts, and excises, in order to pay the debts and provide common defense of the Union. "I am heartily tired with the continued and repeated claims of this General Welfare," he ended. If a fellow congressman "be right in his principles of construction, taking the clause which gives general legislation to Congress—making, as he does, the sovereignty reside in the Government," added Virginia congressman James Johnson, "it squints not only at monarchy, but at despotism—despotism as absolute as ever wielded." By using the terms "common defence" [sic] and "general welfare," Johnson acknowledged, "to point out the objects for which the specified and enumerated powers had been delegated," Congress instituted a government "of the most indefinite and unlimited powers."[6]

The opponents of slavery restriction likewise assailed the liberal construction of the Necessary and Proper Clause, agreeing ardently with Kentucky's Hardin that it contained no delegation of power, neither adding to nor diminishing the powers of Congress. The clause, he believed, "was evidently introduced first to prevent those who were hostile to the General Government from alleging that it had no powers incidental to those expressly granted," and which were "necessary to be exercised to effectuate the objects for which the Constitution was framed and adopted." By employing the word "necessary," therefore, the framers intended "to restrict and prevent" Congress from taking "too great a latitude" in its selection and adoption of the means "to carry into full effect the powers already granted." The prevailing doctrine that Congress can enact any law it considers "needful and necessary for the health and prosperity of the General Government," Hardin concluded, "is a most dangerous one," and if this movement persisted, then it "must lead to the complete consolidation of this Government."[7]

Yet, a third potent congressional power—that over the regulation of commerce—entered the fray as well, accompanying the Necessary and Proper and the General Welfare clauses as a legitimate tool for Congress to stop the spread of slavery. The Commerce Clause became a favored weapon in this struggle by the supporters of restriction in Missouri. Again, Pennsylvania's Sergeant represented the prevailing perspective proffered by his fellow restrictionists. "Slaves are every where [sic] articles of trade, the subject of traffic and commerce, bought and sold, from place to place, and from hand to hand, by public sale or by private sale, as suits the convenience or interest of the owner, and in all respects treated as property," he declared, and, therefore, the general power to regulate commerce included a power to regulate "this kind of commerce." If the power to regulate commerce "with foreign nations" gave Congress the power to prohibit the importation of slaves into the United States, Sergeant conjectured, then how could it be doubted that the power to regulate commerce "among the States" authorized Congress, "when in their opinion the 'general welfare' or the 'common defence' [sic] require it," to prohibit the transportation of slaves from state to state."[8]

Again, as with the broad interpretation of the Necessary and Proper and the General Welfare clauses, anti-restrictionist congressmen argued otherwise, promoting a strict construction of congressional authority over interstate commerce and proffering the position that the commerce powers did not authorize the Tallmadge Amendment. Maryland congressman Samuel Smith assailed the assumption that Congress held the power to "prohibit slaves passing from one State to another" under the Commerce Clause. If Congress had no power to prohibit the produce of Maryland from being sent to Boston, nor to prevent the cotton of the South passing to New York for sale, he conjectured, then that body could not have the power "to prohibit the slaves of the South, under the power to regulate commerce, from being sent to Missouri, either with or without their masters." If deemed to be property, then Congress possessed no authority to prohibit the interstate movement of slaves, unless Congress had the power to prohibit other property, and few claimed it did. "It has been said that Congress have [sic] power to regulate commerce among the several States, and therefore may prohibit carrying slaves into Missouri," surmised Virginia's Smyth. "I answer, that a power to regulate commerce is not a power to prohibit commerce." Congress maintained the power to regulate *interstate* commerce, he added, but the proposed restriction affected only a single state, Missouri. "No preference is to be given by any regulation of commerce," therefore, "to the ports of one State over those of another." Congress had no right to implement any regulation applying to one state, agreed Delaware's Louis McLane. It had to be general among the whole, as all must share the advantages or disadvantages of the regulation. "Partial regulations of commerce," he assumed "was precisely the evil which the power vested in the Congress was intended to guard against." Kentucky's Hardin concurred. Congress, he rightly admitted, could not prevent him from taking his property from one state to another. The framers inserted the Commerce Clause in order for the states to "divest themselves of all power to embarrass and trammel each others' trade and commerce" from state to state. The proposed restriction on Missouri could not be justified under the commerce powers, Hardin reasoned, "for it is not general; it is not applicable to the whole United States; it is only to bind Missouri." Can it ever be pretended, then, that under the powers to regulate commerce between states, Congress could free slaves? "No one certainly has the hardihood to assert it," declared Holmes, concurring heartily with his Southern colleagues.[9]

This apparent drift inclining to a more liberal interpretation of congressional power clearly alarmed Southerners, for this perceived pattern indicated a movement that could eventually allow Congress the authority to interfere with a domestic institution and undermine the reserved powers overall. No group of individuals despaired more over the trend of broad construction of the Constitution than the Jeffersonian Old Republicans, who, nearly to a man, hailed from Virginia. They feared above all the adverse precedent established by their Northern colleagues who invoked the Necessary and Proper, General Welfare, and Commerce clauses in terms that gave Congress powers seemingly not expressly delegated in the Constitution. The danger of precedent became their watchword, and they lectured others consistently about it, chiding their fellow congressmen for justifying the Tallmadge Amendment simply because they believed Congress had regulated slavery in the admission of new states in the past. The Virginians constantly corrected what they deemed an errant view of the history of congressional actions regarding new states and the issue of slavery, admonishing in the same voice the dangers of precedent.[10]

But if the opponents of restriction feared the dangerous precedent established by a broad interpretation of Article I, Section 8, of the Constitution, they were completely unnerved when some New England congressmen invoked another section of the Constitution in defense of expansive congressional authority—the preamble. "Here, sir, the great objects of this Constitution unfold," surmised New Hampshire's Clagett, "and, in construing it, these objects should be kept steadily in view." Massachusetts representative Joshua Cushman suggested that, in a legislative sense, the term "Congress shall have power" applied "to all the articles and clauses" of Section 8 of the Constitution and "is to be inferred from the nature of the case as well as from the correspondence to the language used in the preamble, where the expression is more full and definite, and the object more clearly stated." Cushman called the preamble "music to my ear" and justified it in the cause of eliminating slavery. Although Connecticut congressman Henry Edwards believed the preamble did not confer power, he did consider it "a direction as to the manner in which the powers conferred in the [Constitution] are to be exercised." The preamble, he continued, "expresses nothing more than would have been implied without it," but the "wise men who framed that instrument have relieved us from the necessity of resorting to implication." The "general object" of the framers, declared Timothy Fuller of Massachusetts, was to preserve the citizens of the United States in all their rights against foreign and domestic violence, and "to all this its provisions were intended to be subservient," and the "interpretation of any section or clause must always keep this paramount purpose in view." These general objects of union—the preamble—gave Congress the right to place a restriction regarding slavery on any new state entering the Union.[11]

By employing the preamble to justify broad powers of Congress, especially as it pertained to congressional authority to regulate slavery, these New Englanders presaged Civil War-era scholars, such as William Whiting and Timothy Farrar, who espoused the "Adequacy of the Constitution" theory. Such theorists promoted in the early 1860s the idea that the Constitution was not a limiting authority placing a restraint on the reach of the Federal government; they emphasized instead a Constitution replete with positive commandments allowing the Federal government to do just about anything in the name of preserving the Union. The Constitution thus empowered Congress to take the necessary steps to secure the general purposes of the framers as outlined in the preamble. New England congressmen during the Missouri debates were some of the earliest progenitors of this theory.[12]

Southerners, obviously, countered. All concurred with Tennessee congressman Francis Jones when he chastised his colleagues for resorting to the preamble as a means of promoting the policy of slavery restriction. He despaired that "more than one gentleman would have resorted to this as a source of power," and that "their arguments speak but little in favor of the good sense of the framers of the Constitution." If in the preamble, he concluded, "a power be granted to do whatever, in the estimation of humanity, of religion, of conscience, may be calculated to promote the general welfare," then the preamble itself "would have been a sufficient Constitution," for it "gives [Congress] unbounded powers, and there the framers of the Constitution ought then to have stopped."[13]

For congressmen opposed to slavery restriction in Missouri, the 10th Amendment to the Constitution became the keystone for justifying and enforcing strict limitations on the powers of Congress, specifically, for denying congressional authority to impose the Tallmadge Amendment on Missouri. Few rarely bypassed the opportunity to invoke the amendment in defense of the reserved powers. "The tenth article of the amendment preserves every power not surrendered," declared one congressman, plain and simple. This amendment, considered by the friends of states' rights and limited government to be the most potent of the Bill of Rights, legitimated the sovereignty of the states and empowered them to do anything that was not in violation of the powers expressly surrendered to the Constitution. In fact, Congress could "load Missouri with as many conditions as you will, and on her admission she can throw them off," declared Maine's Holmes. "She may alter her Constitution the next day after her admission, abolish your restriction, and intrench [sic] herself within the tenth article of the amendments, and you cannot assail her." Many defenders of Missouri asserted, moreover, that the 10th Amendment "has as positively reserved to the States the power to establish or prohibit slavery, as if it had been expressed in the very words." The 10th Amendment proclaimed, according to Kentucky's Hardin, "that Congress can do nothing which they are not authorized to do, and that the States can do every thing [sic] that is not delegated to Congress, or which they are forbid to do." Has the power to legislate over slavery been delegated to Congress, queried Smyth of Virginia? It has not, he responded. "Has it been prohibited to the States? It has not. Then it is reserved to the States, respectively, or to the people. Consequently, it is reserved to the State of Missouri, or to the people of that State. And any attempt by Congress to deprive them of this reserved power, will be unjust, tyrannical, unconstitutional, and void." Kentucky senator Richard M. Johnson summed up the popular appeal for the 10th Amendment. "Keep in mind the theory of our General Government," he avowed. "We act as an agent would under a special power of attorney; and the Constitution is the charter by which we act. The powers delegated are there defined. Those not expressly delegated, are reserved to the States, or to the people. To transcend the powers prescribed by the Constitution, is to violate the rights of the States and of the people." Congress possessed no delegated power under the Constitution to impose a restriction like this upon any of the states, he concluded, "nor can it be pretended, unless by that kind of legerdemain construction which would make Congress omnipotent, and render the sovereignties a mere shadow, that this text book of the American statesman contains a single clause even hinting at the delegation of this power."[14]

Anti-restrictionist congressmen invoked other portions of the Bill of Rights in the effort to limit congressional authority. Opponents of restriction in Missouri cited the 9th Amendment to the Constitution as an additional limitation on the powers of the federal government to trample on those reserved to the states and to the people. Southerners often attached the 9th Amendment to the 10th as an added guarantee that Congress could go no further than those powers expressly delegated to it. "Hence, it will follow, that the several States retain every power not delegated by the Constitution to the General Government," concluded Georgia congressman Reid, after quoting the 9th Amendment, "or, in other words, that in all enumerated cases, the several States are left in the full enjoyment of their sovereign and independent jurisdictions." Missouri's John Scott could not agree more: "Congress had no powers but those expressly given, or those inferrible [sic], as being absolutely necessary and proper to enable them to carry those given into effect. The ninth and tenth articles of the amendments to the Constitution settled this question." These same men also appealed to the 5th Amendment, namely the protection to property rights. The Tallmadge Amendment, according to opponents of restriction, forced Missourians to "give up their property" in violation of the 5th Amendment, and it did so without providing any compensation. Even the 1st and 2nd Amendments to the Constitution appeared in the debates, mentioned again only by the opponents of restriction as additional proof of the Constitution's sundry limitations on the powers of Congress.[15]

In their reassessment of the proper boundaries between the reserved and delegated powers, Congress necessarily delved into an exploration of the nature of the Union itself. Was the United States a compact of states, a confederation of equal sovereigns, or had the adoption of the Constitution inaugurated a national, consolidated government? Certainly the Webster-Hayne debates arguably attract the greatest attention as the most celebrated exploration of the nature of the Union during the antebellum period, specifically the contest between states' rights and nationalism, but congressmen a full decade prior had already explored the nature of the Union quite thoroughly. Opponents of restriction, Southerners overwhelmingly, endorsed the concept of the Union as a confederation of equal states, which had surrendered certain enumerated powers to a weaker, smaller central government on behalf of the whole. "What is that Union?" asked Maryland senator William Pinkney. "A confederation of States equal in sovereignty, capable of every thing [sic] which the Constitution does not forbid, or authorize Congress to forbid. It is an equal Union between parties equally sovereign." If there was any point on which the American people universally agreed, surmised Virginia senator James Barbour, then it was to restrain the general government within its "prescribed limits" and to guard against any encroachments on the power of the states, "and thereby prevent a consolidation which has been universally considered as a synonym with monarchy." A consolidated national government, operating exclusively on the people of the nation as a whole rather than on behalf of a compact of sovereign states, was outright anathema to Southern congressmen.[16]

A solid majority of the proponents of restriction in the North likewise viewed the American republic in such terms, an indication of the ideological unity of the Republican party on this particular subject. Pennsylvania's Sergeant, a staunch supporter of slavery restriction in Missouri, defined the Union in terms all Southerners assumed to be gospel. "The Constitution of the United States, though in form the work of the people, . . . was a compact between States," he assumed to be accepted political coin. "It was made by delegates chosen by the States. The votes in the Convention were given by States. It was submitted to the States for their ratification; and its existence depended upon the sanction of a certain number of States. . . . Their sovereignty extended to every thing [sic] within their limits, and to every thing [sic] else, but the few powers . . . which were conceded to the Congress of the Union. Nevertheless, it was a confederation, which comprehended all who were parties to it, and excluded all others." Pennsylvania's Walter Lowrie, another supporter of the Tallmadge Amendment, reflected as well on state sovereignty, "believing that our political salvation depends upon it" and that "a consolidation of this extended empire must end in the worst kind of despotism."[17]

But a coterie of Northern congressmen asserted as ardently that the creation of the Constitution had introduced a strong central government, one with consolidated powers representing a nation of people, not a compact of sovereign states. "Since the adoption of the Constitution," declared New York congressman Ezra Gross, "so far as its federal powers extend, the United States may be regarded as an individual nation, and as a consolidated Government." He further argued that Congress should be the judge of its own powers, that the "safety of our Republic" demanded "constructions which give to the General Government a national form and energy." In language and tone that most certainly rattled states' rightists (but would have surely inspired Daniel Webster), Gross concluded the "integrity of the Union" and the harmony of the people "imperiously demand that the proud aspiring States should be taught to know their distance, to lower their lofty crests, to revolve in their humble orbs around the National Government, the sun of the system, and lose their dazzling radiance in the superior splendor of his beams." Another New Englander, Rhode Island senator James Burrill, felt it clear that "the States are limited sovereignties, and that the supremacy is vested by the people of these United States in the Federal Government." The several states, therefore, were "restrained and limited" and thus "must act in subordination to the general will, that is to say, the federal will."[18]

Inextricably intertwined in this extensive exploration of the nature of the Union was the location of sovereignty itself. All placed ultimate sovereignty in the people. "The fundamental principle of this and of every republican Government is, that the sovereign power resides, and is inherent in the people, and not in the Government," proclaimed Delaware's McLane, voicing the prevailing opinion of his colleagues. "Upon the principles of our Government, all the sovereignty is in the people—they are the foundation whence it all flows, and the General Government has no other power than what the people have delegated to it for Federal purposes." The powers exerted by the state governments, as well, he concluded, "are in the virtue of the sovereign power of the people."[19]

But congressmen diverged often, adopting various approaches, as to what governmental entities, state governments or the federal government, held the people's trust and wielded authority on their behalf. Most took a balanced view, adopting the attitude of Ohio congressman William

Trimble, who found federal and state sovereignty to be absurd, for the country "knows no sovereign but the people, who are the legitimate source of all power." The people created their governments, he contended, which they had every right to modify or abolish as their interests required. "One portion of power was given to the State government; another portion of power was given to the Federal Government," Trimble concluded, in the more widely accepted viewpoint. "The power which was not given to the State government or the Federal Government, remains with the people; these governments are, therefore, limited—neither of them can be sovereign." Still, New Englanders, obviously acquiescing in the mantra of popular sovereignty, deemed the federal government the responsive authority. Joshua Cushman of Massachusetts, for example, agreed with all that "the real sovereign of our country is the people," but maintained that "Congress are but the ministers of this sovereign," and "this absolute sovereignty resides, not in minute portions or States, but in the whole people, whose will, expressed by their Constitutional organs, is the law, and must be obeyed."[20]

Southerners and their Northern ally, the Maine District congressman, disagreed with Cushman, again confirming the idea that all sovereignty resided in the people, but contending that it was exercised through the state governments before the general government. The lone New Englander who supported Missouri's admission sans restriction, John Holmes, declared that the Constitution never took sovereignty from the States, but merely "confirmed, or at least recognised [sic] it," and that sovereignty "remained in the States after the adoption of the Constitution." Mississippi congressman Christopher Rankin expressed the typical Southern, anti-restriction perspective. "In our Government, all admit sovereignty of the people; but, if the arguments of gentlemen who advocate this restriction be correct, Congress possesses absolute sovereignty, and the people are their servants," he conjectured. "There is no sovereignty in Congress, known to the Constitution, except such as is expressly delegated; the limits of which are clearly marked and defined by that instrument." Even the state governments, he continued, which derived their powers "immediately from the people," stood as but "a portion of natural liberty or absolute sovereignty, delegated to rulers, to be exercised for the common welfare." The federal government, however, "emanating from the States" and "wielding an authority regulating and protecting the community of States, is one degree farther removed from the source of power."[21]

All these exhaustive and disparate ideological approaches reinterpreting the Constitution and the federal system of government, in the pursuit of confirming or denying congressional authority to place restrictions on Missouri's admission, necessarily involved the specter of slavery. The lure to delve into diatribes and jeremiads about the evils of slavery captivated many a Northern congressman, forcing slaveholders in Congress to defend, most often rather uncomfortably, the efficacy of their domestic institution. Most Southerners simply avoided any commentary about slavery, stating instead that the practice, regardless of any moral turpitude, was beyond the authority of Congress; slavery existed only through municipal law and fell completely within the reserved rights of the states themselves to allow or disallow. Congressmen from both sides of the aisle beseeched their comrades to avoid inflammatory rhetoric and divisive polemics based on overt emotional appeals addressing the nature of slavery per se. "Let us discard from this high Constitutional question, all those extrinsic considerations which have been forced into its discussion," pleaded Maryland senator Pinkney. "Let us endeavor to approach it with a philosophic impartiality of temper, with a sincere desire to ascertain the boundaries of our authority, and a determination to keep our wishes in subjection to our allegiance to the Constitution." Virginia congressman Philip Pendleton Barbour summed it up best: "The question is not, then, whether slavery is, in itself, an evil, but whether, supposing it to be such, we have the power to correct it, in relation to Missouri?" Yet even if congressmen succeeded in bypassing the philosophical, ideological, moral, religious, and emotional arguments for or against slavery, they still could not avoid the constitutional aspects inherent in the institution. Congressmen from both North and South, East and West, struggled with the question of whether the Constitution recognized, or even sanctioned, slavery. Was slavery protected by the Constitution, or did that document prohibit altogether any interference with it? On this question—strictly constitutional—Congress had to decide, for the whole question of whether Congress could require restrictions, namely regarding slavery, on states entering the Union was at stake.[22]

Opponents of restriction in Missouri split over this constitutional conundrum. Some, like Virginia's Philip Pendleton Barbour, adamantly maintained that Congress had no relationship with the institution. The states maintained full authority "by a law of their own enactment, to authorize it—to call it into existence whenever they shall think fit," and states prohibiting slavery "in the exercise of their legislative power, have willed that it shall be so." State legislatures only could abolish slavery, "because to them appertains the whole business of municipal legislation, and this regulation would be embraced within it." Delaware's McLane agreed. Congress, he argued, possessed "no municipal powers, no power to interfere in the local concerns of a State," neither could that body "establish rules respecting the rights of property," and thus Congress had absolutely no power to affect slavery, in Missouri or anywhere for that matter. "It is a domestic relation in every State of the Union in which it exists, and the subject of their municipal power." But what about clauses in the Constitution clearly touching upon slavery? As for the Fugitive Slave Clause, McLane qualified that "this provision is a complete exposition of the whole spirit of the Constitution," that is, "it admits the right in each State to make its own regulations upon this species of property; to tolerate or to abolish." Without this clause, he surmised, "it would have been in the power of each State to abolish slavery, and prevent the owner even of an absconding slave from claiming him as such," and thus the probability of the adoption of such a policy in free states necessitated the inclusion of the clause in the Constitution. "All the power, therefore, in Congress, over the slaves, legitimately brought here, is a protecting power for the benefit of the owner, and a protecting power merely against conflicting policy of State regulations, of which it is the peculiar object." But, as soon as slavery was deemed property, slavery became subject to municipal authority.[23]

Other Southerners intimated that the Constitution indeed touched slavery, yet in a manner that not only confirmed its existence but even protected it from congressional interference. Georgia congressman Robert Reid stated that "the right of the citizen to possess slaves is expressly recognised [sic] by the instrument of which we speak," and he listed the pertinent sections in the Constitution, from the Three-Fifths Clause to the Migration and Importation Clause to the Fugitive Slave Clause. Jones of Tennessee also believed the Constitution "recognised [sic] the existence of slavery." Mississippi senator Walter Leake argued that "as to the particular species of property which is the subject of the present discussion," the Constitution "has clearly recognised [sic] this," citing the Fugitive Slave Clause as proof.[24]

Northern congressmen likewise appeared fragmented in their approach to the question of slavery and the Constitution. As the chapter herein by John R. Van Atta on [Article IV, Section 3, Clause 1] explores in-depth, many Northern congressmen cited the history of the admission of new states as incontrovertible evidence that Congress had indeed legislated on slavery, and thus, by precedent, it maintained that authority to place and enforce restrictions on Missouri. On this tack, supporters of the Tallmadge Amendment were united and consistent. "In every instance, some restriction or curtailment of legislative authority, more or less extensive," claimed Pennsylvania's Sergeant, "has been imposed and assented to, with universal approbation." As John Eastman also demonstrates in his chapter on the Guarantee Clause [Article IV, Section 4], Northern congressmen deemed slavery to be contradictory with a republican form of government, and thus Congress could restrict slavery by invoking the Guarantee Clause.[25]

Others seemingly confirmed the views of Southerners, claiming no connection between the peculiar institution and the Constitution. "The right to hold slaves guarantied [sic] by the Federal Constitution! No, sir," proclaimed Cook of Illinois. "The right to hold slaves, therefore, is not created by the Constitution. Nor is it a federal right; it is a State right." Again, what of the clauses of the Constitution addressing slavery? These proved "only a necessary regulation" growing out of the "previous existence of slavery in the Union, and does not therefore create the right to hold slaves." The practice of slavery, agreed New York's Gross, "depends solely on the positive regulations of the individual States," and this "custom" of some states enslaving human beings was, "in the spirit of amity and compromise, left untouched by any provisions in the Constitution."[26]

Other sections of the Constitution randomly entered into congressional debates as well. Responding to congressmen who claimed that the Constitution was a creature of the original states, and thus subsequent states stood in an unequal manner to the Constitution, Holmes of Maine referred his colleagues to Section 10 of Article I, which contains prohibitions on the states, and asked them if these applied only to the states that formed the Constitution. If so, he pondered, could the states admitted afterwards then declare war, enter into treaties, coin money, and so on?

Such a construction, Holmes concluded, "would be dangerous, absurd, and destructive of the uniformity and safety of the whole system." Other opponents of restriction seized the opportunity to inquire of the nature of Section 10. Kentucky congressman Richard Anderson flipped Holmes's argument, asking if Congress could impose restriction on Missouri, based on the contention that she was not party to the original compact, then could Congress demand other concessions from states that entered the Union after ratification, in disregard of Section 10? "If Congress can make this clause the mean [sic] of exacting from a State the relinquishment of any privilege or right," he declared, "there is no limit to the control which she may acquire." Virginia's Johnson went so far as to suggest that the prohibitions in Section 10 were not absolute, that in the case of an armed invasion of a state, for example, it could "derive the power to keep troops and ships of war" in order to defend its citizens if the federal government delayed in coming to its defense. In relation to the federal government, the states occupied the same ground as individuals. "Whenever a government is unable to defend the citizen, the right of self-defence [sic], a natural right, recurs to him," he contended. "When the General Government is unable to defend the States, the natural and inalienable right of self-defence [sic] reverts to the States, and authorizes them to defend and preserve themselves."[27]

After a series of compromises, orchestrated by Speaker of the House Henry Clay, the House and Senate finally passed the Missouri Bill on March 3, 1820, admitting the "state" on an equal footing with the other states and authorizing the "state" to form a constitution and create a state government—and without any restriction on slavery. When President Monroe signed the Missouri Bill into law on March 6, 1820, the long and divisive episode seemingly ended, but Missouri quickly renewed the struggle by inciting another intense constitutional debate. A section of the new state's constitution, written and adopted in the summer of 1820, empowered the state legislature "to prevent free Negroes and mulattoes from coming to and settling in this State, upon any pretext whatsoever." That phrase alone touched off a firestorm of debate in Congress and across the nation, brought into question Missouri's legitimacy as a state, and provoked another ardent anti-Missouri movement. A whole host of constitutional considerations and questions arose immediately, mainly concerning Article IV, Section 2, Clause 1—the Privileges and Immunities Clause.

Nearly three and a half decades before the infamous *Dred Scott* decision, congressmen in the spring of 1821 thoroughly explored what citizenship meant in the United States. They struggled to arrive at a definition of a "citizen." They asked which entity, federal or state, determined just who is a citizen. As expected, restrictionists adopted one approach and anti-restrictionists another.

Missouri's nebulous standing in the Union—that is, whether it was a member of the Union or not—inspired another hotly contested constitutional debate. Was Missouri officially and formally—and thus finally—admitted into the Union when Congress passed the Missouri Bill and the president signed it into law, thus making it a sovereign state? Restrictionists replied in the negative; anti-restrictionists responded in the positive. For that matter, what was Congress's role and authority regarding a state's constitution? Must it approve a state constitution as the pretext for formal admission? If so, what was the basis of that approval, the Guarantee Clause in Article IV, Section 4? Did Congress even possess the plenary power to approve or disapprove? Restrictionists replied in the positive; anti-restrictionists responded in the negative. Was this a question for Congress or for the courts? Advocates of restriction supported the former, while opponents of restriction claimed the latter.

In the meantime, Missouri had created a state government in the summer of 1820. The people elected delegates to the first General Assembly and a governor and lieutenant governor to the first executive branch; the state legislature passed a series of laws, and a newly appointed state supreme court and an inferior state court system adjudicated numerous cases. The citizens likewise elected their first U.S. representative and two U.S. senators. From all appearances, Missouri was indeed a sovereign state in the federal Union. But Congress refused to seat or to recognize officially the representatives Missourians sent to Washington, not while debate continued over the state's constitution, specifically the meaning of that repugnant phrase. When the presidential election of 1820 arrived, Missouri's electoral votes came under intense scrutiny, and a compromise was introduced and quickly rejected to count them. Although the state's electoral votes had absolutely no bearing whatsoever on the outcome of the presidential contest—which there was none—counting or not counting them ultimately determined the status of statehood. Again, restrictionists refused to seat

Missouri's elected representatives and count the votes; anti-restrictionists pushed to open the doors to Missouri's federal representatives and accept their votes. Missouri's Territorial Delegate, John Scott, now duly elected by the citizens of Missouri to be that state's first representative in the U.S. House, refused to respond when congressmen called upon Missouri's territorial delegate and not its official congressman.

Another compromise finally terminated this most unpleasant and controversial chapter in U.S. constitutional history. The House, again with the influence of Speaker Clay, accepted the Senate's solution, known more popularly as the Eaton Proviso, a proposal of Tennessee senator John Eaton, which stipulated: "That nothing herein contained shall be so construed as to give the assent of Congress to any provision in the Constitution of Missouri, *if any such there be*, which contravenes that clause in the Constitution of the United States which declares that 'the citizens of each State shall be entitled to the privileges and immunities of the citizens of the several states.'" Simply put, Missouri will be admitted into the Union after its state legislature enacted legislation declaring that if the state ever did pass such a law, that it would be nonbinding. In one last bit of irony fitting to the whole Missouri crisis—and again a strictly constitutional one—Missouri would officially become a recognized state when its apparently unrecognized state legislature accepted the conditions—but if Missouri was not a state, then how could it have a state legislature, and, moreover, one that Congress mandated to pass a law? The Missouri "state" legislature quickly passed the "Solemn Public Act" Congress demanded, and President Monroe finally ended the whole matter via presidential proclamation on August 10, 1821, recognizing Missouri as the 24th state in the Union. The State of Missouri repudiated its part of the bargain on several occasions prior to the Civil War. Congress apparently never cared.

As did the previous generation of statesmen who justified revolution, independence, and a new order for the ages, congressmen throughout the Missouri debates recurrently cited a comprehensive body of literature and a wide-range of prominent political thinkers, from classical times to the founding era, in order to support their various political and philosophical positions and bolster their interpretations of the Constitution. Publius became their mainstay. All three of the authors of the *Federalist Papers*—James Madison, Alexander Hamilton, and John Jay—frequently appeared in the debates as validation of claims for and against restriction. Mississippi's Rankin shared the commonly accepted view of this work, referring to "that most able commentary on the Constitution of the United States, called the Federalist, which is known to be the joint production of Mr. Madison, General Hamilton, and 'that great civilian, Mr. Jay'." Missouri's delegate to Congress, John Scott, quoted Madison's *Federalist* No. 43 and No. 45 in support of Missouri's right to decide its own privileges. Georgia's Reid quoted a passage from Madison's *Federalist* No. 39 to defend state sovereignty; Pennsylvania senator Jonathan Roberts used the same number to locate the proper definition of a republican government. Maine's Holmes decided that "a very able advocate of the Federal Constitution apprehended that there would be more danger from faction in the members [states] than from power in the Federal head." Delaware's McLane also used *Federalist* No. 45 to promote states' rights, along with a reference to Madison's *Federalist* No. 42, also a favorite of Rankin. Delaware senator Nicholas Van Dyke quoted Madison in *Federalist* No. 45 and No. 46, as well as Hamilton in *Federalist* No. 84. Philip Barbour quoted Madison's *Federalist* No. 38, as "the most unquestionable authority" in defense of the Confederation Congress, while elder brother in the U.S. Senate, James Barbour, cited Hamilton's *Federalist* No. 11, stating at another juncture that "I will call to my aid the work so frequently referred to—the Federalist." Kentucky's Anderson used Madison's *Federalist* No. 40 in defense of the "transcendent and precious right" of a state to create and alter its own constitution, and in another instance condemned Alexander Hamilton, declaring "that it was not his intention to give a definition of a republic, but if Mr. Hamilton, in the Federalist, had not been grossly wrong in stating that clause in the Constitution, declaring that Congress should guaranty [sic] to every State in the Union a republican form of government, it would well support his position." Plenty of other congressmen continued to cite the "authors of the Federalist" to sustain their particular perspectives.[28]

After Publius, Emer de Vattel served as one of the favored sages of political wisdom. Kentucky's Hardin cited the Swiss thinker on several occasions in his exposition covering the character of nation states and the treaty-making powers. Pennsylvania's Joseph Hemphill countered with his own take on Vattel. Yet no individual in Congress turned to Vattel like Missouri's Scott, who quoted the *Law of Nations* for hours of debate, filling numerous pages with quotes from Vattel's famous work. Virginia's Smyth relied on Vattel's mentor, Dutch jurist Hugo Grotius, to explain the treaty rights of sovereign powers. New York congressman Henry Meigs extensively employed "the celebrated" Montesquieu's *Spirt of the Laws.*[29]

Few solons of the history of republicanism failed to make the list, whether used to impugn or uplift—from Creon, Euripides, Theseus, Homer, Virgil and Caesar, to John Milton, James Steuart, Thomas Malthus, Edmund Burke, and to Luther Martin, John Taylor of Caroline, St. George Tucker, Benjamin Franklin, and John Marshall. Congressmen alluded to Napoleon and Cromwell to chastise their opponents and label them as eminent threats to American republicanism. Even Abraham made an appearance. When individuals proved inadequate, history served the purpose. Entering the fray came ancient and modern confederacies, from Greek and Roman, to German, Dutch, and Swiss. Prominent state papers and other widely-read literature of American history consistently entered into the deliberations—Thomas Jefferson's *Notes on Virginia,* the Declaration of Independence, the Articles of Confederation, George Washington's Farewell Address, the Alien and Sedition Acts, the Virginia and Kentucky Resolutions. One congressman compared restriction and all its adverse constitutional consequences to the French Reign of Terror. Southerners rarely missed an opportunity to remind all concerned of New England sedition at the Hartford Convention, noting that the proposed changes to the Constitution proffered in 1814 differed from the changes those same New England congressmen were calling for just six years later in 1820.

Although the Ratification debates occurred three decades prior to the Missouri debates, that seminal founding moment was not all that distant for the 15th and 16th Congresses. Three former U.S. presidents, who were central figures in the inauguration of the new government in 1789, closely monitored the ongoing crisis. James Madison, the ascribed "Father of the Constitution," was alive and well, and commenting publicly on the original intent of the Founding Fathers, at least from his perspective and memory. Although not in attendance at the Philadelphia Convention, former presidents John Adams and Thomas Jefferson still stood as monuments in the creation and subsequent development of the American republic and its new constitutional system. Both men had reconnected several years before the first petition seeking statehood emanating from Missouri. In their now celebrated correspondence, Adams and Jefferson monitored and commented on the Missouri debates in Congress—Adams uncharacteristically more sanguine about Missouri's admission and Jefferson considerably more frightened about the future of the young republic with Missouri coming into it with slavery.

Yet, even more closely associated with the founding moment, that is, the Philadelphia Convention itself, two members of Congress actively engaged in the Missouri debates had attended the Constitutional Convention. One of the more ardent proponents of slavery restriction in Missouri (and throughout all U.S. territory, for that matter), Rufus King, a U.S. senator from Massachusetts and the last Federalist candidate for U.S. President, served as a key figure in Philadelphia in 1787 and in his state's ratification of the U.S. Constitution the following year, and continued his prominent antislavery position in Congress more than three decades later. Charles Pinckney, the U.S. representative from South Carolina, also attended the Constitutional Convention, and with a fellow delegate from South Carolina authored the Fugitive Slave Clause of the Constitution. Pinckney fought the Tallmadge Amendment in the U.S. House as vehemently as King defended the restriction measure in the U.S. Senate. During the Missouri debates, fellow congressmen turned, moreover, to each of these two distinguished American statesmen to glean the real intentions of the framers—and each offered differing renditions.

In sum, the admission of Missouri quickly became a constitutional crisis of the first order, and congressmen of the day knew full well of this fact. Whether they were aware that their extensive and elaborate exploration of the Constitution arguably rivalled only that of the state ratification debates three decades earlier, no one ever publicly admitted. But the Missouri debates most certainly must be considered as one of the more exhaustive reappraisals of the federal system of government and a comprehensive reinterpretation of the Constitution in the history of the early republic. Indeed, the Missouri admission crisis ranks with other intense antebellum constitutional controversies, from Hamiltonian Finance and the struggle between England and France bitterly pitting Jeffersonian Republicans against Hamiltonian Federalists during the 1790s, to the American System (the Nullification Crisis especially) consuming the Age of Jackson, and, ultimately, to secession, disunion, civil war, and reconstruction. The essays in the pages that follow recount the intensity of the constitutional crisis the young republic faced from 1819 through 1821.

NOTES

1. *Annals of Congress,* U.S. House of Representatives, 16th Congress, 1st Session, 967, 1033, 1076, 1357, 1383.

2. James Monroe to Spencer Roane, February 16, 1820, *Congressional Globe,* 30th Congress, 2d Sess., Appendix, 76; Speech of Senator Westcott of Florida, *Congressional Globe,* 30th Cong., 2d Sess., Appendix, 56.

3. *Annals of Congress,* House, 16th Cong., 2d Sess., 508, 517, 530–31, 1163.

4. *Annals of Congress,* House, 16th Cong., 1st Sess., 1093, 1179, 1398.

5. *Annals of Congress,* House, 16th Cong., 1st Sess., 970–71.

6. *Annals of Congress,* House, 16th Cong., 1st Sess., 998, 1076-77, 1358–59.

7. *Annals of Congress,* House, 16th Cong., 1st Sess., 1077, 1078.

8. *Annals of Congress,* House, 16th Cong., 1st Sess., 1199, 1200.

9. *Annals of Congress,* House, 16th Cong., 1st Sess., 942, 971–72, 996, 1080, 1162, 1240.

10. *Annals of Congress,* House, 16th Cong., 1st Sess., 1187, 1526.

11. *Annals of Congress,* House, 16th Cong., 1st Sess., 1037, 1294, 1306, 1441, 1468.

12. Massachusetts congressman Joshua Cushman contended that "the power which is claimed for the Constitution is inherent in every body politic which has within it the principles of its own preservation. . . . This power is conferred on Congress in stronger terms than by the decree of the Roman Senate which conferred power on the Consul. In the literal sense, this decree only gave the power to ward off injuries. But the Constitution is more explicit; in unequivocal language it confers a power on Congress not only to secure the commonwealth from harm, but also to procure for it good—to provide for the common defence and promote the general welfare." *Annals of Congress,* House, 16th Cong., 1st Sess., 1295–96.

13. *Annals of Congress,* House, 16th Cong., 1st Sess., 1459.

14. *Annals of Congress,* House, 15th Cong., 2d Sess., 1185, 1196; *Annals of Congress,* House, 16th Cong., 1st. Sess., 933, 969, 975–76, 977, 995, 1025, 1037–38, 1075, 1227, 1249, 1274–75, 1297, 1333–34, 1459, 1499; *Annals of Congress,* Senate, 16th Cong., 1st Sess., 165, 197, 316, 358.

15. *Annals of Congress,* House, 15th Cong., 2d Sess., 1197; *Annals of Congress,* House, 16th Cong., 1st Sess., 979, 998, 1025, 1083, 1122, 1227, 1229, 1261, 1333–34, 1367–68, 1499, 1521.

16. *Annals of Congress,* Senate, 16th Cong., 1st Sess., 316, 397.

17. *Annals of Congress,* House, 16th Cong., 1st Sess., 1179-80; *Annals of Congress,* Senate, 16th Cong., 1st Sess., 202.

18. *Annals of Congress,* House, 16th Cong., 1st Sess., 1252, 1294–98; *Annals of Congress,* Senate, 16th Cong., 1st Sess., 214.

19. *Annals of Congress,* House, 16th Cong., 1st Sess., 1149, 1150.

20. *Annals of Congress*, Senate, 16th Cong., 1st Sess., 202, 288; *Annals of Congress*, House, 16th Cong., 1st Sess., 1294–95.

21. *Annals of Congress*, House, 16th Cong., 1st Sess., 976, 1333.

22. *Annals of Congress*, Senate, 16th Cong., 1st Sess., 394; *Annals of Congress*, House, 16th Cong., 1st Sess., 1220.

23. *Annals of Congress*, House, 15th Cong., 2d Sess., 1185, 1187; *Annals of Congress*, House, 16th Cong., 1st Sess., 1082, 1219–20, 1152–53, 1153–54.

24. *Annals of Congress*, House, 16th Cong., 1st Sess., 1028, 1458; *Annals of Congress*, Senate, 16th Cong., 1st Sess., 196–97.

25. *Annals of Congress*, House, 15th Cong., 2d Sess., 1181, 1182; *Annals of Congress*, House, 16th Cong., 1st Sess., 1188, 1189–90, 1191, 1303, 1468–69.

26. *Annals of Congress*, House, 16th Cong., 1st Sess., 1104, 1251–52.

27. *Annals of Congress*, House, 16th Cong., 1st Sess., 975, 1260, 1366–67.

28. *Annals of Congress*, House, 15th Cong., 2d Sess., 1196, 1197–98; *Annals of Congress*, House, 16th Cong., 1st Sess., 977, 1025, 1222, 1257, 1258, 1275, 1336, 1343; *Annals of Congress*, Senate, 16th Cong., 1st Sess., 308, 320, 322, 339.

29. *Annals of Congress*, House, 16th Cong., 1st Sess., 944, 946, 947, 1007, 1074, 1075, 1081, 1116, 1493–98, 1509–12.

CHAPTER TWO

The Privileges and Immunities Clause

Christopher Childers

> **"The citizens of each state shall be entitled to all privileges and immunities of citizens in the several states."**
>
> [Article IV, Section 2, Clause 1]

WHEN THE 16TH Congress passed the Missouri Compromise on March 3, 1820, and President James Monroe signed it into law three days later, most Americans breathed a collective sigh of relief that leaders had averted disunion. The debates over slavery in Missouri, and the entire Louisiana Purchase, had reawakened tensions over the issue of slavery and westward expansion. Not since the ratification of the Constitution had the slavery issue posed such a threat to the Union. Missouri's admission to the Union had punctuated the tranquility of the Era of Good Feelings by dividing Americans into antislavery and proslavery camps. The compromise seemed to offer a return to domestic tranquility and good feelings after almost thirteen months of political turmoil. "If the Union must be dissolved, slavery is precisely the question upon which it ought to break," Secretary of State John Quincy Adams wrote in his diary on March 3. "For the present however the contest is laid asleep."[1]

All that remained was for Missouri to draft its constitution and formalize the process of statehood. But when Missouri submitted its constitution to Congress in November of 1820, the controversy reawakened with fury. The framers of the Missouri constitution, defiant in their opposition to federal control over slavery in the territories, made a statement in favor of slavery and states' rights by prohibiting the emancipation of slaves and by directing the legislature to pass legislation barring free people of color from entering the state. Though repugnant, the former clause did not violate the U.S.

Constitution, but the latter clause did. By prohibiting free people of color from entering Missouri, the drafters of the state's proposed constitution provoked a discussion over race and law that the 16th Congress had tried to avoid. Most politicians during the Missouri debates had limited their opinions to the constitutionality of restricting slavery, rather than tackle the broader issues of slavery and race in American society. By barring free blacks from the state, the proposed Missouri constitution forced Congress to confront momentous issues concerning race, slavery, and the meaning of citizenship in the Union.

Excluding free people of color from Missouri violated the Privileges and Immunities Clause of the U.S. Constitution, which declares that "the Citizens of each State shall be entitled to all the Privileges and Immunities of Citizens in the several States." Presumably, as citizens of one state, free blacks had the right to free movement within any other state in the Union, as guaranteed by Article IV, Section 2, of the Constitution. Now Missouri threatened to violate a basic right of U.S. citizenship, as well as the principle of interstate comity, by barring a certain class of citizens from the state by virtue of their race. Antislavery Northerners who opposed the compromise that had just become law in the previous session of Congress now saw a new opening to deny Missouri's bid for statehood. Proslavery Southerners, on the other hand, demanded the immediate acceptance of Missouri's constitution and its immediate admission to the Union. By December 1820, the battle lines had been drawn for another round of acrimonious debate that ended in the so-called second Missouri Compromise.

Throughout the renewed debate, the meaning of the Privileges and Immunities Clause and how it applied to the issue of free people of color in Missouri took center stage. As a matter of constitutional interpretation, the dispute seemed easy to solve. The proposed Missouri constitution violated the clause by denying a group of citizens, in this case free people of color, the right to enter the state of Missouri. Therefore, Missourians must remove the offending clause and recognize the principles of interstate comity for free blacks before the territory could become a state. The problem with this solution, however, stemmed from the contentious history of Missouri's bid for statehood. Presumably Congress would compel the drafters of the Missouri constitution to remove the offending language or risk jeopardizing statehood itself. The power to compel a prospective state to meet certain conditions in order to obtain statehood had been at the heart of the first Missouri debate, when New York congressman James Tallmadge had proposed forcing Missouri to adopt gradual emancipation as a condition of statehood. Missourians had fought congressional authority then, and they would surely fight it now, in November 1820, should Congress force them to alter their proposed constitution.

The second Missouri debate, however, had an added dimension that further complicated how it played out in Congress and in the court of public opinion. Beyond constitutional interpretation lay the issue of America's longstanding history of racial discrimination. Significant ambiguities in how Northerners and Southerners approached the issues of race and citizenship complicated the admission of Missouri to the Union, all of which had the potential to destabilize America's racial order if politicians or the public started questioning them. For example, antislavery Northerners could and did decry Missouri's blatant violation of the U.S. Constitution, but in actuality Northern states had long sought to restrict the privileges and immunities of free blacks. Conversely, proslavery Southerners lined up in defense of Missouri's right to draft a constitution of its choosing, one that barred free people of color, yet Southerners had a clear history of recognizing the citizenship of free blacks.

But were free blacks truly citizens of the United States? Put another way, did race play a role in determining American citizenship? Proslavery and antislavery politicians alike quickly realized that the debate had shifted to the issue of race and citizenship. On the one hand, if free people of color were U.S. citizens then the Missouri constitution violated the Privileges and Immunities Clause and must be stricken from the document as a condition of statehood. If on the other hand, free people of color were not citizens, then Missouri's draft constitution could stand as written. Until the time that Missouri submitted its constitution to Congress, slavery had driven the disputes in the Missouri controversy. The advocates of restriction had generally prevailed in moral arguments over the extension of slavery. Southerners had not yet formulated the argument that slavery was a positive good for society. Across the nation, remnants of the Revolutionary-era hope that slavery would disappear remained—however faint those sentiments had become. Now, however, the issue of race became the driver of political discourse, and as much as restrictionists opposed slavery, many if not most of them did not oppose racial prejudice. In North and South alike, free people of color frequently found their rights in jeopardy. And as it turned out, defending the rights of free people of color proved more difficult than defending restriction of the extension of slavery.[2]

A conversation between Secretary of State John Quincy Adams and Secretary of War John C. Calhoun at the end of the first Missouri debate illustrates the difference well. When Congress passed the first Missouri Compromise on March 3, 1820, President James Monroe summoned the members of his cabinet to answer two questions about the bill. First, Monroe asked his cabinet if Congress had the right to prohibit slavery in a territory. Second, he asked if the congressional prohibition of slavery in the bill applied after statehood or only during the territorial period. Both Adams, an antislavery Massachusetts native, and Calhoun, a proslavery South Carolinian, agreed that Congress possessed the right to restrict slavery in a territory. After the meeting, Calhoun and Adams walked home together, and as they strolled off Capitol Hill they engaged in a discussion over Missouri and slavery in general, a conversation remarkable for its breadth and for its civility. The Calhoun of 1820 remained a nationalist, not yet having transformed into the ardent states' rights proponent he would become within a decade. Adams, on the other hand, held to antislavery beliefs, though perhaps not as strongly as he would in his post-presidential career as a congressman and the chief instigator of the Gag Rule controversy.

As they walked and talked, Adams pressed the Southerner on the evils of slavery, on its degradation of manual labor and how it made the Southern master class look down upon their Northern brethren who engaged in manual labor. Calhoun politely disagreed, disputing Adams's notion that slavery degraded labor. Calhoun himself, he noted, had held the plow. "Manufacturing and mechanical labour," Calhoun responded, "was not degrading. It was only manual labour—the proper work of Slaves—No white person could descend to that." Throughout the discussion between these two friends, however, the heart of American slavery and the crux of the issue that provoked the second Missouri debate became clear. According to Calhoun, the great principles of liberty and equality that Adams and antislavery Northerners espoused "were always understood as applying only to white men." Calhoun illustrated his point with a particularly striking example: even if he was the most popular man in his district, if he hired a white house servant his reputation would be "irretrievably ruined." Servitude and manual labor in the South, according to Calhoun, belonged to the black person by virtue of that person's race. The racial line divided the South into a free white class and an enslaved black class, which produced the "best guarantee to equality among the whites."[3]

Adams balked at Calhoun's characterization because, to his mind, it conflated servitude and labor with slavery. Perhaps because of his own prejudice, because it seemed self-evident, or for other unexplained reasons, Adams missed Calhoun's conflation of race and slavery. Race defined American slavery, which made the presence and status of free people of color in the United States even more of an anomaly. The racial issue, lurking in the first round of debates over Missouri's statehood, subsumed the second round of debates as Northern and Southern congressmen argued over whether the proposed Missouri constitution violated the Privileges and Immunities Clause of the U.S. Constitution and whether free people of color even had the right to citizenship and its protections.

Understanding how the Privileges and Immunities Clause played a role in the Missouri crisis involves three significant issues that Americans had to address. First, the development of the clause in the Constitutional Convention of 1787 and what vision the framers had for it, proves crucial to explaining how it provoked the second Missouri crisis. Though the notion of original intent leads to spirited debate in modern politics, it plays a significant role in understanding the Missouri controversy. Second, analyzing how congressmen debated the meaning of the Privileges and Immunities Clause reveals that Northerners and Southerners disputed the original intent of the framers. Third, behind the differing interpretations of the clause among Northern and Southern congressmen rested a fundamental disagreement about citizenship itself, one that the framers had either failed to anticipate or simply ignored.

The framers of the Constitution developed the Privileges and Immunities Clause out of necessity. In a union composed of sovereign states, the matter of rights collided with the inevitability of mobility. In other words, could a citizen of one state have the expectation of similar rights in another state? The Articles of Confederation answered in the affirmative by providing that "the people of each state shall have free ingress and regress to and from any other state, and shall enjoy therein all the privileges of trade and commerce, subject to the same duties, impositions and restrictions as the inhabitants thereof respectively." The Constitution of 1787 simplified and refined the previous document by stating that "The Citizens of each State shall be entitled to all Privileges and Immunities of Citizens in the several States."

By declaring that citizens of one state had rights in the other states, the Constitution created a national citizenship of sorts that prevented states from discriminating against citizens from other states or by favoring one state's citizens over those of another. As U.S. Supreme Court justice and constitutional lawyer Joseph Story explained in 1840, the Constitution had "wisely created, as it were, a general citizenship."[4] James Madison, writing as Publius in *The Federalist* No. 42, likewise implied that the United States needed a general citizenship lest naturalization law become a jumble of conflicting state laws. And though national citizenship remained maddeningly undefined until after the Reconstruction Amendments, the Constitution nonetheless provided for some form of citizenship that transcended state lines.

The Constitutional Convention of 1787 wrote the Privileges and Immunities Clause to prevent a state from discriminating against the rights of citizens of another state. Because the clause stipulated that it protected the privileges and immunities of state citizens, the questions of how states confer citizenship and who was eligible for citizenship immediately arose. The clause itself sought to standardize, to some degree, how government conferred citizenship. Alexander Hamilton explained in *The Federalist* No. 80 that state citizenship implies citizenship "in the union." Because of that, Hamilton asserted that the federal judiciary should resolve disputes between citizens of different states.[5] More important, however, to the discussion of how the Privileges and Immunities Clause played a role in the Missouri controversy, the clause requires a precise understanding of who possessed or could possess citizenship. On this point turned the entire debate over Missouri's proposed constitution and its odious provision that excluded free people of color from the state.

By the time of the Missouri crisis, the legal status of free people of color in the United States had changed—usually not for the better—as state legislatures in the North and South sought to restrict their rights. Especially in the South, the presence of free blacks undermined the idea of racial slavery that, contrary to the professed hope of some of the founding generation, had strengthened rather than weakened in the forty-five years since independence. Regardless of developments in the early nineteenth century that threatened the legal status of free people of color, the Constitution of 1787 included them in the Privileges and Immunities Clause. The clause's language cited the "Citizens of each State" without reference to color. Indeed, historical evidence makes clear that free people of color possessed citizenship. In several states, they exercised the right to vote. Constitutional precedent also suggested that the clause encompassed free people of color. The Articles of Confederation's version of the Privileges and Immunities Clause uses no qualifying language for race that would have excluded free people of color, whereas other parts of the document distinguish between white citizens and free blacks. During the debate over the Articles of Confederation, delegates from South Carolina recognized the significance of not excluding free people of color and moved to insert the word "white" before the phrase "free inhabitants." Their motion failed, but it implies that Southerners must have recognized that the clause not only recognized the citizenship of free blacks but that it also granted them certain rights on an equal basis with white citizens.[6]

Additional evidence implies that free people of color enjoyed citizenship rights, even in slaveholding states. The state of Virginia, for example, in 1783 repealed a law that excluded free blacks from state citizenship, stipulating that "all free persons born within the territory of this commonwealth" possessed "all the rights, privileges, and advantages of citizens."[7] In that same year, Congress debated an amendment to the Articles of Confederation, the first introduction of the notorious three-fifths ratio that fractionally apportioned the slave population for purposes of taxation, that referred to "white and other free citizens."[8] When the Constitutional Convention met in Philadelphia in 1787, it simplified the language of the Privileges and Immunities Clause, but the delegates did not alter the definition of citizens to exclude free people of color. That free blacks had served in the Continental Army likely played a role in preventing changes.

Overall, in the post-Revolutionary era, American leaders avoided efforts to restrict the rights and citizenship of free people of color. Even as late as 1803, Congress implicitly recognized the citizenship of free blacks. In that year, it passed a law that prohibited the importation of black seamen who were not "a native, a citizen, or registered seaman of the United States."[9] Language in the congressional debates further corroborates the idea that Congress recognized the citizenship of free people of color.

The historical record of the Revolutionary era and early nineteenth century contains many examples of legal recognition of free black citizenship, but Congress and state legislatures also restricted the rights of free blacks in other instances. In other words, one cannot assume that free blacks enjoyed full and undisputed citizenship rights during this period. To the contrary, American political leaders in the early republic viewed blacks—free or enslaved—as racially inferior. A contrasting body of evidence proves the point. The Naturalization Act of 1790, for example, limited citizenship to free white people.[10]

In the years after American independence politicians wrestled with the competing notions of universal freedom and equality on the one hand and the system of racial slavery that created a color line in America on the other. The Revolutionary moment pushed leaders toward an expansive definition of rights and citizenship while the uncomfortable realities of slavery pulled them away in other instances from the radicalism of the Revolution itself. Clearly, free blacks possessed citizenship, but what that citizenship meant in practice was contested throughout the years between independence and the Missouri controversy.

That citizenship did not have to mean common rights for all citizens complicated matters further. Gender provides the most obvious example of the inequality of rights among citizens. Women and men alike shared citizenship, but as citizens men enjoyed more expansive rights than did women. Men could vote and enter into contracts; women generally could not. Again, because citizenship lacked a precise definition it becomes difficult to define what privileges and immunities a citizen might enjoy. It depended on age, gender, religion, property owned, and, of course, color.

The relationship between race and citizenship became more problematic by the year 1820, not only because of the revolutionary spirit of freedom and liberty, but also because of the practical reality that the free black population had increased significantly in the previous thirty years. A growing free black population led to a corresponding increase in discriminatory legislation primarily at, but not limited to, the state level. Indeed, on the eve of the Missouri debate several states wrestled with the issue of rights for free people of color. In Kentucky, for example, the legislature enacted a law in 1798 stipulating that "if any negro, or mulatto, or Indian, bond or free, shall at any time lift his or her hand in opposition to any person not being a negro, &c." that person could be punished with thirty lashes.[11] In 1820, the Kentucky Court of Appeals heard a case that dealt with the now-repealed law, but declared, nonetheless, that the law violated the state's constitution on the basis that it unfairly discriminated against free people of color. Yet the court's decision opined that certain forms of discrimination were indeed legal. Free people of color, Justice Benjamin Mills argued in the opinion, "are certainly, in some measure, parties" to the political compact of the state. "Although they have not every benefit or privilege which the Constitution secures, yet they have many secured by it. We need not take the trouble of inquiring how far they are or are not parties."[12]

Not everyone could deflect the question so easily, however. As much as the citizenship of free people of color seemed established in law, just as many competing examples proved that Americans did not agree on the nature of free black citizenship. By 1820, politicians and jurists alike seemed willing to recognize a limited form of citizenship for free blacks, but the bounds of those limits remained in contest. The Missourians, in drafting their constitution, seemed at the vanguard of a movement to restrict citizenship rights on the basis of race.

Other states had enacted provisions like the prohibition in the Missouri constitution through legislation. By 1820, at least six Southern states and one Northern one had enacted laws prohibiting the immigration of free people of color between 1793, when Virginia enacted its law, and 1819, when the Mississippi legislature barred free blacks from the state.[13] In sum, other states had set a precedent that Missouri took to an even higher legal level in 1820 when it banned free blacks in its constitution. Conversely, at least four states, New York, Massachusetts, North Carolina, and Tennessee, recognized the citizenship of free blacks. Other states may not have barred free black immigration, but they sought to deter it by enacting laws restricting the rights of free people of color. In Indiana, Illinois, and Kentucky state law prohibited free blacks from voting, marrying white people, testifying in court against whites, or attending public schools. Given the acrimonious debate over Missouri's admission to the Union, however, its efforts to enact a constitutional ban on the immigration of free blacks would not go unchallenged. Northerners who had supported restriction and opposed the compromise passed through Congress in 1820 saw a potentially successful opportunity to challenge Missouri's entry into the Union as a slave state.

During the first round of the Missouri debates, antislavery Northerners had illustrated their willingness to use whatever political means necessary in order to stop the advance of slavery into Missouri and the remainder of the Louisiana Purchase. The issue of whether Congress could restrict slavery in the territories had passed with the first compromise, but Missourians had provided another opening for a challenge. Northern restrictionists believed that it had to come from the question of citizenship since it represented the most solid basis on which to mount an offensive against Missouri's statehood. As citizens, free people of color could claim protection under the Privileges and Immunities Clause. Therefore, proslavery leaders had to attack the parameters of free black citizenship in order to uphold their racial regime. Because Southern leaders saw the presence of free blacks and their exercise of political power as a subversive threat to slavery, the master class would likely defend Missouri's proposed constitution.

The congressional response to Missouri's ban on free blacks erupted predictably along sectional lines, but to leave the description at those simple terms obscures the dramatic debate over slavery and race that emerged once Congress again took up the Missouri issue in November 1820. In speech after speech, congressmen laid bare the unsettled nature of free black citizenship in America. Southerners inched closer to a defense of slavery as a positive good. Northerners revealed the limits of their sympathy for free and enslaved blacks. By focusing on the privileges and immunities of free people of color, Congress delved into the realm of natural law and equality, revealing that "the phrase 'all men are created equal' was not a historical truth but a value judgment still struggling to transform itself into fact."[14]

Much of the debate played out in the U.S. Senate, where a select committee had examined Missouri's proposed constitution and recommended admission to the Union, with a banal proviso authored by John Eaton of Tennessee that declared that "nothing herein contained shall be so construed as to give the assent of Congress to any provision in the Constitution of Missouri, *if any such there be*, which contravenes" the Privileges and Immunities Clause of the U.S. Constitution.[15] Of course, the words "if any such there be" identified the crux of the dispute: did Missouri have the constitutional right to restrict the immigration of free blacks? If free blacks were citizens, then no; if not, then yes. And so the debate raged. Senator James Burrill, a Rhode Island Federalist, answered that "there was nothing in the Constitution of the United States which recognized distinctions" of color with respect to citizenship.[16] Accordingly, if a free person of color possessed citizenship in Massachusetts, that person had rights that Missouri must recognize. The ban was plainly unconstitutional. "The States of this Union were not distinct and independent nations," Burrill argued, "but a confederacy of kindred republics" that had formed their union under the banner of "we the people of the United States."[17] No other state could legally enforce Missouri's ban and, therefore, Congress had a duty to reject it.

Politicians from the kindred republics of the North raised an important—and unimpeachable—constitutional point, but the way in which Northern states themselves treated free people of color under the law hurt the legitimacy of their case. Sensing hypocrisy, Southern senators examined Northern state laws and found plenty. South Carolina senator William Smith delivered a damning speech in which he detailed Northern treatment of free blacks under the law.[18] Ohio and Connecticut excluded free blacks from suffrage. Massachusetts prohibited intermarriage between blacks and whites. Indiana barred blacks from testifying against whites in court. Free blacks could not serve in the state militias of Vermont and New Hampshire. Smith's investigation, though it did not directly address the point of free black citizenship, exposed the ways in which Northern states excluded blacks from the attributes of citizenship—privileges and immunities that white citizens would have enjoyed under state law. It showed that as much as Northerners might object to the institution of slavery, they seemed to subscribe to the racist belief that African Americans were a degraded class of people under the law.

The restrictionists could hardly muster a defense because they believed in the inferiority of African Americans. Even one of the most progressive restrictionists, Senator David Morril of New Hampshire, could not entirely escape that conclusion. Morril boldly stated that "Color does not come into the consideration [of citizenship], and it has no share in characterizing an inhabitant or citizen. On this exposition I shall rest my argument."[19] Yet Morril undercut his statement by conceding Smith's point that New

Hampshire prohibited African Americans from serving in the state militia. "Custom has made a distinction between them and other men," Morril added, "but the Constitution and laws make none."[20] Other Northern senators joined Morril in defending their states' discriminatory laws. Harrison Gray Otis of Massachusetts defended his state's ban on intermarriage. As a "very small minority," free people of color had no right to argue against laws like Massachusetts's restriction because the "vast majority" had seen fit to impose the ban with the "desire of transmitting to posterity its blood pure and unmixed."[21]

Southern senators like Smith had touched a raw nerve by exposing Northern racism. Southerners argued that at the least free people of color held an inferior form of citizenship to whites and, at the most extreme, they did not have the right to citizenship at all. To prove the point, or at least to undermine the Northerners' credibility, senators like Smith of South Carolina had responded with evidence showing how Northern states placed free people of color in an inferior status as citizens. On this point, Northern senators had no effective response, so Northerners looked anew at challenging their interpretation of the Constitution. Southerners had argued that Congress's approval of the constitution was a *pro forma* matter; that the sovereign people of Missouri had spoken and that Congress must accede to their will. Northerners demolished that point by noting that the Constitution gave Congress the right and responsibility to ensure that new states created a republican form of government. By violating the Privileges and Immunities Clause, Missouri's constitution did not meet the constitutional test of a republican form of government.

Senators offered intense volleys of arguments for and against Missouri's constitution, but the debated ended quickly. On December 12, 1820, the Senate passed the resolution admitting Missouri to the Union with John Eaton's meaningless proviso that Missouri's constitution could not conflict with the federal constitution. From there the proceedings pivoted to the House of Representatives, where congressmen waited to engage in their own version of the debate. Speaker of the House John W. Taylor of New York, one of the most vocal restrictionists in the previous session of Congress, referred the matter to a select committee, which presented a resolution on November 23. The terminally ill South Carolinian William Lowndes presented the resolution to Congress with his own ringing endorsement, and with a curious provision of his own concerning the legality of Missouri's ban on free people of color. Lowndes argued that any dispute over the ban "should be remitted to judicial cognizance."[22] By deferring to the power of judicial review on the question of the legality of Missouri's prohibition on free people of color, Lowndes articulated an idea that reappeared periodically during the antebellum era. In 1821, Lowndes wanted the Supreme Court to decide the question of whether a state could ban free people of color; in 1848, the so-called Clayton Compromise called on the court to define popular sovereignty with respect to slavery in the territories. And Lowndes was not alone in calling for a court ruling, as other congressmen echoed his sentiments.

Meanwhile, Southern representatives echoed their colleagues across the Capitol building in accusing Northerners of hypocrisy on the race question. South Carolina's Charles Pinckney, who had switched to the House from the Senate for the 16th Congress, delivered a strong speech in favor of prompt admission for Missouri. Pinckney called out the "unexpected and inexcusable opposition" of Northern restrictionists for instigating the latest crisis over Missouri as a disingenuous ploy to prevent the creation of another slave state, one that threatened the future of the Union.[23] More memorably, Pinckney, who had participated in the Constitutional Convention, claimed that he had authored the Privileges and Immunities Clause. "I must know, or perfectly recollect, what I meant by it," he stated. "At the time I drew that constitution," Pinckney continued, "I perfectly knew that there did not then exist in the Union such a thing as a black or colored citizen; nor could I then have conceived it possible that such a thing ever could have existed in it; nor, notwithstanding all that is said on the subject, do I now believe that one does exist in it."[24]

The question then, as Pinckney framed it, was "what is a citizen of the United States?" In South Carolina, Pinckney answered, all whites held citizenship. Race, in other words, played a determining role in citizenship. Pinckney admitted that even among whites, the rights of citizenship varied. Women, for example, could not vote. Clergy could not serve in the state legislature. Pinckney did not address the Palmetto State's extreme property requirements for voting, but the point would have corroborated his claims, even if it would have laid bare the slaveholders' oligarchy in his state. But blacks could not be citizens.

After denying that any African American could hold citizenship, Pinckney turned to the now-familiar argument of Northern hypocrisy on the race question. He recalled the discriminatory restrictions imposed on free blacks in the North. As for the right of suffrage that some Northern free blacks enjoyed, Pinckney dismissed it and them as pawns of white leaders. "These degraded beings are frequently, in a most improper state, dragged to the polls, with tickets in their hands which they cannot read, compelled by men under whose influence they are obliged to act, to disgrace, in the most shameful manner, the highest privilege our Republic boasts."[25] Pinckney's argument rested on two points: first, that Northern law recognized free people of color as inferior and second, that their right to vote degraded the franchise itself.[26]

Belief in the racial inferiority of African Americans undergirded Pinckney's entire argument. Though he accused Northerners of hypocrisy for circumscribing the rights of free blacks, he did not disagree with their reasoning. To Pinckney, and to these Northerners, race made free people of color inferior under the law. In 1821, the South Carolinian's argument stood at the extreme of proslavery rhetoric, but in the coming decades it would become mainstream. The debate over Missouri's constitution and the second Missouri compromise advanced the proslavery ideology far beyond the bounds of the necessary evil argument and speeches from politicians like Pinckney in the House and Smith in the Senate proved the point.

Pinckney's speech, delivered on February 13, 1821, came at a moment when the Missouri statehood resolution remained in peril in the House of Representatives. In two previous roll call votes, the House had rejected the resolution; a third vote to advance the resolution after Pinckney's speech likewise failed on a close vote of 82 to 88. The next day in the House brought one of the most surreal, and vitriolic, debates during the entire crisis as Congress prepared to count the electoral votes for president and vice-president. Southerners, claiming that Missouri was already a state, demanded that its electoral votes count in the election while Northerners claimed the opposite. Only through the legislative acumen of Henry Clay did the dispute end and the votes get counted.

Still, the problem of Missouri's statehood remained, and once again Henry Clay's parliamentary skills came to the rescue. On February 22,

Clay moved to appoint a joint congressional committee to consider Missouri's application for admission to the Union. Three days later, the committee advanced a new resolution that largely followed the evasive course that Senator John Eaton had proposed earlier in the session. The new resolution admitted Missouri to the Union "upon the fundamental condition" that the clause directing the state legislature to prohibit the immigration of free blacks to the state "shall never be construed to authorize the passage of any law . . . by which any citizen of either of the States of this Union shall be excluded from the enjoyment of any of the privileges and immunities to which such citizen is entitled under the Constitution of the United States."[27] By the terms of the congressional resolution, Missouri had to assent to this "fundamental condition," which it did on July 26—sort of. Any astute observer could see the absurdity of Missouri stating that its constitution did not do something that it plainly did. Given the irreconcilable issues involved and the stakes of the debate, however, this was not the time for clarity. On August 10, 1821, President Monroe issued a proclamation declaring Missouri the twenty-fourth state in the Union. The Missouri crisis had ended with this second compromise.

The resolution, expertly shepherded through Congress by Clay, elevated political evasion to an art form. Missouri's Thomas Hart Benton declared the Kentuckian the "*Pacificator* of ten millions of Brothers," but pacification came in the most absurd of forms. In one sense the resolution said nothing, as everyone knew that if free blacks were citizens of the United States then Missouri's constitution clearly violated the federal constitution. Yet the resolution left the question of citizenship open, for it did not judge whether free blacks held citizenship or not. Presumably future congresses, or more likely the courts, could decide later. The crisis passed and many people forgot the constitutional clash over the privileges and immunities of free blacks. Missourians, however, did not entirely forget. In 1825, the state legislature passed a law that prohibited African Americans and mulattoes from entering the state unless they could verify their citizenship, an impossible condition. Twenty-two years later, an even more defiant legislature nullified the resolution of 1821.

On February 28, 1821, the day the Senate approved the resolution admitting Missouri to the Union, John Quincy Adams offered a postmortem of the crisis in his voluminous diary. "In the progress of this Affair," he wrote, "the distinctive character of the inhabitants of the several great divisions of this Union have been shewn more in relief than perhaps in any National transaction since the Establishment of the Constitution." Adams conceded that the proslavery interests has amassed the most talent and influence in advancing their position. "They have threatened and intreated, bullied and wheedled, until their more simple adversaries have been half coaxed half frightened into a surrender of their principles for a bauble of insignificant promises."[28] Adams predicted a future conflict over the slavery issue though he did not offer details on how he thought it would come or which side would win. Regarding the notion of equality and citizenship for free people of color, however, Northerners had not as much surrendered their principles as they had revealed their belief that African Americans did not have the right or the capacity to exercise the privileges and immunities of white citizens. In the coming decades between the Missouri crisis and the Civil War, the idea of African American citizenship would not disappear. The second Missouri crisis forced the issue into the political arena and therefore no discussion of its impact on constitutional interpretation would be complete without a consideration of how the Missouri Compromise framed the issue in succeeding decades.

The debate over the Privileges and Immunities Clause in the Missouri controversy had long lasting ramifications for the issue of citizenship in the early republic, but after 1821 the location of the discussion shifted from Congress to the courts. Congress rarely addressed the issue of free black citizenship in the forty years between the Missouri debates and the Civil War. Instead, it became the subject of legal battles based on competing interpretations of law. Months after Missouri's admission to the Union, the Monroe administration addressed the question of black citizenship when Secretary of the Treasury William Crawford asked for the opinion of Attorney General William Wirt on whether a free person of color could command a ship leaving Norfolk, Virginia. Regulations required that only U.S. citizens could command oceangoing vessels. Wirt argued that they could not, as "no person is included in the description of citizens of the United States who has not the full rights of a citizen in the State of his residence."[29] Wirt made two legal points that would have long-term significance: first, that state citizenship determined federal citizenship and, second, that free people of color in Virginia possessed neither state nor federal citizenship. Theoretically, if a state recognized free black citizenship, and a few New England states in 1821 did, then perhaps that person could claim U.S. citizenship. Nevertheless, because so few states recognized free black citizenship the vast majority of free people of color would have been excluded under Wirt's opinion.

Wirt's opinion, along with the aftermath of the Denmark Vesey slave insurrection six months later, foreshadowed the direction of the argument that had come out of the Missouri crisis. After Vesey's failed rebellion, South Carolina enacted strict laws regulating the movement of African Americans, including the Negro Seamen Law, which required that black crew members of ships docking in any South Carolina port be arrested and jailed until their ship left port. A Supreme Court justice on circuit duty ruled the law unconstitutional in 1823 and Attorney General Wirt concurred, but South Carolina continued to enforce the law, which remained an issue into the 1830s. By 1832, other Southern states had enacted similar legislation, causing something of an uproar in diplomatic circles, since Great Britain employed black seamen on its ships. In that year, President Andrew Jackson's Attorney General, Roger Brooke Taney, issued a legal opinion on the law and addressed the subject of black citizenship. According to Taney, "the African race in the United States even when free, are everywhere a degraded class, and exercise no political influence. The privileges they are allowed to enjoy, are accorded to them as a matter of kindness and benevolence rather than of right." Based on that argument, Taney concluded that free people of color "were evidently not supposed to be included by the term *citizens*. And were not intended to be embraced in any provisions of that Constitution but those which point to them in terms not to be mistaken."[30] Twenty-five years later, Taney, then Chief Justice of the United States, used the same logic in his opinion in *Dred Scott v. Sandford*.

One of the most odious Supreme Court decisions in American history traced its legal origins to the Missouri controversy and involved, at least in part, the discussion of the Privileges and Immunities Clause that arose in the second debate. By 1857, the issue of citizenship among free people of color remained unclear but a sort of consensus had emerged among legal experts and politicians. First, most people agreed that federal citizenship derived from state citizenship. Second, given the first legal point it remained possible that free blacks could be U.S. citizens. Nevertheless, the courts had not pronounced definitively one way or the other. The Dred Scott case changed that. Roger Taney's sweeping decision—many called it *obiter dicta*—reiterated the opinion that he had issued in 1832 regarding the Negro seamen acts. As "beings of an inferior order," Taney argued, African Americans could not possess U.S. citizenship because "they had no rights which the white man was bound to respect."[31] On this basis, Taney denied Dred Scott's citizenship and, therefore, his standing to sue in federal court.

Taney's ruling violated established legal precedent on several issues. Case law made clear that states had indeed recognized state citizenship for free people of color. On that point alone, Scott should have had legal standing to sue under the diversity of citizenship clause in the Constitution. Taney's ruling also ignored precedent on the issue of free black citizenship that suggested that federal citizenship derived from state citizenship. In sum, Taney's ruling took the most extreme proslavery, racist position on the issue of black citizenship and attempted to enshrine it in law through judicial review. Taney's revisionist opinion on the issue of citizenship, coupled with his invalidation of the Missouri Compromise line, provoked an uproar in the North that had significant ramifications for the coming of the Civil War.

Taney's decision in *Dred Scott v. Sandford* attempted to conclude a national conversation over race and citizenship that had erupted during the Missouri debates of 1820 and 1821. Forty-seven years earlier, Northern congressmen had attempted to stall Missouri statehood by rejecting its constitution, a document that clearly violated the Privileges and Immunities Clause of the U.S. Constitution by excluding free people of color from the state. Southerners, sensing the long-term ramifications of a debate over slavery, race, and citizenship, responded by strengthening the defenses of their regime by denying black citizenship. The issue remained unsettled, though in the intervening years state governments slowly eroded the rights of free blacks. Finally, in 1857, the Supreme Court's ruling in the Dred Scott case finished what the proslavery regime started years earlier in the second Missouri controversy.

NOTES

1. David Waldstreicher, ed., *John Quincy Adams: Diaries, I: 1779–1821*, 2 vols. (New York: Library of America, 2017), I: 545.

2. Robert Pierce Forbes, *The Missouri Compromise and Its Aftermath: Slavery and the Meaning of America* (Chapel Hill: University of North Carolina Press, 2007), 110–11.

3. For the conversation between Adams and Calhoun, see Waldstreicher, ed., *Diaries*, I: 543–45.

4. Joseph Story, *A Familiar Exposition of the Constitution of the United States* (New York: Harper & Brothers, 1840), 242.

5. Alexander Hamilton, "The Federalist No. 80," in Jacob Cooke, ed., *The Federalist* (Middletown, CT: Wesleyan University Press, 1961), 537.

6. Jonathan Elliot, *The debates, resolutions, and other proceedings in convention, on the adoption of the federal Constitution, as recommended by the general convention at Philadelphia*, 4 vols. (Washington: n.p., 1827-1830), 1:90.

7. Don E. Fehrenbacher, *The Dred Scott Case: Its Significance in American Law and Politics* (New York: Oxford University Press, 1978), 65.

8. *Journal of the Continental Congress, 1774–1789*, 34 vols. (Washington, D.C.: Government Printing Office, 1904–1937), XI: 652.

9. Richard Peters, ed., *The Public Statutes at Large of the United States of America* (Boston: Charles C. Little and James Brown, 1845), II: 205.

10. Peters, ed., *The Public Statutes at Large*, I: 103, 414.

11. John Codman Hurd, *The Law of Freedom and Bondage in the United States*, 2 vols. (Boston: Little, Brown & Company, 1858–1862), II: 14.

12. Hurd, *Law of Freedom and Bondage*, II: 14n1.

13. Hurd, *Law of Freedom and Bondage*, II: 5, 20, 78, 95, 117, 146, 158.

14. George Dangerfield, *The Awakening of American Nationalism, 1815–1828* (New York: Harper and Row, 1965), 130.

15. *Annals of Congress*, Senate, 16th Cong., 2d Sess., 26. Italics added.

16. *Annals of Congress*, Senate, 16th Cong., 2d Sess., 48.

17. *Annals of Congress*, Senate, 16th Cong., 2d Sess., 48.

18. *Annals of Congress*, Senate, 16th Cong., 2d Sess., 51–77.

19. *Annals of Congress*, Senate, 16th Cong., 2d Sess., 105.

20. *Annals of Congress*, Senate, 16th Cong., 2d Sess., 113.

21. *Annals of Congress*, Senate, 16th Cong., 2d Sess., 96.

22. *Annals of Congress*, House, 16th Cong., 2d Sess., 455.

23. *Annals of Congress*, House, 16th Cong., 2d Sess., 1134.

24. *Annals of Congress*, House, 16th Cong., 2d Sess., 1134.

25. *Annals of Congress*, House, 16th Cong., 2d Sess., 1135–36.

26. Forbes, *The Missouri Compromise and Its Aftermath*, 114.

27. *Annals of Congress*, House, 16th Cong., 2d Sess., 1228.

28. Waldstreicher, ed., *Diaries*, I: 596.

29. *Official Opinions of the Attorneys General of the United States* (Washington: Government Printing Office, 1852), I: 506–09.

30. Quoted in Fehrenbacher, *The Dred Scott Case*, 70.

31. For Taney's opinion, see Benjamin C. Howard, *Report of the Decision of the Supreme Court of the United States and the Opinions of the Judges Thereof in the Case of Dred Scott versus John F. A. Sandford* (Washington: C. Wendell, 1857), 5-60; quoted material appears on 13.

CHAPTER THREE

The Guarantee Clause

John Eastman

> "The United States shall guarantee to every State in this Union a Republican Form of Government, and shall protect each of them against Invasion; and on Application of the Legislature, or of the Executive (when the Legislature cannot be convened) against domestic Violence."
>
> [Article IV, Section 4]

ONE OF THE key arguments raised during the debate in Congress over the admission of Missouri was whether the Republican Guarantee Clause of Article IV, Section 4 of the Constitution allowed (or even *required*) Congress to deny admission if Missouri's Constitution permitted slavery. Or, phrased differently, would the existence of slavery mean that the new government being proposed would not be "republican" in form, and therefore a violation of the constitutional guarantee that the United States was obligated to make?

Missouri was not, of course, the first territory that permitted slavery to have sought admission to the union, and neither was it the first to seek admission as a slave state; ten other states had been admitted prior to it, including five that expressly allowed or acknowledged slavery.[1] Kentucky, Mississippi, and Alabama went so far as to prohibit the legislature from passing laws emancipating slaves without the consent of their owners, or preventing emigrants from bringing slaves with them into the state.[2] It is therefore a bit odd that the argument over whether the Constitution's Guarantee Clause actually prohibited Congress from admitting a new state that permitted slavery first arose in the debate over Missouri's admission. The delicate compromises over slavery made in order to effect the adoption of the federal Constitution in 1787 can help us understand why that was the case. A full exploration of this aspect of the Missouri admission debate can also help one understand the distinction between the *principles* of the Constitution and its *compromises,* and the compatibility of the former, though not the latter, with the principles of the nation's founding charter, the Declaration of Independence.

The Declaration is therefore an appropriate place to begin. It's famous maxims, rooted in both "the Laws of Nature and of Nature's God,"[3] define the theoretical foundations of the American regime. The fact that "all men are created equal" is asserted as a self-evident truth.[4] What that meant, for Jefferson as well as the other founders who universally subscribed to this revolutionary principle, was that no man was so superior to another as to have a warrant to rule the other without his consent. Or, as Jefferson wrote with his characteristic flair on the eve of his death on the fiftieth anniversary of the signing of the Declaration of Independence, "the mass of mankind has not been born with saddles on their backs, nor a favored few booted and spurred, ready to ride them legitimately."[5] For that reason, and as a necessary corollary to the self-evident truth of human equality, the "just powers" of government must be derived "from the consent of the governed," and the only legitimate purpose of government is to secure the "unalienable rights" with which each equal human being is endowed by his "Creator," including the rights to "life," to "*liberty,*" and to "the pursuit of happiness."[6]

Slavery is the antithesis of equality and consent—self-evidently so. And it denies to a class of human beings their God-given equal entitlement to liberty. This was well understood by the entirety of the founding generation, even those leading lights like Jefferson, Washington, and Madison who themselves owned slaves, an ignominious inherited patrimony from their colonial forebears. But to see how the mandate of consent, derived from the self-evident truth of human equality, found its way into the Constitution's Republican Guarantee Clause, where it was relied on by slavery's opponents during the Missouri admission debate, requires a bit of historical foundation.

In 1783, after years of wrangling over the disposition of the western lands, Virginia ceded to the United States her claims to all land northwest of the Ohio River, a tract of land that would eventually become the states of Ohio, Indiana, Illinois, Michigan, and Wisconsin. The terms of the Virginia Act of Cession, which were scrupulously followed by Congress in the years to come, included this provision: "that the States so formed shall be distinct *republican* States."[7]

"The distinguishing feature" of a republican form of government, the Supreme Court would later acknowledge, "is the right of the people to choose their own officers for governmental administration, and pass their own laws in virtue of the legislative power reposed in representative bodies, whose legitimate acts may be said to be those of the people themselves."[8] In other words, in an extended territory, republican government is the *means* by which the Declaration's *principle* of consent by the governed is implemented. And because the principle of consent is mandated by the self-evidence of the proposition that all men are created equal, the constitutional guarantee of a republican form of government is analytically incompatible with the existence of slavery. As James Madison, himself a slave-owner, stated early in the federal constitutional convention of 1787, "Where slavery exists the Republican Theory becomes still more fallacious."[9]

This conclusion, logically compelled by the nature of the matter, was given effect in the Northwest Ordinance, the ordinance adopted by the Continental Congress on July 13, 1787, "for the government of the territory of the United States northwest of the river Ohio" or, in other words, for the territory that had been ceded to the United States by Virginia in 1783. Article VI of that Ordinance provided:

> There shall be neither slavery nor involuntary servitude in the said territory, otherwise than in the punishment of crime, whereof the party shall have been duly convicted. . . .[10]

The preamble to the Ordinance makes clear that the prohibition on slavery was not adopted simply because, as some historians would later argue, the soil and climate of the region would not support a slave economy. On the contrary, the preamble demonstrates that the antislavery provision was mandated both by the requirement in the Virginia Act of Cession that the new states be "republican," and by the *principles* upon which the nation and existing states had been founded, namely, the principles of the Declaration of Independence:

> And for extending the fundamental principles of civil and religious liberty, which form the basis whereon these republics [i.e. the existing states], their laws and constitutions, are erected; to fix and establish those principles as the basis of all laws, constitutions, and governments, which forever hereafter shall be formed in the said territory; to provide, also, for the establishment of States, and permanent government therein, and for their admission to a share in the Federal councils on an equal footing with the original States, at as early periods as may be consistent with the general interest: It is hereby ordained and declared, by the authority aforesaid, that the following articles shall be considered as articles of compact, between the original States and the people and States in the said territory, and forever remain unalterable, unless by common consent. . . .[11]

In other words, the antislavery article, like the other of the Ordinance's six articles, was to be considered an "article of compact" that was "forever . . . unalterable" unless by the common consent of the original States and the people and States in the new territory because it was mandated by the *fundamental principles* of civil and religious liberty upon which the existing States were founded and which were to serve as the foundation of government in the new States as well. Significantly, this provision was unanimously supported by the States at the time, slave-holding as well as free.[12]

When the eastern portion of the territory petitioned for statehood in 1802, Congress mandated in the Ohio Enabling Act both that the new State's constitution and government "shall be republican, and not repugnant to the ordinance of the thirteenth of July, one thousand seven hundred and eighty-seven, between the original States and the people and States of the territory northwest of the river Ohio."[13] The people of Ohio (and subsequently the people of each of the other States carved out of the Northwest Territory) complied with that mandate by incorporating into Article VIII, Section 2 of their new constitutions the requirement that "[t]here shall be neither slavery nor involuntary servitude in this State, otherwise than for the punishment of crimes, whereof the party shall have been duly convicted."[14] This provision was necessary, according to the Ohio constitution, in order "That the general, great, and essential principles of liberty and free government may be recognized, and forever unalterably established."[15] Section 1 of the same Article contained a litany of principles drawn from the Declaration of Independence: the equality of all men; the doctrine of inalienable rights, including the rights to life, liberty, property, and the pursuit of happiness; the requirement of consent; and the right to alter or abolish governments when necessary to effect the legitimate ends of government. Moreover, section 1 expressly tied these principles to the idea of "republican" government, which was the mandate in the Virginia Act of Cession:

> That all men are born equally free and independent, and have certain natural, inherent, and unalienable rights, amongst which are the enjoying and defending life and liberty, acquiring, possessing, and protecting property, and pursuing and obtaining happiness and safety; and every free republican government being founded on their sole authority, and organized for the great purpose of protecting their rights and liberties and securing their independence; to effect these ends, they have at all times a complete power to alter, reform, or abolish their government, whenever they may deem it necessary.[16]

In short, the mandate in the Virginia Act of Cession that any new States formed in the northwest territory be "republican" was rooted in the Declaration's statement of principles of human equality, inalienable rights, and the necessity of the consent of the governed. That mandate was then subsequently codified in the Northwest Ordinance's prohibition on slavery, and more broadly in the Constitution's Republican Guarantee Clause, as we will see.

The force and full import of the Northwest Ordinance was not long in coming, particularly in the South. When North Carolina ceded its western lands—present-day Tennessee—to the United States in 1789, it did so on condition that Congress would govern the area "in a manner similar to that which they support in the government west of the Ohio," protecting "the inhabitants against any enemies" and never barring or depriving them "of any privileges which the people in that territory west of the Ohio enjoy."[17] Unlike the Virginia cession of several years earlier, though, the North Carolina cession contained a proviso: "*Provided always,* That no regulations made or to be made by Congress shall tend to emancipate slaves."[18] Congress accepted North Carolina's conditions, and promptly provided by law for territorial government in the areas south of the Ohio River that followed the Northwest Ordinance "except so far as is otherwise provided in the conditions expressed" in the North Carolina cession—in other words, except for the prohibition on slavery.[19]

The condition for protecting slavery contained in the North Carolina cession was repeated by South Carolina and Georgia when those states ceded land that would eventually become the states of Alabama and Mississippi. The Georgia cession, for example, specifically required that the Northwest Ordinance "shall, in all its parts, extend to the territory contained in the present act of cession, *that article only excepted which forbids slavery*."[20] Following the South Carolina cession, Congress authorized the President to establish a territorial government for the Mississippi Territory, "in all respects similar to that now exercised in the territory northwest of the Ohio, *excepting and excluding the last article of the [Northwest Ordinance]*."[21] As Representative Thomas Forrest of Pennsylvania acknowledged, "This, the State of Georgia had a right to except, the territory being within the chartered bounds of the State of Georgia; and, of course, within the limits of the old United States."[22]

The States admitted to the Union out of these territories—Tennessee, Mississippi, and Alabama, as well as Kentucky, which was originally part of Virginia—were thus all exempted from the antislavery provision of the Northwest Ordinance, yet they were nevertheless admitted as though they were in compliance with the Republican Guarantee Clause. Kentucky was admitted to statehood, for example, despite a provision in Article IX of its 1792 Constitution restricting the ability of the legislature even to emancipate slaves. Kentucky itself dealt with the facial contradiction with the Declaration's equality principle by simply "declaring" in Article XII, section 1 that "all men, *when they form a social compact*, are equal"—a far cry from the self-evident proposition that all men are created equal contained in the Declaration of Independence.[23] Similarly, the Mississippi and Alabama Enabling Acts of 1817 and 1819, respectively, provided that the new governments, "when formed, shall be republican, and not repugnant to the principles of the [Northwest Ordinance], *so far as the same has been extended to the said territory by the articles of agreement between the United*

States and the State of Georgia, or of the Constitution of the United States."[24] Both States complied with the terms of their respective enabling acts with constitutions that, like Kentucky's, not only permitted slavery but severely restricted the ability of the legislature even to emancipate slaves; and both States' own Declarations of Rights recognized only that "all *freemen*, when they form a social compact, are equal in rights."[25]

As should be clear, these subtle restatements of the Declaration's equality principle were made not because slavery was thought compatible with the Declaration, but precisely because it was understood that slavery was *not* compatible with the proposition that all men are created equal. Alexander Stephens would confirm this point in his Cornerstone Speech, delivered after the South had seceded but before the Civil War had begun with the firing on Fort Sumter:

> The prevailing ideas entertained by [Jefferson] and by most of the leading statesmen of the time of the formation of the old constitution, were that the enslavement of the African was in violation of the laws of nature: that it was wrong in principle, socially, morally, and politically.[26]

When Congress admitted Mississippi to statehood in 1817, it noted in the Act of Admission that Mississippi's Constitution was "republican and *in conformity to the principles of the Northwest Ordinance*."[27] Apparently, someone forgot to read all the way through to the end of the Northwest Ordinance, where Article VI expressly prohibited slavery. The mistake was corrected when Alabama was admitted two years later, for in the Alabama Act of Admission, Congress recognized only that the Alabama constitution "is republican, and in conformity to the principles of the [Northwest Ordinance], *so far as the same have been extended to the said territory by the articles of agreement between the United States and the state of Georgia*."[28]

In light of these actions by Congress, one might contend that it simply did not believe that the Republican Guarantee Clause had anything to say about slavery or equality. A better reading—given the countervailing precedent in the Northwest Territory—is that these States, carved as they were out of original States, were all entitled to avail themselves of the Constitution's compromises with slavery to the same extent as were the original States whence they came, and were to that extent exempt from the republican principle that had been applied to the Northwest Territory States. In other words, with respect to these States, Congress was duty bound—constitutionally, as well as contractually by virtue of the cession agreements—*not* to consider the conflict between slavery and the constitutional command that each State have a republican form of government.[29]

James Madison makes the same point, albeit obliquely, in *Federalist* No. 43. There, he contends that the authority given to Congress by the Republican Guarantee Clause "extends no further than to a guaranty of a republican form of government, which supposes a pre-existing government of the form which is to be guaranteed. As long, therefore, as the existing republican forms are continued by the States, they are guaranteed by the Federal Constitution."[30] Congress could not challenge the existing governments' countenance of slavery as un-republican, but had to "suppose," or presume, the contrary. The effect of the several cession acts was to extend that presumption to the new States formed from the original beneficiaries of that presumption.

It appears, however, that Madison himself thought slavery incompatible with the Republican Guarantee Clause, though, later in the same *Federalist* paper, he suggests that the participation of former slaves in the political process would make a government more republican:

> I take no notice of an unhappy species of population abounding in some of the States, who during the calm of regular government are sunk below the level of men; but who in the tempestuous scenes of civil violence may emerge into the human character, and give a superiority of strength to any party with which they may associate themselves.
>
> In cases where it may be doubtful on which side justice lies, what better umpires could be desired by two violent factions, flying to arms and tearing a State to pieces, than the representatives of confederate States not heated by the local flame? To the impartiality of Judges they would unite the affection of friends.[31]

The passage is a model of studied ambiguity. Madison leads his readers to believe, without actually saying, that a slave insurrection would allow a state to call on the national government for assistance, but he also subtly suggests that "justice," and hence the stronger republican claim, would lie with those who emerged from slavery, a condition in which they were treated "below the level of men," into the "human character," which is to say, into a position of natural equality, entitled to the same inalienable rights and requirement that they be governed only by their consent as were the people who formed the existing government. In any event, the passage clearly shows Madison applying the Republican Guarantee Clause to the slavery question.

The same idea is at work in the Northwest Ordinance as well. Its antislavery article, Article VI, contains a proviso, elided over above:

> [P]rovided always, that any person escaping into the same [i.e., the Northwest Territory], from whom labor or service is lawfully claimed in any one of the original states, such fugitive may be lawfully reclaimed and conveyed to the person claiming his or her labor or service as aforesaid.[32]

As the emphasized words make clear, the obligation to return fugitive slaves expressly extended only to slaves escaping from the "original states." Article I, section 9 of the United States Constitution contains a similar limitation: "The migration or importation of such persons as any of the states *now existing* shall think proper to admit shall not be prohibited by the Congress prior to the year 1808."[33]

THE DEBATE OVER THE ADMISSION OF NEW STATES CARVED OUT OF THE LOUISIANA TERRITORY ACQUIRED FROM FRANCE

If the above analysis is correct—that the founders codified the Declaration's principles in the Republican Guarantee Clause, but that those principles had limited operation in the original States because of the Constitution's compromises with slavery—we should expect to see the conflict between the Republican Guarantee *principle* and the slavery *compromise* come to a head as slave-holding States that were not carved from original States began seeking admission to the Union. That came about in short order, once the United States purchased the Louisiana Territory from France in

1803. Because this was new territory rather than territory ceded to the national government by existing States,[34] it was not entitled to the proslavery contractual presumption, derived from the various deeds of cession by existing States, from which Kentucky, Tennessee, Mississippi, and Alabama had benefited (or would soon benefit). Instead, its claim to admission was governed by the terms of the treaty between the United States and France, which provided:

> The inhabitants of the ceded territory shall be incorporated in the Union of the United States, and admitted as soon as possible, according to the principles of the Federal constitution, to the enjoyment of all the rights, advantages and immunities of citizens of the United States.[35]

Just what those *principles* were would soon give rise to one of the most profound debates in American history.

Predictably, the first challenge came when the southern portion of the Louisiana Territory, the Orleans district, sought admission in 1811.[36] Section 3 of the Louisiana Enabling Act authorized the people of that district—present-day Louisiana—to adopt a constitution and to form a State government, "*Provided,* The constitution to be formed, in virtue of the authority herein given, shall be republican, and consistent with the constitution of the United States; that it shall contain the fundamental principles of civil and religious liberty."[37] Section 4 provided that "the said state shall be admitted into the Union upon the same footing with the original states."[38]

Here was the conflict presented in textual terms. Louisiana's new constitution was, on the one hand, to be "republican" and to contain the "fundamental principles of civil liberty," and, on the other hand, the state was to be admitted on an equal footing with the existing states. The guarantee of a republican form of government applied to all the existing States, of course (albeit with the slavery presumption discussed above). But the guarantees of civil and religious liberty were not imposed on the existing States by the federal Constitution (unless, of course, those "fundamental principles" are subsumed under the Republican Guarantee Clause). Was it permissible, then, for Congress to impose such terms as a condition of statehood? Indeed, could it impose *any* terms on new States and still comply with the Equal Footing doctrine?[39]

The admission of Ohio some years earlier stood as strong precedent for an affirmative answer to that question. The Virginia Act of Cession had included the seeds of the equal footing requirement. New States admitted from the ceded Northwest Territory, such as Ohio, were to have "the *same rights* of sovereignty, freedom, and independence as the other States."[40] That condition was codified in the Northwest Ordinance as follows: "whenever any of the said States shall have sixty thousand free inhabitants therein, such State shall be admitted, by its delegates, into the Congress of the United States, *on an equal footing* with the original States, in all respects whatever. . . ."[41] But there was a proviso; "The constitution and government, so to be formed, shall be republican, and in conformity to the principles contained in these articles. . . ." including the article prohibiting slavery.[42] The new States to be formed in the Northwest Territory were thus expressly guaranteed the right to enter the union on an "equal footing" with the original states, but the prohibition on slavery was to remain "unalterable," established as the basis for "all laws, constitutions, and governments" that would thereafter be formed in the territory.[43]

In other words, Congress did not see any incompatibility between the "equal footing" requirement and the requirements that the new State constitutions be "republican" and prohibit slavery. Moreover, it was very strong precedent. As Representative Taylor noted during the Missouri Admission debate, the Northwest Ordinance had, during the Continental Congress, passed unanimously by the States and, tellingly, the antislavery provision was actually introduced by a delegate from Virginia.[44] Those actions proved, he added, that Virginia, which had ceded the territory, did not think prohibiting slavery in any new State formed in the ceded territory was contrary to the additional mandate in the Act of Cession that the new States be admitted on equal terms with the original.[45]

But instead of that precedent being viewed as definitively resolving the question, some members of Congress began to question whether the conditions Congress had imposed on Ohio's admission were themselves constitutional. As Representative Fuller noted, no one had objected to the antislavery conditions at the time they were adopted in 1787, re-adopted in 1789, or included in the enabling acts of Ohio, Indiana, and Illinois in 1802, 1816, and 1818. "Those who now call into question the right of restriction are obliged to contend, as a consequence of their new doctrine, that the ordinance was unconstitutional, and that the restriction of slavery by the States northwest of the river Ohio being stipulated and enacted on such a basis is therefore a mere nullity, and may be rightfully dispensed with at the pleasure of those States."[46] That, ultimately, was the ground on which the Southern argument had to stand. *Any* condition imposed on admission could not be binding after statehood lest the new State be admitted on less than equal terms with the existing States.[47]

During the Louisiana admission debate, the thorny theoretical problem arose not over slavery—which was not addressed in the Louisiana constitution at all—but over some territory known as West Florida,[48] over which the United States and Spain were having a dispute. Congress wanted to include West Florida in the new state of Louisiana, but also wanted to keep its options open should the President reach a settlement with Spain that recognized Spain's claim to some or all of West Florida. Thus, Congress sought to impose two conditions on Louisiana's admission: that the title of West Florida would remain subject to future negotiations, and that the people then living in West Florida would, in the meantime, be entitled to representation in the Louisiana legislature.

Perhaps appreciating the full import of the principle that was about to be applied for the first time to a Southern slave State, South Carolina Representative John C. Calhoun objected on the ground that the "proposed amendment would be ingrafting the principle of Territorial government on a State government, to which it was wholly inapplicable."[49] Congress then shifted gears, imposing the conditions on the grant of land to Louisiana rather than its admission to statehood.[50] Although that left in place the condition regarding civil and religious liberty, and others (such as the requirement that the government be conducted in English), the immediate issue of concern, the status of West Florida, having been resolved, the more fundamental debate was left to another day. Louisiana was admitted in 1812, with a constitution that declared in its preamble that it was adopted "In order to secure to all the citizens thereof the enjoyment of the right of life, liberty and property."[51] In its Act of Admission, Congress simply stated "That the said state shall be, and is hereby declared to be one, of the United States of America, and admitted into the Union on an equal footing with the original states, in all respects whatever."[52]

The next portion of the Louisiana Territory to seek admission to statehood was Missouri. Mississippi and Alabama had by then been admitted, with constitutions permitting slavery that Congress was obligated to recognize because of the terms of the South Carolina and Georgia cessions. Indiana and Illinois had also been admitted, and in the latter case the arguments pro and con about the power of Congress to impose conditions on admission were honed (and brought into line with the politics of slavery).[53]

The Illinois Enabling Act, like its predecessors in Ohio and Indiana, mandated that the constitution and State government adopted by Illinois "shall be republican, and not repugnant to the" Northwest Ordinance, including the prohibition on slavery.[54] But Article VI of the Illinois Constitution of 1818 provided only that "[n]either slavery nor involuntary servitude shall *hereafter* be introduced into this State, otherwise than for punishment of crimes, whereof the party shall have been duly convicted."[55] Moreover, it specifically permitted slave labor to be used in the Shawneetown salt mines for seven years, and it recognized lifelong indentured servitude.[56]

New York Representative James Tallmadge opposed Illinois's admission to statehood because these provisions permitted slavery, in contravention of the condition in the Illinois Enabling Act mandating that the State constitution conform to the principles of the Northwest Ordinance, which he asserted were in turn required by the terms of the Virginia cession in 1783.[57] Mississippi representative Poindexter provided a three-fold response: First, the Illinois provision was not materially different than what had already been approved in Ohio;[58] second, that Illinois "virtually" complied with the terms of the Northwest Ordinance; and third, that Congress could not prevent a state from altering its constitution, even changing provisions that were enacted because required as a condition on admission to statehood.[59] Kentucky representative Anderson weighed in as well, contending that the antislavery provision was imposed by Congress, not the Virginia cession, and could therefore be altered with the consent of Congress. "The conditions reserved by Virginia on making the cession," he argued, "were that a certain number of States should be erected from the Territory, and all existing rights of the people preserved."[60] Among those "rights," he contended, was the right to own slaves, since slavery was already in existence in the Illinois portion of the Northwest Territory at the time of the Virginia cession.[61]

What Representative Anderson failed to mention, of course, was that the Virginia cession also required that the states admitted from the territory were to be "distinct *republican* States."[62] Representative Tallmadge apparently thought that the "republican" condition barred the introduction of slavery, or at the very least the slavery prohibition was a solemn pledge made by Congress so simultaneously given as to amount to a compact with Virginia. Moreover, he contended "that the interest, honor, and faith of the nation, required it scrupulously to guard against slavery's passing into a territory where they have power to prevent its entrance."[63]

Illinois was ultimately admitted to statehood, and the exchange recounted here was too brief to determine definitively whether admission was granted because Congress believed the Illinois constitution "virtually" complied with the antislavery requirement, or that the Virginia cession prohibited an antislavery requirement, or even that Congress was simply without power to impose any conditions on statehood. But in the brief exchange, the conflict between the republican principle and a vested "right" to own slaves was squarely broached. It would soon get a much more complete airing when Missouri knocked at Congress's door.

THE MISSOURI ADMISSION DEBATE

On February 13, 1819, during the second session of the 15th Congress, Representative Tallmadge renewed the effort he had begun during the debate over admission of Illinois with the following proposed amendment to the Missouri Enabling Act:

> And provided, That the further introduction of slavery or involuntary servitude be prohibited, except for the punishment of crimes, whereof the party shall have been fully convicted; and that all children born within the said state, after the admission thereof into the Union, shall be free at the age of twenty-five years.[64]

Although some debate occurred on the day Tallmadge introduced his amendment, including an important speech by Speaker of the House Henry Clay, the Annals of Congress do not include its substance. Two days later, though, the House again resolved itself into a Committee of the Whole House to debate Tallmadge's amendment.

After extensive (and heated) debate, the House eventually approved Tallmadge's amendment,[65] but the Senate refused to go along,[66] and neither house would back down from its position.[67] The dispute over the admission of Missouri was therefore carried over to the 16th Congress, where it was renewed with equal vigor, this time centered on a proposal by New York representative John Taylor to ban slavery in the western territories altogether.[68] During the debates in the 15th and 16th Congresses, which were variously described as "long and animated," "stamped with all the marks of eternity,"[69] that "agitated and convulsed" the House,[70] both sides offered up every conceivable argument under the sun—moral, legal and constitutional, practical, predictive, even borderline extortionate with threats of violence and civil war. Some of the contentions made by advocates on each side were simplistic, self-contradictory, or even frivolous. Some supporters of the restriction on slavery contended, for example, that Congress had the power to impose the restriction by virtue of the "general welfare" language in the Constitution's preamble or in the Spending Clause of Article I, Section 8, a position that would have rendered superfluous the remainder of the carefully-crafted enumerated powers, while opponents of the restriction argued at different times that the strong precedent of the States that had been admitted from the Northwest Territory with an antislavery provision was irrelevant because the Virginia Act of Cession required the clause and, contradictorily, forbade the imposition of any conditions.

Some of the arguments were, however, extremely thoughtful, even profound. The most significant of these centered on whether the discretionary authority to admit new States into the Union, provided to Congress in Article IV, Section 3 of the Constitution, allowed Congress to impose an antislavery condition on admission, and whether the mandate in Article IV, Section 4 that the "United States shall guarantee to every State in this Union a Republican Form of Government" even *required* such a condition.

Representative John Taylor of New York, who would succeed Henry Clay as Speaker of the House a year later, opened the discussion by posing the following two questions:

> First. Has Congress power to require of Missouri a Constitutional prohibition against the further introduction of slavery, as a condition of her admission into the Union?
> Second. If the power exist [sic], is it wise to exercise it?[71]

With respect to the first, he noted that the Congress had the power under Article IV, Section 3 of the Constitution to "make all needful rules and regulations respecting the territory . . . of the United States." It also has the power under the same section to admit the territory to Statehood. These are alternative powers, he claimed, and the decision whether to admit a new State or continue it as a territory "is committed to the sound discretion of Congress." He then drew what he believed to be the logical conclusion from that grant of discretionary authority: "But if Congress has the power of altogether refusing to admit new States, much more has it the power of prescribing such conditions of admission as may be judged reasonable." And he noted that from the admission of Ohio in 1802 forward to the present, that proposition had never been questioned.[72] Ohio, Indiana, and Illinois had all been admitted with the requirement to comply with the conditions contained in the Northwest Ordinance, specifically including the prohibition on slavery, he noted. Representative Timothy Fuller of Massachusetts would subsequently note that conditions were also placed on the admission of Mississippi and Louisiana (though, admittedly, not a condition prohibiting slavery).[73]

Representative Fuller elaborated on Taylor's argument that Congress had discretion whether or not to admit a new State, and explicitly tied the exercise of that discretion to the Republican Guarantee Clause of Article IV:

> We certainly have a right, and our duty to the nation requires, that we should examine the actual state of things in the proposed State; and, above all, the Constitution expressly makes a republican form of government in the several States a fundamental principle, to be preserved under the sacred guarantee of the National Legislature. [Art. IV, sec. 4].[74]

Tallmadge's amendment, he continued, merely required that slavery be prohibited in Missouri, and he asked whether the amendment implied "anything more than that its constitution shall be republican." Like Madison before him,[75] Fuller argued that "[t]he existence of slavery in any State is so far a departure from republican principles." It was contrary to the principles of the Declaration—both the principle of equality and the inalienable right to liberty: "Since . . . it cannot be denied that slaves are men, it follows that they are in a purely republican government born free, and are entitled to liberty and the pursuit of happiness." Although his speech drew immediate objection from Southern representatives, who noted with particular concern that there may have been slaves listening in the gallery, Fuller stated that he referenced the Declaration "to draw from an authority admitted in all parts of the Union a definition of the basis of republican government." His proposition was straightforward and unassailable: "If, then, all men have equal rights, it can no more comport with the principles of free Government to exclude men of a certain color from the enjoyment of 'liberty and the pursuit of happiness,' than to exclude those who have not attained a certain portion of wealth, or a certain stature of body; or to found the exclusion on any other capricious or accidental circumstance."[76] Fuller repeated those arguments in the next Congress. The power to admit new States, he contended, "could not but include a power and a duty in Congress to ascertain whether the proposed State possessed the character and interior qualities, which should entitle her to admission."[77]

Southern State representatives contested each of these propositions, of course, with both factual and legal arguments. Primarily they argued that, except for the requirement that the new State's constitution be "republican," Congress had no power to impose any conditions on statehood (and on this point, they were joined even by a few Northern State representatives, such as John Holmes of Massachusetts[78] and Henry Baldwin of Pennsylvania[79]), because any such restriction would deny Missouri an "equal footing" with existing States. Some, like Representative (and future Speaker of the House and Supreme Court Justice) Philip Barbour of Virginia, conceded that Congress could ban slavery while Missouri was still a territory,[80] while others, such as Representative Francis Jones of Tennessee, disputed even that. Congress's Article IV power to make regulations for the territory could not contravene the Constitution's grant of the right of a master to his slave, he argued.[81]

Representative Holmes—from Massachusetts, no less—claimed that the ban on slavery contained in Article VI of the Northwest Ordinance only limited slavery while the territory was territory, not once it became a state. That argument was simply impossible to square with the actual text of the Northwest Ordinance, however, though not for want of trying on Holmes's part. The requirement in Article V that the new states "shall be republican, and in conformity to the principles contained in these articles" did not extend to the Article VI ban on slavery, he contended, because (circularly) that ban dealt with an internal police matter and therefore could only apply as long as the territory was subject to the police power of Congress, namely, while it was a territory. He apparently overlooked the language elsewhere in the Ordinance specifying that the Ordinance contained "articles of compact between the original States and the people *and States* in the said Territory," which were to "forever remain unalterable, unless by common consent."[82]

Representative Scott, the delegate from the Missouri Territory, argued that Congress had no power under the Constitution, prior practice, or the terms of the treaty with France to impose conditions on admission. Although he acknowledged that Congress had express authority to ensure that a State constitution did not violate the Republican Guarantee Clause, he contended, based on his reading of Madison's statements in *Federalist* No. 43 referenced above,[83] that the clause only forbade "aristocratic or monarchical innovations."[84] Because a prohibition on slavery did not fall under the authority provided by the Republican Guarantee Clause, he argued, the Ninth and Tenth Amendments expressly reserved authority over slavery to the States.[85]

There was the lynchpin of the dispute. Did the power to admit States give to Congress a less-included power to impose conditions on admission? And even if not, did the Republican Guarantee Clause permit (or even require) Congress to prohibit slavery in new States?

As to the first, the members of Congress hotly disputed whether prior precedent supported the proposition. Various arguments were advanced by Southern representatives (and at least one Northerner) to get around the precedential value of the Northwest Territory States, all three of which had been admitted with a "no-slavery" condition. The antislavery condition was imposed by the Northwest Ordinance, which was adopted by the Continental Congress before the Constitution was ratified and was therefore of no effect, contended Representative Barbour of Virginia and Representative Scott, the delegate from Missouri (without acknowledging that the Ordinance was re-adopted by the First Congress after ratification of the Constitution).[86] And it was imposed without support in (or even contrary to) the Virginia Act of Cession, so was *ultra vires*.[87]

But the Southerners were not consistent on this point. Others, such as Representative Francis Jones of Tennessee, conceded that the United States acquired the Northwest Territory from Virginia "on condition that slaves should not be permitted to go there."[88] Representative Scott contended that because the Virginia Cession required the ban on slavery, the Northwest Ordinance was not evidence that Congress otherwise had the power to impose such a condition itself.[89] But Scott was not even consistent with himself on this point, for later in the debate he contended that the Virginia Cession "did not contain any stipulation either for or against the introduction of slaves."[90]

As with much of the debate, the confusion—or, rather, the horns of the dilemma on which the Southerners found themselves—turned on the meaning of "republican" government. The Virginia Cession mandated that any new States must be "republican," but it did not specifically mention slavery one way or the other. If the "republican" requirement did not support or require the antislavery provision in the Northwest Ordinance, then the fact that such a condition was imposed by Congress in the admission acts of Ohio, Indiana, and Illinois was strong precedent that Congress had the power to impose such conditions. If, on the other hand, slavery was incompatible with the "republican" requirement, as Tallmadge, Fuller, and others contended, then the Virginia Cession did mandate the slavery prohibition, and Southerners could argue, as Representative Scott and others did, that the Northwest Ordinance's prohibition on slavery was simply required by the terms of the Virginia Cession and did not serve as precedent for *congressional* authority. But here the dilemma lay: if the requirement of "republican" government in the Cession is what sustained the antislavery condition imposed on the Northwest Territory States, then the Constitution's own guarantee of republican government in Article

IV would likewise sustain such a condition on Missouri's admission. As Representative Fuller noted, those denying that Congress had authority to impose an antislavery condition on new States claimed that the only power Congress had was to ensure that the new State be republican, but for Fuller, that was sufficient "to authorize the restriction of slavery by the Constitution, as nothing is more easily demonstrated than that the establishment of slavery is a direct violation of the first principle of republican government—political equality."[91]

That dilemma for the Southerners had a parallel dilemma for the Northerners. If, as Tallmadge, Fuller, and others contended, slavery was incompatible with "republican" government and therefore a violation of the Republican Guarantee Clause, did that guarantee not apply as much to the existing slave-holding States as it did to new States? And if it did not apply to the original States, was that not a concession on their part that the Republican Guarantee Clause was not a source of authority to ban slavery in new States?

The response to this dilemma was one of the most profound parts of the overall debate, addressed with greatest clarity by Representative Fuller in the 15th Congress, as he confronted the prudential issue that led to the inclusion of slavery protections in the Constitution in the first place. Rejecting the shouted objection that his position would require the elimination of slavery everywhere, he contended, in a foreshadowing of the argument that President Lincoln would later make,[92] that the "National Legislature could not interfere" with slavery in the original states. But he argued that the Constitution's provisions that protected slavery in those states were "concessions" against the general, "predominant" republican principle "that all men are free, and have an equal right to liberty, and all other privileges." The concessions were necessary not only to "effect a concert of interests" in crafting the new Constitution, but to avoid placing the "political existence" of the Southern states in jeopardy, which would have resulted in "the most fatal consequences" for "both masters and slaves." But as concessions against the general republican principle, they were to be narrowly construed and limited to the existing states. "The States then holding slaves," he added, "are permitted, from the necessity of the case, and for the sake of union, to exclude the republican principle so far, and only so far, as to retain their slaves in servitude, and also their progeny, as had been the usage, until they should think it proper or safe to conform to the pure principle by abolishing slavery." "But the attempt to extend slavery to the new States is in direct violation of the clause which guaranties [sic] a republican form of government to all the States."[93]

Tallmadge himself spoke to the same point. Although he had been unable to participate in the debate in the Committee of the Whole House because he had just "returned from a journey long in extent, and painful in its occasion,"[94] namely, to bury his son, he noted with regret the intensity of the arguments that his amendment had caused. But he rejected the false claims about his position that had given rise to such vitriol. He had, he said, declared at the time that his amendment was "intended to confine its operation to the newly acquired territory across the Mississippi," and he also expressly declared that he "would in no manner intermeddle with the slaveholding States, nor attempt manumission in any one of the original States in the Union."[95] Then he drew the important distinction between the first States admitted to the Union and Missouri: "The States of Kentucky and Tennessee [which were admitted as slave States] were taken off from other States, and were admitted into the Union without condition, because their lands were never owned by the United States."[96]

Representative Taylor echoed Fuller's and Tallmadge's arguments during the debate in the 16th Congress over his own version of the Tallmadge Amendment. Congress had no right to interfere with slavery in the *existing* States, he contended, and he had no intention to challenge the initial compromise.[97] But for him, that was the limit of the Constitution's compromise with slavery. "The extent of this concession was supposed to be seen and clearly understood. It was believed that it could not be carried beyond the then existing States, and, possibly, to the territory in dispute between the United States and Georgia. It did not apply to foreign territory.[98] Representative Forrest of Pennsylvania made the same point. The Constitution "was a compromise to prevent disunion," he argued, but "it was a dereliction of first principles upon which the independence of our country was achieved; it was an acquiescence in the bondage of those of our fellow-men in whose services their possessors conceived they had a property. It was a compromise for the sake of peace, and confined wholly to the then United States, and not extended to the territory possessed or to be acquired."[99]

Predictably, the Southern delegations strenuously objected. Representative Alexander Smyth of Virginia articulated the main objection:

> It has been questioned by some, whether a constitution can be said to be republican, which does not exclude slavery. But we must understand the phrase, "republican form of government," as the people understood it when they adopted the Constitution. . . . It would be perfidious toward them to put on the Constitution a different construction from that which induced them to adopt it. The people of each of the States who adopted the Constitution, except Massachusetts, owned slaves; yet they certainly considered their own constitutions to be republican.
>
> * * * * *
>
> Sir, if this proposition is adopted, it will be regarded hereafter as an exercise of the power to guaranty a republican form of government to every State in the Union. You are about to admit a State, and you require her to insert in her constitution a clause against slavery. Will it not seem that you have done this by your authority to guaranty a republican form of government? I think it will; for you have no other power that seems to warrant prescribing in part the form of the State constitution. If, in the exercise of this power, you may require of a new State to insert in her constitution a clause against slavery, you may, under the same authority, require an old State to add such a clause to her constitution. Thus you may require of the old States to exclude slavery, or provide for its abolition. The slaveholding States must make common cause with Missouri; for the recognition of such a power in this Government would be fatal to them.[100]

Representative Holmes (of Massachusetts) had a similar take.

> [A]n original State, having all political powers not surrendered by the Constitution, and the power to establish or prohibit slavery never having been surrendered, and new States, on their admission, standing on the same footing, it follows, consequently and irresistibly, that a new State, on admission, has the political power to establish or prohibit slavery. Missouri, on being admitted into the Union, could say

> to Congress, this power was never delegated to you, nor prohibited to me; I am therefore protected by the Constitution in its exercise.[101]

Representative Barbour raised a similar objection in his effort to avoid the precedent of the Northwest Territory States. Apparently recognizing that the Northwest Ordinance was re-enacted by the First Congress after the Constitution had been ratified (and that his initial argument of irrelevance because adopted by the Continental Congress was therefore fatally flawed[102]), he then argued that the Ordinance's imposition of conditions on statehood admission was wrong, because *Congress* could not impose such a restriction, and *Virginia* had not. But to make this argument, he had to sidestep the fact that the Virginia Cession required that any new States be "republican," and instead focus exclusively on the fact that the Virginia Cession required the recognition of equal sovereignty of new States formed in the territory. Such a recognition would, in his view, prevent the imposition of conditions on the new States lest they not be admitted on an "equal footing" with the original.

Neither Smyth, nor Holmes, nor Barbour, nor anyone else addressed head-on the argument that the Constitution's compromise with slavery was limited to the original States that were its beneficiaries, and therefore need not (indeed, could not) be extended to new States that were not. Nor could they, in logic and principle, rebut that argument.

The same issue, albeit in slightly different terms, divided the competing sides when addressing the importance of the language in the Treaty with France by which the United States acquired the Louisiana Territory. Representative Jones of Tennessee, Missouri delegate Scott, and others contended that the Treaty required that new States "shall be admitted."[103] Delegate Scott even claimed that the Treaty also expressly protected slave property, without any appreciation of the irony of resting such an argument on a clause that "protect[ed] the *inhabitants* [of the territory] in the free enjoyment of their *liberty*, property, and religion."[104] Although the Southerners recognized that the Treaty's language also provided that admission be "according to the principles of the Constitution," they failed to address, much less rebut, Representative Fuller's argument that the guarantee of republican government as a prohibition on slavery in new States (though not in the existing ones) was just such a principle.[105] The Treaty's "principles" clause, Fuller had contended, meant "that the republican principles of our Constitution are to govern us in the admission of this, as well as all the new States, in the national family."[106] Then, forcefully rebutting Delegate Scott's claim that the Treaty protected a slaveowner's "property" right in his slaves, Taylor argued: "Is it then pretended that, notwithstanding the declaration in our bill of rights, 'that all men are created equal,'[107] one individual can have a vested property not only in his fellow man, but also in generations not yet called into existence?" Or was it really the case that Congress "cannot provide for the gradual abolition of slavery within its limits, nor establish those civil regulations which naturally flow from self-evident truth?" He thought the answer to those questions had long since been decided by "the practice of nations and the common sense of mankind."[108]

Tallmadge's amendment in the 15th Congress, and Taylor's in the 16th, carried the day in the House, but the Senate, with its equal divide between slave and free states, refused to go along. Even appeals such as that made by Representative Arthur Livermore of New Hampshire, to avoid hypocrisy, were unavailing. "If there is any sincerity in our profession, that slavery is an ill, tolerated only from necessity," he argued, "let us not, while we feel that ill, shun the cure which consists only in an honest avowal that liberty and equal rights are the end and aim of all our institutions, and that to tolerate slavery beyond the narrowest limits prescribed for it in the Constitution, is a perversion of them all."[109]

In the end, the House bowed to the Senate's recalcitrance and adopted the compromise that allowed Missouri to be admitted as a slave State (counterbalanced by the admission of Maine as a free State). Representative Kinsey of New Jersey, who had been a House delegate to the Conference Committee, argued in support of the compromise that it banned slavery in 90 percent of the Louisiana Territory, which he believed was a good result.[110] But it was an unholy compromise. Slavery opponents compromised on the *principle* that the Republican Guarantee Clause forbade the extension of slavery into new States not protected by the Constitution's original compromise with slavery or that imposing such a restriction was otherwise within Congress's authority; Section 4 of the Act required that the new State constitution "shall be republican, and not repugnant to the constitution of the United States," while Section 8 expressly allowed for slavery in the State while otherwise barring it from the rest of the Louisiana Purchase *territory*.[111] Slavery's proponents, on the other hand, could (and eventually would) argue that they had merely acceded to the proposition that most of them had not disputed, namely that Congress could restrict slavery in the territory *as long as it remained a territory*. The arguments that such conditions could not carry over to statehood unfortunately remained as viable after the Missouri Compromise as before, now strengthened by the precedent of Missouri itself—all but guaranteeing that they would come to a head again, as they did thirty years later with the Kansas-Nebraska Act. While the House conferees may have thought they had avoided a calamity, all they really had done was lose what may well have been the best and last opportunity for a peaceful resolution and gradual elimination of the scourge of slavery. Tallmadge's statement near the end of the debate in the 15th Congress highlighted what was at stake: "Now is the time. It must now be met, and the extension of the evil must now be prevented, or the occasion is irrecoverably lost, and the evil can never be contracted."[112] Perhaps the die was already cast by the time Missouri sought admission. Representative Tucker of Virginia claimed toward the end of the debate that the effort to ban slavery in Missouri threatened "not only the peace and welfare of Virginia, in common with all the slaveholding States, but their very political existence."[113] Regardless, Congress did not heed Tallmadge's prescient warning, with catastrophic consequences but forty years later.

NOTES

1. Kentucky in 1792, Tennessee in 1796, Louisiana in 1812, Mississippi in 1817, and Alabama in 1819. *See* Kentucky Constitution of 1792, Article IX, Section 1, reprinted in Francis Newton Thorpe, *The Federal and State Constitutions, Colonial Charters, and other Organic Laws of the States and Territories now or heretofore forming the United States of America*, Vol. III (Washington: Government Printing Office, 1909), 1272; Tennessee Constitution of 1796, Art. III, Sec. 1 (allowing only freemen to vote), Art. XI (Declaration of Rights protecting only "freemen"), in Thorpe, *Federal and State Constitutions*, VI: 3418, 3422; Louisiana Constitution of 1812, Art. II, Sec. 8 (limiting the franchise to freemen), in Thorpe, *Federal and State Constitutions*, III: 1382; Mississippi Constitution of 1817, Art. on Slaves, Sec. 1, in Thorpe, *Federal and State Constitutions*, IV: 2045; Alabama Constitution of 1819, Art. on Slaves, Sec. 1, in Thorpe, *Federal and State Constitutions*, I: 111.

2. Kentucky Const. of 1792, Art. IX, Sec. 1, in Thorpe, *Federal and State Constitutions*, III: 1272; Mississippi Const. of 1817, Art. on Slaves, Sec. 1, in Thorpe, *Federal*

and State Constitutions, IV: 2045; Alabama Const. of 1819, Art. on Slaves, Sec. 1, in Thorpe, *Federal and State Constitutions*, I: 111.

3. Declaration of Independence, paragraph 1.

4. Declaration of Independence, paragraph 2.

5. Thomas Jefferson to Roger Weightman, June 24, 1826, in Paul Leicester Ford, ed., *The Works of Thomas Jefferson*, "Federal Edition," Vol. 10 (New York: G. P. Putnam's Sons, 1904-1905), 390-92.

6. Declaration of Independence, paragraph 2 (emphasis added).

7. Virginia Act of Cession, Sec. 3 (emphasis added), in Thorpe, *Federal and State Constitutions*, II: 955, 956.

8. *Duncan v. McCall*, 139 U.S. 449, 461 (1891).

9. James Madison, June 19, 1787, in Max Farrand, ed., *The Records of the Federal Convention of 1787*, 3 vols. (New Haven: Yale University Press, 1911), I: 318.

10. An Ordinance for the government of the Territory of the United States northwest of the River Ohio (hereinafter Northwest Ordinance 1787), Art. VI in Richard Peters, ed. *The Public Statutes at Large of the United States of America*, 8 vols. (Boston: Charles C. Little and James Brown, 1845), I: 51, 53 note a, readopted 1st Cong., 1st Sess., Ch. VIII, 1 Stat. 50, (Aug. 7, 1789).

11. Northwest Ordinance 1787, Preamble, in Peters, ed., *Statutes*, I: 51, 52 note a.

12. See for example Rep. Taylor's comments on January 27, 1820, in *Annals of Congress*, U.S. House of Representatives, 16th Cong., 1st Sess., 954..

13. Enabling Act for Ohio, Sec. 1, 5, 7th Cong., 1st Sess., in Peters, ed., *Statutes*, II: 173. Congress imposed the same terms on each of the other states that were admitted to the Union from the Northwest Territory: Indiana in 1816, Illinois in 1818, Michigan in 1837, and Wisconsin in 1848.

14. Ohio Constitution of 1802, Art. VIII, Sec. 2, in Thorpe, *Federal and State Constitutions*, V: 2909.

15. Ohio Const., Art. VIII Introduction, in Thorpe, *Federal and State Constitutions*, V: 2909.

16. Ohio Const., Art. VIII, Sec. 1 (emphasis added), in Thorpe, *Federal and State Constitutions*, V: 2909.

17. An Act to accept a cession of the claims of the State of North Carolina to a certain district of western territory, April 2, 1790, in Peters, ed., *Statutes*, I: 106, 108.

18. An Act to accept a cession of the claims of the State of North Carolina, in Peters, ed., *Statutes*, I: 106, 108.

19. An Act for the Government of the Territory of the United States south of the river Ohio, May 26, 1790, Sec. 1, in Peters, ed., *Statutes*, I: 123. It is worth noting that Congress itself, perhaps recognizing that the protection of slavery was contrary to republican principles, did not mention the protection of slavery, but rather chose simply to codify that protection only by referring obliquely to the North Carolina cession document.

20. The Articles of Agreement and Cession [between the United States and Georgia], Art. I, April 24, 1802. In an interesting twist, there was a dispute between Georgia and the United States over ownership of the Mississippi territory.

Pursuant to the U.S. claim of ownership, Congress sought to prohibit the importation of slaves into the Mississippi territory in 1798—ten years before it otherwise would have been allowed to do so under the Importation Clause of Article I, Section 9. See An Act for the amicable settlement of limits with the state of Georgia, and authorizing the establishment of a government in the Mississippi territory, Ch. XXVIII, § 7, April 7, 1798, in Peters, ed., *Statutes,* I: 549, 550 ; see also observations by Rep. Taylor on January 27, 1820, in *Annals of Congress,* House, 16th Cong., 1st Sess., 961.

21. An Act for an amicable settlement of the limits with the State of Georgia, Sec. 3, in Peters, ed., *Statutes,* I: 549, 550. Again, it is worth noting how Congress could not bring itself to mention the word "slavery," but extended the protections mandated by the Georgia and South Carolina cessions only with an oblique reference.

22. *Annals of Congress,* House, 16th Cong., 1st Sess., 1562.

23. Kentucky was even clearer when it adopted a new constitution seven years later, providing, "That all *free* men, when they form a social compact, are equal." Kentucky Const. of 1799, Art. I, Sec. 1.

24. Act of March 1, 1817, in Peters, ed., *Statutes,* III: 348, 349; Act of March 2, 1819, in Peters, ed., *Statutes,* III: 489, 491.

25. Mississippi Const. of 1817, Art. I, Sec. 1 (emphasis added), in Thorpe, *Federal and State Constitutions,* V: 2033; Alabama Const. of 1819, Art. I, Sec. 1 (emphasis added), in Thorpe, *Federal and State Constitutions,* I: 96.

26. "Speech Delivered on the 21st March, 1861, in Savannah, known as 'The Corner Stone Speech,' Reported in the Savannah Republican," in Henry Cleveland, *Alexander H. Stephens, In Public and Private: With Letters and Speeches, Before, During, and Since the War* (Philadelphia: National Publishing Company, 1886), 717–29.

27. Resolution of Dec. 10, 1817, in Thorpe, *Federal and State Constitutions,* IV: 2032.

28. Resolution of Dec. 14, 1819, in Thorpe, *Federal and State Constitutions,* I: 95.

29. During the Missouri admission debate, Representative Tallmadge made the additional argument that Alabama's close proximity to existing slave States, separated only by an "imaginary line," would mean that "the intercourse between slaves and free blacks could not be prevented, and a *servile* war might be the result." He was thus willing to submit to the evil of slavery in Alabama because the evil could not be "safely remed[ied]." *Annals of Congress,* House, 15th Cong., 2d Sess.,1203.

30. *The Federalist* No. 43, in Clinton Rossiter, ed., *The Federalist Papers* (New York: New American Library, 1961), 275.

31. *Federalist* No. 43, in Rossiter, ed. *The Federalist Papers,* 277.

32. Northwest Ordinance, Art. VI, in Peters, ed., *Statutes,* I: 52 n.a.

33. U.S. Const. Art. IV, Sec. 9 (emphasis added). The Constitution's own Fugitive Slave Clause, Art. IV, Sec. 2, cl. 3, is not textually limited to the original states, but the greater power to exclude slaves from new states altogether would render such a protection unnecessary.

34. Territory that was "no part of our ancient domain" is how Representative Taylor described it on January 27, 1820, in the Missouri admission debate. *Annals of Congress,* House, 16th Cong., 1st Sess., 950.

35. Treaty Ceding Louisiana, Art. III, April 30, 1803, in Thorpe, *Federal and State Constitutions*, III: 1359.

36. Indeed, the lines of argument began even earlier, when Congress first sought to establish a provisional government for the new area. As David Currie thoroughly detailed in his book, *The Constitution in Congress: The Jeffersonians, 1801–1829*, (Chicago: University of Chicago Press, 2001), 99–114, Northern Federalists appealed to the Republican Guarantee Clause and to the "spirit" of the Constitution in opposing the plan for temporary government in the territory, which essentially combined legislative, executive, and judicial power into the hands of a single governor appointed by and serving under the direction of the President. In n. 189, Currie cites a speech by Rep. Elliott in *Annals of Congress*, House, 11th Cong., 3d Sess., 1056;and Everett S. Brown, ed., *William Plumer's Memorandum of Proceedings in the United States Senate, 1803–1807* (New York: Macmillan, 1923), 136. Ironically, it was the Southern Democrats who argued that Congress had plenary power over the territories, a position that they would soon repudiate when Congress set its plenary power sights on slavery.

37. Act of Feb. 20, 1811, Sec. 3, in Peters, ed., *Statutes*, II: 641, 642.

38. Act of Feb. 20, 1811, Sec. 4, in Peters, ed., *Statutes*, II: 642.

39. See, *e.g.*, *United States v. Alaska*, 521 U.S. 1, 5 (1997); *Lessee of Pollard v. Hagan*, 44 U.S. (3 How.) 212, 228–29 (1845).

40. Virginia Act of Cession, Sec. 3, in Thorpe, *Federal and State Constitutions*, II: 955, 956.

41. Northwest Ordinance 1787, Preamble, (emphasis added), in Peters, ed., *Statutes*, I: 52 n.a.

42. Northwest Ordinance 1787, Art. V, in Peters, ed., *Statutes*, I: 53 n.a.

43. Northwest Ordinance 1787, Preamble, in Peters, ed., *Statutes*, I: 52 n.a.

44. *Annals of Congress*, House, 16th Cong., 1st Sess., 954; Rep. Plumer of New Hampshire made the same point:"The ordinance of 1787 received the support of the Southern States; and the restriction on slavery, contained in its sixth article, was introduced on the motion of Virginia." *Annals of Congress*, House, 16th Cong., 1st Sess., 1430.

45. *Annals of Congress*, House, 16th Cong., 1st Sess., 959.

46. *Annals of Congress*, House, 16th Cong., 1st Sess., 1475.

47. Delegate Scott of the Missouri Territory made the argument in *Annals of Congress*, House, 15th Cong., 2d Sess., 1198, 1201.

48. Presently, the portion of the Florida panhandle west of the Apalachicola River, as well as the southern portions of Alabama and Mississippi and the southeast portion of Louisiana along the Gulf Coast west to the Mississippi River.

49. *Annals of Congress*, House, 12th Cong., 1st Sess., 1225.

50. *Annals of Congress*, House, 12th Cong., 1st Sess., 1254.

51. Louisiana Const. of 1812, Preamble, in Thorpe, *Federal and State Constitutions*, III: 1379.

52. Act of April 8, 1812, Sec. 1, in Peters, ed., *Statutes*, II: 701, 703.

53. A similar concern led to an important difference between the Mississippi admission in 1817 and the Alabama admission in 1819. In the former, certain conditions

regarding federal tax exemptions and free navigation were imposed as a condition on statehood; in the latter, the same conditions were imposed as a condition on grants of land rather than statehood. As David Currie has noted, "The great Missouri debate had already begun, and Southern Congressmen had seen the dangers that inhered in broad authority to impose conditions on the admission of new states." Currie, *The Constitution in Congress*, 232.

54. Act of April 18, 1818, Sec. 4, in Peters, ed., *Statutes*, III: 428, 430.

55. Illinois Const. of 1818, Art. VI, Sec. 1 (emphasis added), in Thorpe, *Federal and State Constitutions*, II: 980.

56. Illinois Const. of 1818, Art. VI, Sec. 2, in Thorpe, *Federal and State Constitutions*, II: 980.

57. *Annals* of Congress, House, 15th Cong., 2d Sess., 306–07.

58. In this, Representative Poindexter was mistaken. Ohio's Constitution of 1802 provided: "There shall be neither slavery nor involuntary servitude in this State, otherwise than for the punishment of crimes, whereof the party shall have been duly convicted; nor shall any male person, arrived at the age of twenty-one years, nor female person, arrived at the age of eighteen years, be held to serve any person as a servant, under the pretence of indenture or otherwise, unless such person shall enter into such indenture while in a state of perfect freedom, and on condition of a *bona-fide* consideration, received, or to be received, for their service, except as before excepted. Nor shall any indenture of any negro or mulatto, hereafter made and executed out of the State, or, if made in the State, where the term of service exceeds one year, be of the least validity, except those given in the case of apprenticeships." Ohio Const. of 1802, Art. VIII, Sec. 2, in Thorpe, *Federal and State Constitutions*, V: 2908.

59. *Annals of Congress*, House, 15th Cong., 2d Sess., 308.

60. *Annals of Congress*, House, 15th Cong., 2d Sess., 309.

61. *Annals of Congress*, House, 15th Cong., 2d Sess., 309.

62. Representative Barbour would make the same omission in his argument during the Missouri admission debate. *See infra* at p. 73.

63. *Annals of Congress*, House, 15th Cong., 2d Sess., 310.

64. *Annals of Congress*, House, 15th Cong., 2d Sess., 1166, 1170.

65. *Annals of Congress*, House, 15th Cong., 2d Sess., 1214–15.

66. *Annals of Congress*, Senate, 15th Cong., 2d Sess., 273. The Senate rejected the Tallmadge Amendment by a vote of 22 to 16.

67. See, *e.g.*, *Annals of Congress*, Senate, 15th Cong., 2d Sess., 282.

68. *Annals of Congress*, House, 16th Cong., 1st Sess., 732.

69. *Annals of Congress*, House, 16th Cong., 1st Sess., 1491.

70. *Annals of Congress*, House, 16th Cong., 1st Sess., 1579.

71. *Annals of Congress*, House, 15th Cong., 2d Sess., 1171.

72. *Annals of Congress*, House, 15th Cong., 2d Sess., 1171–72.

73. *Annals of Congress*, House, 15th Cong., 2d Sess., 1182.

74. *Annals of Congress*, House, 15th Cong., 2d Sess., 1180.

75. Farrand, ed., *Records of the Federal Convention*, I: 318.

76. *Annals of Congress*, House, 15th Cong., 2d Sess., 1181.

77. *Annals of Congress*, House, 16th Cong., 1st Sess., 1468.

78. *Annals of Congress*, House, 16th Cong., 1st Sess., 804, 967.

79. *Annals of Congress*, House, 16th Cong., 1st Sess., 1489.

80. *Annals of Congress*, House, 15th Cong., 2d Sess., 1185; see also *Annals of Congress*, 16th Cong., 1st Sess., 736. Rep. Mercer of Virginia noted that he had voted to prohibit slavery in the territories, because that was within Congress's constitutional authority, but he did not think they could impose conditions on a new State except that it be republican.

81. *Annals of Congress*, House, 16th Cong., 1st Sess., 1459.

82. Northwest Ordinance 1787, Art. I, Sec. 14, in Peters, ed., *Statutes*, I: 52; see also Massachusetts representative John Holmes's comments in *Annals of Congress*, House, 16th Cong., 1st Sess., 980-84.

83. *Federalist* No. 43, in Rossiter, ed., *Federalist Papers*, 275..

84. Representative Plumer of New Hampshire rejected the contention that slavery was even compatible with this limited interpretation of the "republican" requirement, contending that a system in which "one man is born to labor, and another to enjoy the fruits of that labor; that one is born with a right to govern, and another bound to obey; the one a master, the other a slave" is "the very essence of kingly government." *Annals of Congress*, House, 16th Cong., 1st Sess., 1439.

85. *Annals of Congress*, House, 16th Cong., 1st Sess., 1196..

86. *Annals of Congress*, House, 15th Cong., 2d Sess., 1187, 1196–97.

87. *Annals of Congress*, House, 15th Cong., 2d Sess., 1187.

88. *Annals of Congress*, House, 16th Cong., 1st Sess., 1460.

89. *Annals of Congress*, House, 15th Cong., 2d Sess., 1198.

90. *Annals of Congress*, House, 16th Cong., 1st Sess., 1506.

91. *Annals of Congress*, House, 16th Cong., 1st Sess., 1468–69.

92. *In his* First Inaugural Address, March 4, 1861, Lincoln said, "I have no purpose, directly or indirectly, to interfere with the institution of slavery in the States where it exists. I believe I have no lawful right to do so, and I have no inclination to do so." https://avalon.law.yale.edu/19thcentury/lincoln1.asp.

93. *Annals of Congress*, House, 15th Cong., 2d Sess., 1181–82.

94. *Annals of Congress*, House, 15th Cong., 2d Sess., 1204.

95. *Annals of Congress*, House, 15th Cong., 2d Sess., 1203.

96. Tallmadge was somewhat mistaken on this claim. Although Kentucky and Tennessee were both admitted without the antislavery condition, other conditions—namely, an agreement not to tax non-resident lands at a higher rate than resident lands, and to leave the navigation of the Ohio river free to all U.S. citizens—were imposed on Kentucky, as Representative Plumer of New Hampshire noted later in the debate. *Annals of Congress*, House, 16th Cong., 1st Sess., 1418.

97. *Annals of Congress*, House, 16th Cong., 1st Sess., 951–52.

98. *Annals of Congress*, House, 16th Cong., 1st Sess., 965.

99. *Annals of Congress*, House, 16th Cong., 1st Sess., 1559–60.

100. *Annals of Congress*, House, 16th Cong., 1st Sess., 993, 1004.

101. *Annals of Congress*, House, 16th Cong., 1st Sess., 976.

102. *Annals of Congress*, House, 15th Cong., 2d Sess., 1196-97.

103. *Annals of Congress*, House, 15th Cong., 2d Sess., 1199; for Scott's remarks, see *Annals of Congress*, House, 16th Cong., 1st Sess., 1508; for Jones's remarks, see *Annals of Congress*, House, 16th Cong., 1st Sess., 1459.

104. *Annals of Congress*, House, 16th Cong., 1st Sess., 1508, 1511.

105. *Annals of Congress*, House, 16th Cong., 1st Sess., 956–57.

106. *Annals of Congress*, House, 15th Cong., 2d Sess., 1184.

107. This language is from the Declaration of Independence and not the Bill of Rights, of course, but the idea that the principle of equality is inherent in the Constitution was subsequently adopted by the Supreme Court in *Bolling v. Sharpe*, 347 U.S. 497 (1954). See also *Adarand Constructors, Inc. v. Pena*, 515 U.S. 200, 240 (1995) Justice Thomas, concurring in part, wrote, "There can be no doubt that the paternalism that appears to lie at the heart of this [race-based affirmative action] program is at war with the principle of inherent equality that underlies and infuses our Constitution," and cited the Declaration of Independence; but see *Troxel v. Granville*, 530 U.S. 57, 91 (2000) in which Justice Scalia asserted in his dissent that "The Declaration of Independence . . . is not a legal prescription conferring powers upon the courts."

108. *Annals of Congress*, House, 15th Cong., 2d Sess., 1173–74.

109. *Annals of Congress*, House, 15th Cong., 2d Sess., 1192.

110. *Annals of Congress*, House, 16th Cong., 1st Sess., 1579.

111. Missouri Enabling Act Sec. 4, 8 (Mar. 6, 1820) (emphasis added), in Peters, ed., *Statutes*, III: 545, 547, 548.

112. *Annals of Congress*, House, 15th Cong., 2d Sess., 1206.

113. *Annals of Congress*, House, 16th Cong., 1st Sess., 1526.

CHAPTER FOUR

Rules of Membership: The Missouri Crisis and the Power to Admit New States

John R. Van Atta

> **"New States may be admitted by the Congress into this Union; but no new States shall be formed or erected within the Jurisdiction of any other State; nor shall any State be formed by the Junction of two or more States, or Parts of States, without the Consent of the Legislatures of the States concerned as well as of the Congress."**
>
> [Article IV, Section 3, Clause 1]

THE CRISIS BEGAN on February 13, 1819, when James Tallmadge, a first-term Jeffersonian-Republican from New York, proposed an amendment to the House bill to make Missouri the twenty-third member of the United States (after Alabama). That proviso and the antislavery men behind it would have required the new state's constitution to ban—or "restrict"—any further entry of slaves within its borders and allow all human chattels born there after 1819 to become free at age twenty-five. Northern restrictionists argued that Congress had the implied authority, under the first clause of Article IV, Section 3 of the Constitution—the power to admit new states—to deny Missouri's application unless it agreed to these conditions. Further, and key to the controversy, they wanted restriction like Missouri's to become a rule of membership for all further new states west of the Mississippi in the years to come. Southern leaders, mostly proslavery, opposed this unprecedented stipulation and argued that the Union consisted of *equal* states, each entitled to determine its own *internal* policy regarding slavery and other things, without congressional interference. The question was clear: Just how much constitutional power did Congress hold over the admission of new states?[1]

From the 1770s on, a seed of potential destruction—the issue of slavery—had lain at the heart of national politics. In the first decades of the republic, a tacit understanding between North and South had kept the slavery question relatively (but not entirely) quiet. Northerners, in whose states slavery was dying via gradual emancipation, would respect the property rights and geographical boundaries of Southern slavery and slave owners. Enlightened Southerners, in turn, would try to "ameliorate" the institution while looking for ways to get rid of it. The U.S. Constitution in 1787 had granted slaveholders' protection within a framework of compromises meant to join disparate states and promote common values that North and South otherwise shared. But at some point a reckoning might come. Prophetically, at the New York Ratification Convention in 1788, Melancton Smith observed that in "less time than 25 years, the government will receive its tone. What the spirit of the country may be at the end of that period, it is impossible to foretel [sic]." With regard to slavery, the first major test of that spirit and tone would come within thirty years: Missouri.[2]

As years passed and the nation expanded, the bargain between the North and South became increasingly difficult to sustain. Although party competition between Federalists and Jeffersonian-Republicans highlighted ideological issues that worked, up to a point, to avoid divisive sectional ones, the Federalist Party had declined after the War of 1812. Meanwhile, the populating of distant lands west of the Appalachians had moved apace, despite early governmental intentions to restrain it. Then, the Louisiana Purchase in 1803, an event that none of the Constitution's framers could have imagined, would change the way that Americans conceived of "the West" by extending U.S. territorial limits far beyond what some had thought manageable in a two-mile-an-hour world, especially for a republic that still mostly forswore imperial intentions. In an empire, like that of the British, some parts easily could be regarded as unequal to others, always subservient to a metropolitan center. But could it be so in a federated American republic?[3]

*****

Historians of the early republic have largely neglected the question of the admission of new states—the rules of membership in the old, pre-1865 Union. Compared to other, more dramatic issues, that one did not seem so important until the time of Missouri's application for statehood in 1818 and the foreboding sectional dispute that followed. Looking closely, one finds that *state sovereignty* was the most prominent thread running through the fabric of new-state admissions, especially the new *slave* states, prior to the Missouri debate—and afterward, too, until the Civil War. This principle also proved to be the political value most cherished by the white South and its leaders, the one they perceived as most jeopardized by the Tallmadge Amendment and its "free-state" supporters. In the end, the preservation of state sovereignty, still intact and free from Northern threat, stood as a major sectional victory for the South and the most important outcome of the Missouri crisis.[4]

Apart from its overarching themes of liberty and equality, the American Revolution had asserted the right of newly independent states to govern themselves, meaning they would control their own internal affairs and defend their property rights, including those of slaveholders. Prominent white Southerners, then and in years to come, would speak of this "sovereignty"—which they sometimes also expressed as "states' rights" or "self-government"—as a fundamental part of the Revolutionary heritage, promised both to their own states and all additional ones to follow. New members of the Union, they further insisted, should enter on an "equal footing" with the older ones—equal with regard to constitutional provisions such as rights of representation, the three-fifths compromise, return of fugitive slaves, Bill of Rights protections, and all else. In the early Union, however, "equal footing" resulted not from constitutional provision but from conflicting North-South sectional interests and ground-level politics in the new regions themselves. To the politically active inhabitants of the Missouri Territory in 1819, as in the other new states admitted before, equality of status under the Constitution seemed a *sine qua non* of their joining, one they believed Congress, for all its power, had little choice but to recognize. The alternative might have been for Missourians to break away from the American republic, never to return.[5]

After the original states began ceding their western land claims to the United States, beginning with Virginia in 1784, the Confederation Congress addressed the question whether it would permit slavery to expand farther westward. Its leaders rightly assumed that the land and government policies they adopted for the West—then *only* the region from the Appalachians to the Mississippi—would determine the social and economic destiny of the nation. That same year, a committee of Congress chaired by Thomas Jefferson proposed a land ordinance that would have guaranteed all new states an "equal footing" with the original ones, a far more republican vision of American "empire" than that of the British. More important, it would have prohibited slavery and other forms of involuntary servitude throughout the West after the year 1800. Representatives of New England, New York, and Pennsylvania supported this, but Southern congressmen combined to defeat the slaveholding prohibition by a single vote. Had the proposal succeeded, there would have been no Missouri crisis in 1819 and possibly no Civil War in the decades afterward.[6]

As it was, however, some progress toward limiting slavery west of the Appalachians did occur during the Confederation period. The Northwest Ordinance of July 13, 1787, superseded the 1784 Ordinance, also departing significantly from past British norms. Instead of colonies, permanently dependent on a metropolitan center, frontier provinces of the new Northwest were to evolve into full, equal members of the Confederation—or, later, the Union. The policy called for the westward expansion of republicanism, freedom of worship, trial by jury, and public support for education. In addition, its Article VI at least nominally prohibited slavery north of the Ohio River. An appointed governor, operating with the advice of an executive council, was to be joined by an elected legislature (based on strictly limited suffrage) when the free-adult-male population reached 5,000. Statehood would come eventually to at least three and no more than five parts of the Northwest, but only when the population of free whites in a given part reached 60,000. When new states did enter, it was to be "on an equal footing with the original states." The "equal footing" provision and the prohibition on slavery in the Northwest Territory would most strongly influence the admission of new states north of the Ohio River. These two elements also carried the greatest potential for controversy later, if extended (or not) to the Louisiana Purchase.[7]

In the meantime, the Constitutional Convention that same summer in Philadelphia furnished little more clarification on the terms of sovereignty for new states or the power of Congress to admit them. The framers provided only sparse wording in the first clause of Article IV, Section 3: "New States may be admitted by the Congress into this Union; but no new States shall be formed or erected within the Jurisdiction of any other State; nor any State be formed by the Junction of two or more States, or Parts of

States, without the Consent of the Legislatures of the States concerned as well as of the Congress." At the time of the Tallmadge Amendment in February 1819, the implications and extent of this congressional power remained vague—and largely untested. Nothing in the wording of this Admissions Clause limits it to the original territory of the United States, incapable of extension. Nor, however, does it clearly imply a scope of influence as proposed in the Tallmadge Amendment. The practical meaning would first emerge not from the text of the Constitution or from judicial interpretation but in the more chaotic arena of political conflict among competing regions, sections, interests, and beliefs.[8]

"May be admitted," the clause says, not "must be." The power is discretionary. Technically, Congress was not *required* to admit Missouri.[9] For that matter, the Constitution's framers may not have supposed the steady expansion of the United States to be as inevitable as the 1784 and 1787 ordinances had implied. They did not, after all, think in terms of "Manifest Destiny." Nothing had been preconceived about the physical dimensions of the republic. No one knew how far the "federative principle" extended or that James Madison was right, and Montesquieu wrong, that a republic *could* work in such a large country—larger still after 1803. Doubts about that had surfaced, in fact, at the Philadelphia Convention, where Nathaniel Gorham of Massachusetts, as chair of the Committee of the Whole, reportedly wondered: "Can it be supposed that this vast Country including the Western territory will 150 years hence remain one nation?"[10]

Nor did all, at that time, take it for granted that new states carved from that western region would enter the Union on an "equal footing" with the first thirteen. That consideration, too, had been left undetermined in the Constitution. Some question remained whether the new Congress, under no obligation to the defunct Confederation, would repass—or incorporate—the Northwest Ordinance into federal law. It *would*, it turned out, in 1789. At that time, and afterward, the banning of slaveholding specifically in the Northwest probably signified legal protection of it in the Southwest. But no policy at all, implicit or not, applied for territory to be added later.[11]

In fact, a proposal that new members of the Union "shall be admitted on the same terms with the original States" had been struck *down* at the Philadelphia Convention by a vote of nine states against two (Maryland and Virginia). Delegates Gouverneur Morris and Rufus King of New York feared that the political influence of new Western states might overwhelm that of the East. John Langdon of New Hampshire agreed, on grounds that "circumstances might arise" making it "inconvenient" to admit new states on terms of equality. Virginia delegates, especially Madison and George Mason, objected. The Western states ought not submit to "a union which degraded them from an equal rank," Madison insisted. Further, as Mason had cautioned earlier, "They will have the same pride & other passions which we have, and will either not unite with or will speedily revolt from the Union, if they are not in all respects placed on an equal footing with their brethren." Had a de facto policy of "equal footing" not developed (mostly for Mason's reason) in the early 1790s, followed by more explicit stipulations, beginning with Tennessee in 1796, then the history of westward expansion—and the antebellum relations between North and South—might have evolved quite differently.[12]

On the expansion or restriction of slavery, most framers of the Constitution favored *neither* side, assuming the question to be a state matter. It had always been so before. As of 1787, four Northern states had embarked on gradualist abolition programs: Pennsylvania in 1780, Massachusetts in 1783, and Connecticut and Rhode Island in 1784. As revolutionary fervor cooled, New York and New Jersey, home to the majority of Northern slaves, would wait until 1799 and 1804, respectively.[13]

This state-by-state approach to emancipation also had carried into the ratification debates and newspaper commentary of 1788–1789. Everyone then understood the original states to retain sovereignty over their internal operations, including slave owning, apart from powers shared with or surrendered to the federal government. "The practice of slavery among our confederates ought to be regreted [sic] by us, but is it evidently beyond our control," no matter how "repugnant to our notions of justice," wrote the pseudonymous Mark Antony in the Boston *Independent Chronicle* of January 10, 1788. General William Heath of Roxbury, Massachusetts, an antislavery Continental Army veteran, echoed that view at the Massachusetts Ratifying Convention: "I ardently hope that . . . the southern States will view it [slavery] as we do, and put a stop to it, but to this we have no right to compel them." Would this principle apply in full to new states? Heath thought not: "The federal Convention went as far as they could, the migration or importation [of slaves] is confined to the States now *existing only*, new States cannot claim it." Later development, however, would prove otherwise, and Missouri would further test Heath's proposition.[14]

* * * * *

As of 1789, then, the "equal footing" of new states stood as specified in the Northwest Ordinance, omitted from the new Constitution, and little explored in the ratification debates. Yet federal lawmakers, from the First Congress until the start of the Missouri crisis, came to take the principle as given in a republican system, in contrast with an imperial one. In years to come, standard procedure for statehood would be for a territory to attain roughly 60,000 free white inhabitants, as per the Northwest Ordinance, whereupon the territorial assembly sent a petition to Congress for admission to the Union. Congress then passed an "enabling act," signed by the president, authorizing such territory to submit a constitution. Finally, Congress approved that proposed constitution, thus completing the process, again pending presidential signature. After the original thirteen states, eight new states entered the Union before 1819, four slave and four free: a first round of additions through 1803, including Vermont (free), Kentucky (slave), Tennessee (slave), and Ohio (free); then, Louisiana (slave), Indiana, (free) Mississippi (slave), and Illinois (free) from 1812 to 1818. Alabama (slave) would follow in December 1819, as expected, after the Missouri crisis had begun.[15]

The 1791 addition of slavery-free Vermont—"as a new and entire member"—required the settling of border and land-claim disputes between New York, New Hampshire, and the militant, well-armed citizens of the "Vermont Republic" located in between. Meanwhile, separatist movements in Kentucky, inspired partly by ill feelings toward the Confederation government, nearly cost the United States a part of its 1783 treaty windfall from the British. Kentucky's bitterness had resulted from New Yorker John Jay's willingness, in the Jay-Gardoqui negotiations with Spain (1786), to sacrifice Mississippi River trade access in favor of northeastern shipping interests. Kentucky's eventual admission in 1792 continued an informal practice of North-South balance, again without federal conditions and "as a new and entire member," its slavery unchallenged. Already rebellious in mood, Kentuckians, like the Vermonters, might have refused anything but "equal footing," never mind the absence of that actual wording. Tennessee then entered, in 1796, without federal limitations—the first state with an explicit promise of "equal footing with the original States in all respects whatever"—and, again, no worry in Congress over its new state constitution recognizing the right to own slaves.[16]

When, in 1802, Ohio Territory voters on the verge of statehood elected delegates for their constitutional convention, they unequivocally chose Jeffersonian-Republican candidates pledged to uphold the Northwest Ordinance and oppose the establishment of slavery in any form, including a practice of quasi-slavery that more resembled lasting indentured servitude. The Ohio Enabling Act, which Congress approved in 1802, still allowed voters to embrace slavery in years to come, but most Ohioans, many having migrated from the Northeast, would hear nothing of it.[17]

While the slave-state admission of Louisiana (1812) and Mississippi (1817) had seemed, in effect, a geographical fait accompli (as would Alabama in 1819), the unfolding of late-frontier politics in Indiana and, especially, Illinois foreshadowed the controversy over Missouri's admission. The Northwest Ordinance's ban had less direct effect on the expansion of slavery, it turned out, than Confederation lawmakers expected. At the end of the French and Indian War, the 1763 Treaty of Paris between France and Great Britain had safeguarded the property, including slaves, of French settlers who lived in the Northwest. When Virginia ceded its claim to the region in 1784, its act of transfer also required that existing property rights be honored. The Northwest Ordinance, in turn, had provided for "the just preservation of rights and property," and it protected "private contracts or engagements" from legal infringement. But no one could be sure what influence territorial legislation or further developments might have on the will of Congress after 1789.[18]

In their territorial phases, Indiana and Illinois consequently developed into a cultural no-man's-land as far as slaveholding versus free labor was concerned. In the absence of congressional action to the contrary, both territorial governments could protect slavery while avoiding explicit violations of the Northwest Ordinance. In Illinois, these de facto subterfuges included rental contracts, a system of long-term indentures (slavery except in name), and various means of enforcement that fixed the status of slaves present before 1787. The large influx of settlers into the Northwest after the War of 1812 included many from slave states, their slaves with them.[19] Indiana territorial governor William Henry Harrison, Virginia-born and proslavery, believed that Congress should repeal the ban on slavery to stimulate economic growth. Only after antislavery Hoosiers managed to take over the territorial legislature, calling themselves "yeoman farmers" against the "Virginia aristocrats," did Indiana lawmakers agree on a state constitution in 1816 that officially prohibited slavery.[20]

As for Illinois, admitted two years after Indiana, slaveholding would last in one form or another until 1848, when it ended finally by state constitutional revision. The Illinois Country grew dramatically right after the War of 1812. Most settlers who lived in the southern part by 1818 had come from the slave states, like many who simultaneously migrated to Missouri lands across the Mississippi River. Many Southern yeomen, uninterested in King Cotton, had abandoned the South in favor of fertile lands north of the Ohio River. Those who aspired to become slaveholding planters themselves differed markedly from the cotton magnates of the Deep South. Some came with small numbers of slaves, gambling that Congress, never mind the Northwest Ordinance, might admit Illinois without restriction on slave labor.[21]

As it turned out, well-connected former Southerners and slaveholders would lead the push for Illinois statehood in 1818, making that state's admission a strange prelude to the Missouri crisis. The issue influenced the selection of delegates to the Illinois constitutional convention, where a provision in favor of slavery failed just barely. Illinois slaveholding interests then advocated a compromise: no new slaves, but those then living there would remain, including "French-owned slaves," whose masters had been protected under Virginia's 1784 act of cession. The race-based indentured servant system—blacks "contracting" indefinitely to work for whites—would continue, but the male children of those "indentured" would gain freedom at age twenty-one, females at eighteen. That, of course, would give owners time to sell off their human property or relocate perhaps to the Missouri side of the Mississippi. Besides, any or all of this could still change, at the behest of Illinois lawmakers themselves, after Congress granted statehood. Because the Illinois constitution of 1818 prohibited slaves from being "introduced" without freeing any there already, antislavery Northern critics vented their contempt. As one said, "After Slavery has been established, it is a serious evil, which claims some indulgence in the manner of treating it. But to begin wrong, has no excuse."[22]

That autumn of 1818, the U.S. House of Representatives addressed a resolution to admit Illinois as the twenty-first state under a proposed state constitution much less clear on slavery than those of Ohio and Indiana before it. Right off the bat, its most vigorous opponent proved to be James Tallmadge of New York, whose personal antislavery roots went back at least to his late 1790s student days at Brown University. In Rhode Island, Quaker abolitionists had pressured through the legislature a gradual emancipation statute little more than a decade before. Meanwhile, the Empire State's first embracing of gradual emancipation in 1799 coincided with young Tallmadge's opening of his law practice in Dutchess County. Having freed his own two servants in 1817, Tallmadge entered Congress that year intent on being a moral reformer and a liberator of slaves. Akin to antislavery Northerners who, as historian Susan-Mary Grant has said, used the South to help clarify their own identity, he would try to influence Illinois, and then refashion Missouri, in keeping with his rapidly changing New York, which in 1817 had pledged anew to end its own slavery completely by 1827.[23]

In the House, Tallmadge claimed, correctly, that Illinois Territory contained fewer than the number of inhabitants required by the Northwest Ordinance for statehood and that the document it had submitted could be interpreted as justifying slave trading. Southerners, including George Poindexter of Natchez, Mississippi, replied that Illinois, like Ohio and Indiana, had "virtually" conformed to the requirements of the 1787 Ordinance. In any case, fairness in the rules demanded that Illinois be admitted with no less "a sense of expediency" than all previous new states. Tallmadge retorted that a congressional obligation to prohibit slavery in Illinois constituted "a tie not to be broken," and if the issue required "a sense of expediency," then he regarded "that tie ten thousand times stronger." To that, William Henry Harrison, now an Ohio congressman, replied tellingly that no earlier provisions, including those of the Northwest Ordinance, could have stripped the people of Illinois of their "sovereign authority."[24]

This time, only a handful of congressmen, mostly Northeasterners, joined in protesting Illinois's admission, 34 voting against and 117 in favor. After a unanimous Senate vote, President James Monroe ushered Illinois into statehood on December 3, 1818. Out-of-doors, however, Tallmadge won the admiration of the antislavery press. The *Hartford Times* noted the "unexpected" and "spirited" debate on the admission of Illinois and praised Tallmadge as "a liberal republican, and a gentleman of fine talents." Indiana, the *Times* writer stressed, had not only banned slavery but added a special clause in its constitution prohibiting any amendment ever being made to restore it afterward. Illinois had not. Tallmadge had faced the fact that "while in one hand we hold the torch of freedom, we in the other are brandishing the whip of the slave driver."[25]

* * * * *

The pattern of Southern expansion in the late eighteenth and early nineteenth centuries easily accounts for the establishment of slaveholding in the Missouri Territory by 1819. Whatever its authority, Congress would have had difficulty reversing the effects of previous policies that long had shaped settlement, trade, and labor in the Ohio, Mississippi, and Missouri Valleys. Yet Tallmadge and his cohorts still proposed to end the further expansion slavery by the power to admit new states. The well-settled areas south of the Ohio River and west of the Mississippi River all featured thriving slavery-based societies before federal governance much affected them. The United States had little choice but to accept the rights of slaveholders as a condition of extending its control over these regions between 1783 and 1819. That federal acceptance—even protection—of the preexisting labor system had helped to keep slaveholding Westerners loyal to the early United States rather than carrying their allegiance to neighboring powers or asserting their own independence.[26]

Put another way, as historian John Craig Hammond has observed, Americans since the Revolution had not so much *created* an empire for slavery as they had *acquired* one, all the more so with the Louisiana Purchase. Prior to 1760, slaveholding in the trans-Mississippi West had spread throughout the environs of New Orleans and had scattered inland. With the expansion of Caribbean plantation-style agriculture in the 1770s, along with the reordering of imperial possessions after the French and Indian War, slave labor proliferated from the Mississippi Delta northward into the Ohio and Missouri River regions. Spain and Great Britain both granted land generously to settlers, rewarded production to supply their Caribbean island holdings, and promoted the further importation of slaves. White planters from Saint-Domingue, upended there by the slave revolution of

1791, found refuge in the future state of Louisiana, where they transplanted their slaveholding and sugar-growing.[27]

Between 1763 and 1800, the population growth of the lower Mississippi Valley had exploded. As it had for Kentucky and Tennessee, Congress admitted the new states of the lower-Mississippi region—Louisiana, Mississippi, and Alabama—accepting the "slave societies" there as already deeply rooted. By that time, cotton planters in the southeastern United States looked westward for their lucrative future, while others in the Southwest moved up the Mississippi—the "river of dark dreams"—toward slaveholders' wealth beyond their wildest imaginings.[28]

In 1804, the Missouri Country already hosted a small but profitable "society with slaves," with French, British, and even Native American inhabitants relying on their blacks in fur trading, lead mining, and salt production as well as agriculture. The 1787 prohibition of slavery in the Northwest Territory had chased some additional French slaveholders and other proslavery settlers over to the west side of the Mississippi, where river towns welcomed them and cheap land beckoned. The 1796 Treaty of San Lorenzo with Spain, which delivered the Western trading rights that the 1786 Jay-Gardoqui negotiations threatened to deny, had further encouraged westward movement.[29]

Article III of the 1803 Louisiana Purchase Treaty had implicitly guaranteed the property-holding rights of French slave owners. Of still greater relevance to the issue of Missouri statehood, it also provided that the inhabitants of the new territory "be incorporated in the Union of the United States and admitted as soon as possible according to the principles of the federal Constitution," including enjoyment of all "rights, advantages and immunities of citizens of the United States." To that vocal contingent, mainly Northeastern Federalists, who had doubted the constitutionality of the Purchase in the first place, the question also had arisen whether the Admissions Clause of the Constitution applied at all to territory acquired after 1789. If not, then the above wording of the Purchase Treaty meant nothing. As it was, in January 1804, Federalist Senator James Hillhouse had anticipated Tallmadge in trying to forestall the expansion of slavery. Hillhouse, of New Haven, Connecticut, not only abhorred slavery but had opposed ratification of the Louisiana Treaty. His 1804 plan included prohibiting the direct importation of slaves into the Louisiana Territory, limiting service of slaves brought in from other states to just one year of their adulthood, barring from the territory slaves of recent import, and permitting only actual settlers to bring in new ones.[30]

Southern senators responded that slavery west of the Mississippi could not be reversed. "[N]either laws moral or human can do it," contended Georgia's James Jackson. "Men will be governed by their interest, not the law." During the Missouri debate, Senator David L. Morril of New Hampshire would perceptively, if sadly, echo that point: "The people of this country are fond of property. It is impossible to restrain them within legal bounds, when you present to them a pecuniary advantage." Because sectional lines on slavery expansion did not stand as firmly in 1804 as they would by 1820, Hillhouse's three proposals involving the slave trade passed the Senate easily, but the most radically antislavery one, restricting a slave's obligation to just one year of adulthood, went down by a vote of 17 to 11. In 1805, when Congress split the Louisiana Territory into two separate parts, it left slaveholding alone. So, while the Northwest evolved into free states, the entire trans-Mississippi West remained open to slaveholders.[31]

Given the above, Tallmadge's initiative of February 13, 1819, could only have come across to Missourians as more radical than it may have seemed to him or would appear today. It looked that way to others, too: "a wider scope of operation than, on the *face* of it, would be supposed," observed the *National Intelligencer*. Its reform thrust reflected more than just New York's expanded commitment to emancipation. It also mirrored an early flowering of abolitionism in the Northeast for a decade or so earlier. Congress had never tried to restrict the *internal* social and economic practices of new states, much less dictate the future limits of slaveholding within a state. But now the Tallmadge Amendment advanced a condition for admission to the Union other than anything stated or clearly implied in Article IV, Section 3 of the Constitution. It was, as the *Intelligencer* correctly added, the "first instance of such a restriction being imposed on the new states," as opposed to new territories.[32]

While Tallmadge's amendment was not the first attempt to restrict slavery expansion into the upper part of Louisiana, earlier ones, following Hillhouse's, had failed for various reasons, especially the factor of timing. In 1811, as the House considered elevating Missouri to second-stage territorial status, Pennsylvania Republican Jonathan Roberts had introduced a proposal to prohibit any further introduction of slaves. Others at that moment, however, persuaded him that the approaching war with Britain took precedence over divisive sectional concerns. Besides, when early Western settlers already questioned distant authority, giving further incentive to join a foreign rival—Spain, at that time—seemed unwise. In 1812, Abner Lacock, another Pennsylvania Republican, had tried again against wartime odds, mustering only 17 House votes in favor. In April 1818, New Hampshire Republican Arthur Livermore had proposed a constitutional amendment to bar admission of any more slave states, but with Alabama statehood on the horizon, the House defeated that, too.[33]

When the state of Louisiana entered the Union in 1812, its southernmost location within the Louisiana Purchase, along with its heavily creole population, dominant plantation-style economy, and dependence on a "slave society," had seemed to foreordain its becoming the first slave state west of the Mississippi. In the case of the Missouri Territory, however, geography carried different implications. To preserve slavery there would be to fortify the institution as far as two hundred miles north from the mouth of the Ohio River, by 1820 the unofficial dividing point between freedom and slavery. That might invite further rooting of the institution to the west and northwest, beyond Missouri's borders, no matter any congressional attempts to stop it.

*****

The Tallmadge Amendment not only reflected a growth of free soil/antislavery sentiment over the previous few decades but also asserted a construction of federal powers that seemed to threaten the South more than ever. For that reason, it provoked an intense defensive reaction, drawing heavily on "Old Republican" beliefs and revealing concerns beyond just the admission of Missouri. Southern representatives sensed anti-Southern as well as antislavery conviction behind the Northern attack. As Georgia's Thomas W. Cobb saw it, the amendment would deprive Missouri "of one branch of sovereignty not surrendered by any other state in the Union, not even those beyond the Ohio." Cobb, a Jeffersonian-Republican from small-town Greensboro, in Greene County, would later gravitate to William H. Crawford's strict constructionist, states-rightist faction of the party. Following the "Old Republican" playbook, Cobb insisted that no one could properly show the Constitution as providing this prerogative to Congress, either expressly or by inference[34]

Other Southern congressmen stressed the considerable difference between the cases of Missouri and Illinois. Slavery had never been outlawed in the former. No territory open legitimately to slavery had ever been denied statehood on its own terms. Even if Congress *could* dictate conditions for a new state, other than it be "republican" in form, that power would be "nugatory," said House Speaker Henry Clay of Kentucky. Once admitted, he thought, any state had the right to amend its constitution and govern itself as its people saw fit. If entering under the exacting provisions of the Tallmadge Amendment, however, Missouri's slavery most likely would be dealt a death blow before the time came when state legislators could do much to revive it.[35]

When the debate escalated a few days later, antislavery Northerners sidestepped the question of state sovereignty in favor of their moral vision for westward expansion. "Our votes this day," declared New York's John W. Taylor, a nationalist Jeffersonian from upstate, "will determine whether the high destinies of this region . . . shall be fulfilled, or whether we shall defeat them by permitting slavery, with all its baleful consequences, to inherit the land." As for the Constitution, Taylor maintained that both the territorial clause and the power to admit new states gave Congress sufficient antislavery authority. Another restrictionist, Timothy Fuller of Massachusetts, who had studied law with abolitionist Levi Lincoln, added that slavery could not fit with the higher American ideals of the time. Emphasizing the "discretionary" power of Congress to admit new states, Fuller added, federal lawmakers had "to examine the actual state of things in the proposed State . . . to ascertain that her constitution or form of government is republican." For Missouri, he found otherwise. New Hampshire's Livermore, a former Federalist judge now turned Jeffersonian-Republican, reinforced Fuller's view. Beyond politics, said Livermore, lawmakers faced a moral turning point for American civilization, a chance "if not to diminish, at least to prevent, the growth of a sin which sits heavy on the souls of every one of us."[36]

On the Southern side, Virginia's Philip Pendleton Barbour insisted that Congress could not dictate terms of admission without infringing on the sovereignty of Missouri and, later, that of other new states. Barbour had studied law under St. George Tucker at the College of William and Mary, and it showed. Orange County planter, slaveholder, and future U.S. Supreme Court justice, the "Old Republican" Barbour consistently had taken the anti-nationalist, strict-constructionist side on major economic questions. He stood hostile to the national bank, protective tariffs, and internal improvements funding. State sovereignty, he now emphasized, provided the bulwark against overreaching federal authority. In the Admissions Clause, Barbour contended, the term "State" carried "a fixed and determinate meaning; in itself, it imports the existence of a political community, free and independent, and entitled to exercise all the rights of sovereignty, of every description whatever." That included all the rights of sovereignty that had applied for the original states. While slavery no longer existed in some of those states, Barbour asserted, it was because "they themselves, in the exercise of their legislative power," and not that of Congress, "have willed that it shall be so." If, on the other hand, Congress were to usurp Missouri's legislative prerogative, requiring a prohibition of slavery, "then that State could not repeal it, unless, indeed, another opinion [perhaps Clay's or one from the Supreme Court] was correct."[37]

That day, February 15, the Committee of the Whole voted 79-67 to include the Tallmadge Amendment in the Missouri bill. But then, on the 16th, Missouri's territorial delegate John Scott took his feet, his outrage matching that of Southern representatives. The people of his territory, he announced, were "brave and independent in spirit, they were intelligent, and knew their own rights; they were competent to self-government, and willing to risk their own happiness and future prosperity in the legitimate exercise of their own judgment and free will." To impose this "unconstitutional inhibition" on Missouri, he predicted, would invoke memories of the American Revolution, hastening the time "when the General Government might, in turn, undertake to dictate to them on questions of internal policy." Another flurry followed Scott's inflammatory speech. "If a dissolution of the Union must take place," Tallmadge replied, addressing both Scott and Cobb, "let it be so! If civil war, which gentlemen so much threaten, must come, I can only say, let it come!" Standing as the "representative of freemen," Tallmadge added, he knew the will of his New York constituents and, "regardless of consequences," they would "proclaim their hatred to slavery in every shape." If that sounded to Southerners like a further threat to "equal footing," they could be just as sure that many restrictionists in both House and Senate, including Tallmadge and New York senator Rufus King, believed that extending the three-fifths clause to slave states beyond the Mississippi also would violate the original intentions of the Constitution's framers.[38]

Replying further to the antislavery argument, Edward Colston of Virginia had warned that such confrontational words as Tallmadge's could not be contained within the walls of Congress. Reaching the ears of slaves, they could "excite a servile war," endangering the lives of Southern whites and freeing no one in the end. Here, Colston referred to a longstanding boundary between Northern and Southern cultures, not to be crossed. Unlike John Brown a generation later, even the most ardent white anti-Southerners would refrain from fomenting slave insurrection. Recognizing as much, Tallmadge on February 16 denied having meant any such violation. But this traditional courtesy to the South ceased, Tallmadge contended, at the banks of the Mississippi and did not apply regarding "a newly acquired territory, never contemplated in the formation of government."[39]

* * * * *

The Missouri issue also raged far beyond just Washington politics. That fury heightened after the 15th Congress ended in March 1819 without resolving the Missouri problem. Outside the U.S. capital, public opinion on that question circulated everywhere—neighborhoods, county seats, churches, taverns, town halls, and beyond. Popular concern swept through the South and West as well as the North. The *New-Hampshire Sentinel,* among other newspapers, reported in early June 1819 that the "fate" of the Missouri bill had produced "great excitement in the territory proposed for admission, and in the slave-holding States generally." In some of those places, loyalty to the federal government had eroded. As John C. Calhoun would later observe to Andrew Jackson, the Missouri question had "undoubtedly contributed to weaken to some degree the attachment of our southern and western people to the Union."[40]

On the restrictionst side, Theodore Dwight's *New York Daily Advertiser* proclaimed in February 1819 that antislavery Americans now had more reason to hope "that the enterprising and hardy race of men who are settling the new regions of territory will not feel themselves degraded, but elevated, by the idea, that the soil which they own is to be cultivated by *freemen,* not *by slaves.*" Soon after, the New York Manumission Society, headed by New York City mayor Cadwallader D. Colden, resolved on March 9, 1819, that any further introduction of slavery into the West would be "irreconcilable with the genius of our government and institutions, and hostile to the political, moral and social interests of our common country."[41]

If nothing else, the inconclusive first round of the Missouri debate had succeeded at least in promoting the expanded view of congressional power over the admission of new states. Former Supreme Court Chief Justice John Jay, in a widely published November 1819 letter to Elias Boudinot, contended that Congress after 1808 held enlarged authority over slavery, believing that "it ought not to be introduced nor permitted in any of the *new states,* and that it ought to be gradually diminished and finally abolished in all of them." Rufus King, in an 1819 pamphlet that replicated his own restrictionist speeches in the Senate, instructed that newly admitted states "are the extension of the principles of our free government." Unless that object "be promoted by the admission of new states, no such admission can be expedient or justified." On November 16, 1819, a meeting at the City Hotel in Manhattan hosted perhaps the largest public gathering of all on Missouri, some two thousand in attendance. They pledged "to prevent, by all constitutional means," the further extension of the evil, asserting "clear and indisputable [congressional] power . . . to prohibit the admission of slavery into any state or territory hereafter to be formed and admitted into the Union."[42]

Citizens groups all over the Northeast prepared antislavery memorials for the upcoming 16th Congress. A December 2, 1819, public meeting of citizens in Hartford, Connecticut, one of many in the Northeast, declared it "a duty the American people owe to their republican character . . . to prevent the further extension of slavery," which they considered "contrary to the spirit of our free and excellent constitution." The Hartford document also opposed the admission of newly acquired territories on an "equal footing." Congress could force restrictions on new states carved from territory acquired after 1789, it contended, because the compromises made in the federal constitution applied to the original states *only.* Any trans-Mississippi territories lay "out of the limits" pertaining to those original compromises. Similarly, a December 1819 citizens' meeting in Newport, Rhode Island, endorsed a petition opposed to spreading slavery further into *any* state or territory. It argued that making Missouri a slave state, "to say nothing of its utter inconsistency with the genius of our republican institutions," could only worsen illegal slave importation. The *Richmond Enquirer*, summarizing a general reaction of white leaders all around the South, answered that such doctrines as these would "prostrate the powers of the new states" and make them "*hold all their rights* at the fiat of the general government."[43]

Missourians, for their part, now faced another year of territorial status, while their economy, like that of other regions, slumped because of the Panic of 1819. They watched in frustration as the Alabama statehood bill passed without restrictions on slavery. An anonymous correspondent to the *St. Louis Enquirer* surmised, after the 15th Congress closed, that "some timid people, thinking Congress omnipotent and that next year their slaves will be surely lost, will sell off their property at a sacrifice, and remove away" in favor of migrants from the New England states. Perhaps the proslavery majority of Missourians would have more allies next time, men "waked up to the danger" of increasing federal government power. Otherwise, as Scott, too, had intimated, if "the worst came to the worst" and Congress acted in the end "to suit the views of the New England politicians," Missourians would rise up in revolutionary indignation and refuse to submit.[44]

Grand juries and other public meetings in Missouri registered contempt for congressional meddling with the "right" to build their society as they saw fit. In the early republic, county-level grand juries addressed a wide range of public matters. Their decisions then circulated among newspaper editors. At a May 15, 1819, meeting in St. Louis, where the slave population in the surrounding environs neared 20 percent, a group including Alexander McNair, who would become the first governor of Missouri, and David Barton, later one of the state's first two U.S. senators, unanimously declared Congress to possess no right "to control the provision of a state constitution, except to preserve its republican character." Again, if it became necessary, the territory's people had every right to "meet in convention by their own authority," forming a constitution and government of their own, should they "deem it expedient to do so." If the 16th Congress were to deny them again, Missourians could regard that as "an attempt to expel" them from "the federation of the States," justifying a resort to revolution. Another such meeting of irate Missouri inhabitants occurred on September 14, 1819, in the southernmost river county of New Madrid, with a slave population of almost 13 percent. It reached similar conclusions, viewing "with regret and astonishment" the assumption of Congress "to dictate to us on matters of internal policy" and insisting on being admitted "on an equal standing with the original states or not at all."[45]

* * * * *

The now-prolonged crisis entered a new phase when Washington law-makers assembled again in December 1819. More than ever, Jeffersonian-Republicans outnumbered Federalists in the 16th Congress, 30 to 10 in the Senate, 157 to 26 in the House. But key to the Missouri question was the North-South sectional split within the Jeffersonian ranks, especially the handful of cross-sectional votes—free-state "doughfaces," that is, Northern men willing for whatever reasons to vote with the South. Further, Maine's splitting off from Massachusetts, and applying that December for admission as a free state, enabled anti-restrictionists to propose bringing Missouri and Maine into the Union together, both on their own terms.

With the House majority still restrictionist by just a few votes, the center of battle now switched to the Senate. "I fear from what I see that the southern States, by persisting in abetting the claim of Missouri, will more estrange the majority of this & the eastern part of the Confederacy," the Southern-sympathizing Philadelphia editor Robert Walsh, Jr., indicated to James Madison on January 2, 1820. When, a day later, the Missouri bill emerged from the Senate Judiciary Committee *minus* the restrictionist provision, Pennsylvania Senator Jonathan Roberts tried to restore it, losing 27-16 in a floor vote on February 1. Meanwhile, Southerners praised defenders of states' rights and Missouri's sovereignty. Yet some anti-restrictionists, such as Virginia senator James Barbour, brother of Philip Pendleton Barbour, feared that Congress would admit Maine but not Missouri, resulting in no trans-Mississippi gain and, instead, a catastrophic loss for Southern political interests all around.[46]

At last, the long-awaited breakthrough came on February 16, 1820, a full year after the crisis had begun. The Senate agreed by a vote of 23-21 to admit Maine and Missouri together. At that point, Senator Jesse B. Thomas of Illinois proposed what turned out to be the critical compromise amendment to prohibit slavery in the territory north of latitude 36° 30′ (except for Missouri). That option had been discussed earlier but dismissed—for good reason. The anti-compromise *New York Daily Advertiser* had warned that an official geographical division "would be fraught with dangerous consequences," just as likely to "sow the seeds of discord in the government" as the extremism of restrictionists' had been.[47]

On February 17, the Senate, eager to compromise, passed the Thomas Amendment by 34-10, while the Maine-Missouri bill, with the 36° 30′ provision attached, also went through by 24-20. Then, speaker Clay succeeded in substituting the Thomas Amendment for Tallmadge's in the House, where a change of just a few votes could undercut the thin restrictionist majority. There is no doubting Clay's personal motivation in promulgating what would come to be known at the "American System," the doctrinal linchpin of his presidential hopes. But for both political and philosophical reasons, he also leaned toward federal partnership with the states, though stopping short of being full-blown "states'-rightist." In the end, however, President James Monroe and his unionist allies most likely operated behind closed doors to help lure for Clay some of the necessary votes.[48]

The Missouri Compromise consisted of three simple elements: Missouri admitted without restriction on slavery, Maine added as a free state, and a line at 36° 30′ prohibiting slavery in the northern part of the Louisiana Purchase. Southern members backed the 36° 30′ restriction narrowly, 39-37 in the House. The border states (Delaware, Maryland, and Kentucky) voted 16-2 in favor. Virginia, where "Old Republican" views now dominated, stood against it 18-4. The other slave states voted 19-17 in favor. Relieved to have a bill that could hold the Union in one piece, Monroe signed the compromise on March 6, 1820.[49]

Even as the major crisis over Missouri *appeared* to be settled, a further one loomed over the second session of the 16th Congress. Passing the compromise, Congress had in effect agreed to admit the Missouri Territory to statehood on condition of its submitting an acceptable constitution. A defiant Missouri convention, however, produced a document that required the Missouri legislature to prevent free Negroes and mulattos from entering and settling in the state—a violation of Article IV, Section 2 of the federal Constitution, the "Privileges and Immunities" clause. This "second Missouri question," however, raised a simpler constitutional challenge to the rules of membership than the first one had. Any clause in a state constitution, if against that of the United States, "would be a nullity," as the now-aging Madison recognized. Here, as well, Congress could not "vary the political equality of the States, or their Constitutional relations to each other or to the whole," he noted. After months of further bickering and more parliamentary maneuvering in the House, mostly engineered by Clay, congressmen on February 26, 1821, passed a resolution that Missouri's admission be finalized on "equal terms" with the original states. But this depended on the "fundamental condition" that the prohibition against free blacks in its constitution "shall never be construed to authorize the passage of any law . . . by which any citizens of either of the States of this Union shall be excluded from the enjoyment of any of the privileges and immunities to which such citizen is entitled under the Constitution of the United States." However grudgingly, Missourians went along with that. On August 10, 1821, President Monroe *again* declared the question of Missouri statehood put to rest.[50]

* * * * *

In all, the South (and Missouri) got the better of the deal, having "compromised" less than the antislavery North and winning on all points that mattered most to them from the beginning. Tallmadge and his cohorts wanted to prevent the further westward expansion of slavery, which they did, seemingly, for most of the region north of 36° 30′. But to Southerners focused on state sovereignty, the threat of disunion had helped, as it had on earlier occasions. The slave states got what they most valued: a victory of state self-determination and, from their perspective, a defeat of antislavery nation-building designs as represented in the Tallmadge Amendment.

For the time being, of course, antislavery forces had won the battle of the map, that is, the largest territorial share of the Louisiana Purchase. Yet few Southerners regarded the region north of 36° 30′ as promising for plantation-style agriculture or likely to become new states in the very near future. As Rufus King lamented, the Thomas Amendment had given the North only "a prairie, without wood or water, excepting the great River [the Missouri] and its branches," whereas the area south of the line (if adding Texas later) provided room for several new slave states in the fullness of time. And besides, as the Kansas-Nebraska Act in 1854 would show, Congress could with no greater difficulty erase an artificial dividing line between slave and free territory as it could establish one in the first place.[51]

As for slavery, this Southern victory included an implied Northern concession that no federally mandated emancipation would occur in new states. The power to ban slavery could continue to apply only in territorial development. Further, the fate of the institution in the slave states, now including Missouri, remained strictly up to them. Meanwhile, with Missouri entering with Maine, Southern voting power remained unthreatened in the Senate. That arrangement would prove essential for Southern willingness to remain tied to a centralized government that could well, from current appearances, be counted on less to support white Southerners' vital interests than it often had in years past.

If the Missouri Compromise would leave unaltered the customary rules for new-state admissions, the 1820 Thomas Amendment line at 36° 30′ did influence the development of American thinking about the trans-Mississippi frontier by deliberately sectionalizing it. Before that, the "West" had seemed like an unbroken expanse of territory from the Great Lakes to the Gulf of Mexico and, after the Adams-Onís Treaty of 1819, stretching as far westward as the Rockies. The 36° 30′ line would create a more defined "Southwest"—the place beyond the Mississippi, including Arkansas Territory, the yet-unorganized area of Oklahoma, the recently admitted state of Louisiana, and eventually Texas—all open to slavery to the extent that it could work geographically and economically.[52]

On New Year's Day 1845, with the admission of Florida pending, the U.S. Supreme Court under Chief Justice Roger B. Taney would finally address the "equal footing" doctrine with its decision in *Pollard's Lessee v. Hagan*. Unsurprisingly, it found the doctrine to be an implied element of Article IV, Section 3, expanded to pertain not only to the original thirteen states but to all. Equality of all new states to the older ones thus went from being a tradition to a hallmark of antebellum constitutional law. The case involved a dispute between the United States and the state of Alabama regarding issues of sovereignty over the navigable waters of that state. In Justice John McKinley's opinion of the court, Georgia in 1802 had ceded the territory that in 1819 had become the state of Alabama "on the same conditions and restrictions" as those of the 1787 Northwest Ordinance, minus the provision in the ordinance that forbade slavery and including the "equal footing" stipulation. When Alabama then became a member of the Union on the same footing as the original states, said McKinley (an

Alabaman himself), "she succeeded to all the rights of sovereignty, jurisdiction, and eminent domain which Georgia possessed at the date of the cession," except for the public lands therein that remained under control of the United States. Afterward, Congress could exercise no "municipal sovereignty" within a new state: "Such a power is not only repugnant to the Constitution, but it is inconsistent with the spirit and intention of the deeds of cession." That sweeping statement accommodated no exception for regions acquired after 1789, such as the Louisiana Territory or Florida. As a U.S. senator prior to his appointment to the Court in 1837, McKinley had advocated, still more radically, that Congress stood obligated to cede the federally owned public lands, as well, to the new states upon their creation.[53]

The Missouri crisis had challenged but not changed the previously existing relationship between the old, pre-Civil War states and the central government. The antislavery side had disputed white Southern hopes for the social, economic, and political future of the trans-Mississippi West, and the controversy as a whole had presented the first real moment of truth for the Union. Slave-state leaders feared the erosion of their power in Washington, as some Northerners had gone so far as to attack the "equal footing" doctrine by questioning a prospective new state's right to control its own internal affairs and doubting whether the three-fifths and fugitive slave clauses applied to states carved from the Louisiana Purchase. The Missouri fight further tested what remained of the Jeffersonian political alliance between North and South. Many Northerners stuck with Tallmadge, but the Jeffersonian-Republican Party could not indefinitely tolerate a controversy that would split it, and the country, in half. At the national level, once again, political maneuvering overcame sectional conflict. And once again, human rights for African Americans would go begging. Not for nearly another half century, when Abraham Lincoln's very different Republican Party and his Northern armies succeeded in settling the sectional question by force, would the old Union finally give way to the new.

NOTES

1. *Annals of Congress*, House, 15th Cong., 2d Sess., 1170. The classic monograph on the Missouri crisis is Glover Moore, *The Missouri Controversy, 1819–1821* (Lexington: University of Kentucky Press, 1953), while Robert P. Forbes, *The Missouri*

Compromise and Its Aftermath: Slavery and the Meaning of America (Chapel Hill: University of North Carolina Press, 2007) is the primary revisionist study. In different ways, John Craig Hammond, *Slavery, Freedom, and Expansion in the Early American West* (Charlottesville: University of Virginia Press, 2007) and Matthew Mason, *Slavery and Politics in the Early Republic* (Chapel Hill: University of North Carolina Press, 2006) fill in much of the backstory prior to 1819. Gary J. Kornblith's *Slavery and Sectional Strife in the Early American Republic, 1776–1821* (Lanham, MD: Rowman & Littlefield Publishers, 2009) briefly examines Missouri-related issues from the beginning of the nation. For my own perspective, see John R. Van Atta, *Wolf by the Ears: The Missouri Crisis, 1819–1821* (Baltimore: Johns Hopkins University Press, 2015).

2. Melancton Smith, June 21, 1788, quoted from "Melancton Smith and Alexander Hamilton Debate Representation, Aristocracy, and Interests," New York Ratifying Convention, June 17–July 26, 1788, in *The Debate on the Constitution: Federalist and Antifederalist Speeches, Articles, and Letters during the Struggle over Ratification*, edited by Bernard Bailyn, 2 vols. (New York: Library of America, 1993), 2: 757–75, quotation on 764. On "Amerlioration," see Christa Dierksheide, "'The great improvement and civilization of that race': Jefferson and the 'Amelioration' of Slavery, ca. 1770–1826," *Early American Studies* 6 (Spring 2008), 165–97, and Dierksheide, *Amelioration and Empire: Progress and Slavery in the Plantation Americas* (Charlottesville: University of Virginia Press, 2014).

3. On the fragility of republics, see Drew R. McCoy, *The Elusive Republic: Political Economy in Jeffersonian America* (Chapel Hill: University of North Carolina Press, 1980), 5, 13–47. For broader perspectives on empire-building, see Ian Tyrrell, *Transnational Nation, United States History in Global Perspective Since 1789* (New York: Palgrave Macmillan, 2007). On early republic land policy, see John R. Van Atta, *Securing the West: Politics, Public Lands, and the Fate of the Old Republic, 1785–1850* (Baltimore: Johns Hopkins University Press, 2014).

4. On congressional power to admit new states, see Gary Lawson and Guy Seidman, *The Constitution of Empire: Territorial Expansion and American Legal History* (New Haven: Yale University Press, 2004). I am indebted also to François Furstenberg, "Revenge of the Articles: The Unconsidered Problem of New States in the Constitution," paper presented at "'Contrary to the law of nature': The Missouri Crisis and the Politics of Slavery," CUNY Graduate Center, March 22, 2019.

5. See Louis Touton, "The Property Power, Federalism, and the Equal Footing Doctrine," *Columbia Law Review* 80 (May 1980): 817–39.

6. Don E. Fehrenbacher, *The Slaveholding Republic: An Account of the United States Government's Relations to Slavery* (New York: Oxford University Press, 2001), 26–28; Kornblith, *Slavery and Sectional Strife*, 30–31; Merrill D. Peterson, *Thomas Jefferson and the New Nation: A Biography* (New York: Oxford University Press, 1970), 281–84.

7. On the Northwest Ordinance, see Peter S. Onuf, *Statehood and Union: A History of the Northwest Ordinance* (Bloomington: Indiana University Press, 1987) and Paul Finkelman, "Slavery and the Northwest Ordinance: A Study in Ambiguity," *Journal of the Early Republic* 6 (Winter 1986): 343–70.

8. Lawson and Seidman, *Constitution of Empire*, 73–75. On the evolution of constitutional interpretation in the crucible of politics, see especially Jonathan Gienapp, *The Second Creation: Fixing the American Constitution in the Founding Era* (Cambridge, MA: Belknap Press, 2018).

9. The Louisiana Purchase, from which Missouri would be created, had been ratified under the constitutional theory that the treaty-making power, together with the necessary and proper clause in Article I, Section 8, could be used to justify the acquisition of new territory, provided that the acquisition be done in pursuit of one of the specified powers of Congress—in this case, the power to admit new states. This would mean that Congress, by accepting the Treaty in 1803, had pledged to bring into the Union all parts of the Louisiana Territory at some point—or, alternatively, set them free from the United States. Either way, it did not have to act by any particular point in time. See Lawson and Seidman, *Constitution of Empire*, 72–85, 81–83, 202–03.

10. See Jefferson to John Breckinridge, August 12, 1803, in *The Portable Thomas Jefferson*, ed. Merrill D. Peterson (New York: Penguin Classics, 1975), 494–97, esp. 496; James Madison, "*Federalist*, No. 10," in *James Madison Writings*, ed. Jack N. Rakove (New York: Library of America, 1999), 160–67. Lawson and Seidman, *Constitution of Empire*, 79–81, Gorham quoted on 2. See also, James Madison, *Notes of Debates in the Federal Convention of 1787*, ed. Adrienne Koch (Athens: Ohio University Press, 1966), 410.

11. David Waldstreicher, *Slavery's Constitution: From Revolution to Ratification* (New York: Hill and Wang, 2009), 88; Jack N. Rakove, *Original Meanings: Politics and Ideas in the Making of the Constitution* (New York: Knopf Doubleday Group, 1996), 70–73; Pauline Maier, *Ratification: The People Debate the Constitution, 1787–1788* (New York: Simon & Schuster, 2010), 190.

12. Max Farrand, ed., *The Records of the Federal Convention of 1787*, 3 vols. (New Haven: Yale University Press, 1911), 2: 454; 1: 579.

13. Fehrenbacher, *Slaveholding Republic*, 28–33, esp. 33; Kornblith, *Slavery and Sectional Strife*, 24–27, 33–34; Leonard L. Richards, *The Slave Power: The Free North and Southern Domination, 1780–1860* (Baton Rouge: Louisiana State University Press, 2000), chap. 2. See also, Joanne Pope Melish, *Disowning Slavery: Gradual Emancipation and "Race" in New England, 1780–1860* (Ithaca: Cornell University Press, 1998), and Van Atta, *Wolf by the Ears*, 7–8.

14. Mark Antony, "Slavery 'Ought to be Regreted . . . But it is evidently Beyond Our Controul': A Defense of the Three-Fifths Clause," *Independent Chronicle* (Boston), January 10, 1788, and "General William Heath on Slavery," January 30, 1788, in Bailyn, ed., *The Debate on the Constitution*, 1: 737-43, quotation on 740, 915–16.

15. On the idea of "stages" of territorial development and early state admissions, see Jack Ericson Eblen, *The First and Second United States Empires: Governors and Territorial Government, 1784–1912* (Pittsburgh: University of Pittsburgh Press, 1968).

16. For Vermont, see "An Act for the Admission of the State of Vermont into this Union," Feb. 18, 1791, http://avalon.law.yale.edu/18th_century/vt03.asp; for Kentucky, "Act Admitting Kentucky into the Union," February 4, 1791, *The Federal and*

State Constitutions, Colonial Charters, and other Organic Laws of the States and Territories now or heretofore forming the United States of America, ed. Francis Newton Thorpe, 7 vols., (Washington, DC: Government Printing Office, 1909), https://oll.libertyfund.org/titles/thorpe-the-federal-and-state-constitutions-vol-iii-kentucky-massachusetts; for Tennessee, see "An Act for the Admission of the State of Tennessee into the Union," June 1, 1796, TNGenWeb Project, https://www.tngenweb.org/law/17960601.html; Rakove, *Original Meanings*, 27, 70–74, 163–68; Maier, *Ratification*, 237–41, 276–77.

17. Hammond, *Slavery, Freedom, and Expansion*, 78, 76–95; also, Van Atta, *Wolf by the Ears*, 42.

18. "An ordinance for the government of the territory of the United States, North-west of the river Ohio," July 13, 1787, https://www.loc.gov/resource/bdsdcc.22501/?sp=1; Finkelman, "Slavery and the Northwest Ordinance," 347–48.

19. Hammond, *Slavery, Freedom, and Expansion*, chaps. 5–6. See also Nicole Etcheson, *The Emerging Midwest: Upland Southerners and the Political Culture of the Old Northwest, 1787–1861* (Bloomington: Indiana University Press, 1996); Jeremy Adelman and Stephen Aron, "From Borderlands to Borders: Empires, Nation-States, and the Peoples in Between in North American History," *American Historical Review* 104 (June 1999), 814–23.

20. Finkelman, "Slavery and the Northwest Ordinance," 369; Van Atta, *Wolf by the Ears*, 41–43.

21. Hammond, *Slavery, Freedom, and Expansion*, chap. 6; Adam Rothman, *Slave Country: American Expansion and the Origins of the Deep South* (Cambridge: Harvard University Press, 2005), chap. 5. On settlement of the Illinois Country, see John Reda, *From Furs to Farms: The Transformation of the Mississippi Valley, 1762–1825* (DeKalb: Northern Illinois University Press, 2016).

22. *The Essex Register* (Salem, MA), October 3, 1818. On the closeness of the slavery issue in Illinois, see, for example, "Illinois," *Spirit of the Times & Carlisle Gazette* (Carlisle, PA), October, 12, 1818. See also *National Advocate* (New York City), September 30, 1818; *New-York Daily Advertiser*, November 17, 1818.

23. On Tallmadge, I am indebted to Sarah Gronningsater, "New York Antislavery Politics and the Origins of the Tallmadge Amendment," paper presented at "'Contrary to the law of nature': The Missouri Crisis and the Politics of Slavery," CUNY Graduate Center, March 22, 2019. See Susan-Mary Grant, *North Over South: Northern Nationalism and American Identity in the Antebellum Era* (Lawrence: University Press of Kansas, 2000), 4–5, 8–9. Also, generally, David N. Gellman, *Emancipating New York: The Politics of Slavery and Freedom, 1777–1827* (Baton Rouge: Louisiana State University Press, 2006).

24. *Annals of Congress*, House, 15th Cong., 2d Sess., 306–07, 310–11; *The National Messenger* (Georgetown, District of Columbia), November 25, 1818; *New-York Daily Advertiser*, November 28, 1818.

25. "NEW STATE OF ILLINOIS SLAVERY," *The Times* (Hartford, CT), December 8, 1818. For the Illinois vote, *Annals of Congress*, House, 15th Cong, 2d Sess., 311. For more detail on the Illinois controversy, see Van Atta, *Wolf by the Ears*, 43–47.

26. See John Craig Hammond, "Slavery, Settlement, and Empire: The Expansion and Growth of Slavery in the Interior of the North American Continent, 1770–1820," *Journal of the Early Republic* 32 (Summer 2012): 175–206. On the distinction between "slave societies" and "societies with slaves," see Ira Berlin, *Many Thousands Gone: The First Two Centuries of Slavery in North America* (Cambridge: Belknap Press, 1998), 8–9, 7–13, 22, 98, 105–08.

27. Hammond, *Slavery, Freedom, and Expansion*, chap. 3; Rothman, *Slave Country*, chaps 2–3.

28. See Walter Johnson, *River of Dark Dreams: Slavery and Empire in the Cotton Kingdom* (Cambridge: Belknap Press, 2013), chap. 1; also, Edward E. Baptist, *The Half Has Never Been Told: Slavery and the Making of American Capitalism* (New York: Basic Books, 2014), chaps. 1–3.

29. Stephen Aron, *American Confluence: The Missouri Frontier from Borderland to Border State* (Bloomington: Indiana University Press, 2006), 151–52. For Missouri's products and economic needs, see the *Baltimore Patriot*, August 14, 1819.

30. "Louisiana Purchase Treaty, April 30, 1803," General Records of the U.S. Government, Record Group 11, National Archives, https://www.ourdocuments.gov/doc.php?flash=false&doc=18&page=transcript; Lawson and Seidman, *Constitution of Empire*, 73–78; James M. Banner, Jr., "Hillhouse, James" in *American National Biography*, ed. John A. Garraty and Mark C. Carnes, 24 vols. (New York, 1999), 10: 813–14.

31. Jackson, quoted in William Plumer, *Memorandum of Proceedings in the United States Senate, 1803–1807*, edited by Everett Somerville Brown (New York: Macmillan, 1923), 115–16; Morril, quoted in George William Van Cleve, *A Slaveholders' Union: Slavery, Politics, and the Constitution in the Early American Republic* (Chicago: University of Chicago Press, 2010), 236; Kornblith, *Slavery and Sectional Strife*, 46–47.

32. *National Intelligencer*, quoted in the *Mercantile Advertiser* (New York City), February 19, 1819. For Southern perspectives on the Constitution, see Don E. Fehrenbacher, *Sectional Crisis and Southern Constitutionalism* (Baton Rouge: Louisiana State University Press, 1995), *Constitutions and Constitutionalism in the Slaveholding South* (Athens: University of Georgia Press, 1989), and *The Dred Scott Case: Its Significance in Law and Politics* (New York: Oxford University Press, 1978), chaps 1–2. Also, generally, Van Cleve, *A Slaveholders' Union*.

33. John Craig Hammond, "'Uncontrollable Necessity': The Local Politics, Geopolitics, and Sectional Politics of Slavery Expansion," in *Contesting Slavery: The Politics of Bondage and Freedom in the New American Nation*, edited by John Craig Hammond and Matthew Mason (Charlottesville: University of Virginia Press, 2001), 138–60, esp. 147–48.

34. See "Remarks of Mr. Cobb, of Georgia," *City of Washington Gazette* (Washington, DC), March 27, 1819.

35. "Remarks on Tallmadge Amendment," February 15, 1819, in *The Papers of Henry Clay*, edited by James F. Hopkins, et al., 10 vols. (Lexington, KY: University Press of Kentucky, 1959–1992), 2: 670. On the compatibility of slavery and the "American System," see Andrew Shankman, "Neither Infinite Wretchedness nor Positive Good:

Mathew Carey and Henry Clay on Political Economy and Slavery during the Long 1820s," in Hammond and Mason, eds., *Contesting Slavery*, 247–66.

36. Taylor, *Annals of Congress*, House, 15th Cong., 2d Sess., 1170–79, esp. 1170, 1173–74 (on Taylor, see also, Richards, *Slave Power*, 70, 75–81, 89, 95, 122); Fuller, *Annals of Congress*, House, 15th Cong., 2d Sess., 1179–84, esp. 1180; Livermore, 1191–93, esp. 1193.

37. *Annals of Congress*, House, 15th Cong., 2d Sess., 1185–86. For Barbour's speech, 1184–91. On Philip Pendleton Barbour and family, see William S. Belko, *Philip Pendleton Barbour in Jacksonian America: An Old Republican in King Andrew's Court* (Tuscaloosa: University Alabama Press, 2016); and Charles D. Lowery, *James Barbour: A Jeffersonian Republican* (Tuscaloosa: University Alabama Press, 1984).

38. Scott, *Annals of Congress*, 15th Cong., 2d Sess., 1195–1203, esp. 1201–02; Tallmadge, 1203–14, esp. 1204.

39. References to Colston, *Annals of Congress*, 15th Cong., 2d Sess., 1180, 1205; Tallmadge, 1203. The initial House vote on the Tallmadge Amendment, on February 16, 1819, reflected bipartisan support in the North. The first part of the amendment—to forbid the future entrance of slaves into Missouri—passed the House 87-76, Northern Republicans and Federalists voting in favor 86-10, the South 66-1 against. For the vote, *Annals of Congress*, House, 15th Cong., 2d Sess., 1214–15; Senate, 273. The 15th Congress ended on March 4, 1819, and so did Tallmadge's single term in the House. Meanwhile, a parallel debate had unfolded that February over the new Arkansas territory, with slaves making up eleven percent of the population. (In comparison, slaves constituted roughly sixteen percent of Missouri's.) New York's Taylor had played Tallmadge's role this time, pushing a similar amendment in the House to restrict slavery under the congressional power to regulate the territories—a question *different* from the admission of new states. Arkansas qualified "as a more southern country," the *Alexandria Gazette* explained, "and therefore demanding slavery, and looking moreover at present only for a territorial government—not to be a state." The effort failed, but just barely, Taylor's proposal falling 89-87. Northern members voted 86-15 in favor, Southerners 74-1 against. Here, geography apparently mattered more than antislavery conviction, if only a little, as did the unionist acceptance of balance between slave- and free-state territory. Arkansas lay significantly south of the symbolic Ohio River divide. In the Senate, Taylor's restriction lost 19-14, the slave states unanimously opposed. See *Alexandria Gazette*, February 19, 1819; *Annals of Congress*, House, 15th Cong., 2d Sess., 1272–82; Senate, 272–73. Also, Forbes, *Missouri Compromise and Its Aftermath*, 46; William W. *Freehling, Road to Disunion, Volume I: Secessionists at Bay, 1776-1854* (New York: Oxford University Press, 1990), 149–50; *and Moore, Missouri Controversy*, 59–64.

40. *New-Hampshire Sentinel* (Keene, NH), June 5, 1819; Calhoun to Jackson, June 1, 1820, in *The Papers of John C. Calhoun*, edited by Robert L. Meriwether, et al., 28 vols. (Columbia: University of South Carolina Press, 1959–2003), 5: 164–65, quotation on 164. For the view of the crisis as confined to Washington politics, see Moore, *Missouri Controversy*, 65, 170, 342.

41. *New-York Daily Advertiser*, February 20, 1819; "Resolutions of the New York Manumission Society," in the *Spectator* (New York City), March 9, 1819; Van Atta, *Wolf by the Ears*, 77.

42. Jay to Boudinot, November 17, 1819, in James G. Basker, ed., *American Antislavery Writings: Colonial Beginnings to Emancipation* (New York: Library of America, 2012), 223–24; and King, "Observations of Rufus King on the Missouri Bill," in Basker, *American Antislavery Writings*, 225–27, quotation on 225; "THE MEETING AT NEW-YORK," *Daily National Intelligencer* (Washington, DC), November 22, 1819.

43. "Prohibition of Slavery in Missouri," January 18, 1820, in *American State Papers, Miscellaneous*, 28 Volumes (Washington: Gales and Seaton, 1832-1861), Vol. 2, Report No. 481; "Prohibition of Slavery in Missouri," January 12, 1820, in *American State Papers, Miscellaneous*, Vol. 2, Report No. 479; "MISSOURI QUESTION," *Richmond Enquirer*, December 16, 1819, and referring to other such meetings around the Northeast, including Boston and Trenton, November 23, 1819.

44. Letter to editor, *St. Louis Enquirer*, March 31, 1819.

45. Meeting in St. Louis, reported in *The Political Intelligencer* (Fredericktown, MD), June 26, 1819; "New Madrid," *St. Louis Enquirer*, October 6, 1819. For county-by-county slave population percentages in Missouri, see Van Atta, *Wolf by the Ears*, 56–57.

46. Robert Walsh to Madison, January 2, 1820, in *The Papers of James Madison: Retirement Series*, edited by David B. Mattern, et al., 2 vols. to date (Charlottesville: University of Virginia Press, 2009-), 1: 580–81, quotation on 581; James Barbour to Madison, February 10, 1820, in Mattern, et al., *Papers of James Madison: Retirement Series*, 2: 8–9; Moore, *Missouri Controversy*, 92–93, 97–98.

47. *New-York Daily Advertiser*, February 24, 1819. For the Senate vote on the Thomas Amendment, *Annals of Congress*, Senate, 16th Cong., 1st Sess., 428. Also, Forbes, *Missouri Compromise and Its Aftermath*, 46–47. On Thomas's Illinois strategy, see "A REPUBLICAN," *Edwardsville Spectator* (Edwardsville, IL), October 3, 1820, and March 27, 1821; also, Joseph E. Suppiger, "Amity to Enmity: Ninian Edwards and Jesse B. Thomas," *Journal of the Illinois State Historical Society* 67 (April 1974): 201–11.

48. See Forbes, *Missouri Compromise and Its Aftermath*, chap. 3, and for an interesting alternative interpretation on Monroe, see John Craig Hammond, "President, Planter, Politician: James Monroe, The Missouri Crisis, and the Politics of Slavery," *Journal of American History* 105 (March 2019): 843–67. On Clay as a strategist, see Peter B. Knupfer, *Union As It Is: Constitutional Unionism and Sectional Compromise, 1787–1861* (Chapel Hill: University of North Carolina Press, 1991), 21–22, 119–57; James C. Klotter, *Henry Clay: The Man Who Would Be President* (New York: Oxford University Press, 2018), 44–48; Van Atta, *Wolf by the Ears*, 92–96.

49. For analysis of the House vote, see Moore, *Missouri Controversy*, 107–11; and Don E. Fehrenbacher, *The South and Three Sectional Crises* (Baton Rouge: Louisiana State University Press, 1980), 18–19, 69. Also, Freehling, *Road to Disunion*, 144–61.

50. Madison to Monroe, November 19, 1820, in Mattern, et al., *Papers of James Madison: Retirement Series*, 2: 151–53, quotation on 151; Forbes, *Missouri Compromise and Its Aftermath*, 10, 112–19, 125, 207, 118–19, 311–12. For Clay's report, see

"Admission of Missouri into the Union," February 10, 1821, in *American State Papers, Miscellaneous*, Vol. 2, Report No. 502. On Henry Clay's role generally in this "second" Missouri Compromise, see Merrill D. Peterson, *The Great Triumvirate: Webster, Clay, and Calhoun* (New York: Oxford University Press, 1987), 62–65. Some suggested that the antislavery side in Congress hoped to delay Missouri's admission until their allies in Missouri managed to prevail at home: "A main cause for keeping up the question at this session and continuing it in the next," wrote the Washington correspondent for the *Kentucky Reporter*, "is the expectation that the restrictionists will succeed at home if another convention can be got up in Missouri." [reprinted as "TO THE EDITOR OF THE REPORTER," in the *Nashville Gazette* (Nashville, TN), March 17, 1821.]

51. King, quoted in George Dangerfield, *The Awakening of American Nationalism, 1815–1828* (New York: Harper & Row, 1965), 116.

52. On sectionalizing of Jeffersonian expansion, see Robert E. Bonner, *Mastering America: Southern Slaveholders and the Crisis of American Nationhood* (Cambridge: Cambridge University Press, 2009), 11–14. With regard to thinking "sectionally," see Grant, *North over South*, 63–64. On limited knowledge of the trans-Mississippi West, see Peter J. Kastor, *William Clark's World: Describing America in an Age of Unknowns* (New Haven: Yale University Press, 2011).

53. *Pollard's Lessee v. Hagan et al.*, 44 U.S. (3 How.) 212 (1845), 222–24, quotations on 223, 224; J. Mills Thornton III, "McKinley, John," in Garraty and Carnes, eds., *American National Biography*, 15: 120–21.

Figure 1. Henry Baldwin. John Sartain after James R. Lambdin, *Henry Baldwin, LL. D.*, 1861, mezzotint, etching and stipple on buff wove paper, 12 1/4 x 9 3/4 in, Pennsylvania Academy of the Fine Arts.

Figure 2. John C. Calhoun. George Peter Alexander Healy, *John C. Calhoun*, c. 1845, oil on canvas, 45 3/4 x 38 1/2 x 2 3/4 in, National Portrait Gallery, Smithsonian Institution, NPG.90.52.

Figure 3. Henry Clay. John B. Neagle, *Henry Clay*, 1842, oil on canvas, 27 3/4 x 21 3/4 x 1 1/2 in, National Portrait Gallery, Smithsonian Institution, frame conserved with funds from the Smithsonian Women's Committee, NPG.93.476.

Figure 4. William Henry Harrison. Albert Sands Southworth and Josiah Johnson Hawes, *William Henry Harrison*, ca. 1850, daguerrotype, 3 1/4 x 2 3/4 in, The Metropolitan Museum of Art, gift of I. N. Phelps Stokes, Edward S. Hawes, Alice Mary Hawes, and Marion Augusta Hawes, 1937, 37.14.44.

Figure 5. Richard Mentor Johnson. John B. Neagle, *Richard Mentor Johnson*, 1843, oil on canvas, 40 x 34 3/4 x 3 3/4 in, Corcoran Collection (bequest of Mrs. Benjamin Ogle Tayloe), 2015.19.1.

Figure 6. Louis McLane. Engraved portrait of Secretary of the Treasury Louis McLane, U.S. Bureau of Engraving and Printing.

Figure 7. John Sergeant. Thomas Sully, *John Sergeant*, 1811, oil on canvas, 32 1/2 x 26 in, National Portrait Gallery, Smithsonian Institution, gift of Mrs. Craig Wylie, NPG.84.179.

Figure 8. Samuel Smith. Charles Balthazar Julien Févret de Saint-Mémin, *Samuel Smith*, 1798, engraving on paper, 21 5/8 x 15 3/4 in, National Portrait Gallery, Smithsonian Institution, gift of Mr. and Mrs. Paul Mellon, NPG.74.39.4.8.

Figure 9. Alexander Smyth. [Creator unknown], *Alexander Smyth, Brigadier General*, 1880, lithograph, the Miriam and Ira D. Wallach Division of Art, Prints and Photographs: Print Collection, The New York Public Library.

Figure 10. John Taylor. Caroline L. O. Ransom, *John W. Taylor*, 1900, 31 1/2 x 25 in, Collection of the U.S. House of Representatives.

Figure 11. Samuel W. Dana. Charles Balthazar Julien Févret de Saint-Mémin, *Samuel Whittelsey Dana*, 1806, engraving on paper, 21 5/8 x 15 3/4 in, National Portrait Gallery, Smithsonian Institution, gift of Mr. and Mrs. Paul Mellon, S/NPG.74.39.10.5.

Figure 12. Harrison Gray Otis. Chester Harding, *Harrison Gray Otis*, 1833, oil on canvas, 36 x 28 in, National Portrait Gallery, Smithsonian Institution, gift of Emily Morison Beck, NPG.77.30.

Figure 13. Jesse B. Thomas. Photograph from the United States Senate Historical Collection.

Figure 14. Nicholas Van Dyke. Charles Balthazar Julien Févret de Saint-Mémin, *Nicholas Van Dyke*, 1802, engraving on paper, 21 5/8 x 15 3/4 in, National Portrait Gallery, Smithsonian Institution, gift of Mr. and Mrs. Paul Mellon, NPG.74.39.4.14.

Figure 15. Philip Pendelton Barbour. Etching from J. A. C. Chandler et al., eds., *The South in the Building of the Nation* (Richmond, VA: Southern Historical Publication Society, 1909).

Figure 16. Benjamin Hardin. Etching from Lucius P. Little, *Ben Hardin: His Times and Contemporaries with Selections from His Speeches* (Louisville, KY: The Courier-Journal Job Printing Co., 1887), frontispiece.

Figure 17. Henry Meigs. Etching from Henry B. Meigs, *Record of the Descendants of Vincent Meigs, Who Came from Dorsetshire, England to America about 1635* (Baltimore, MD: John S. Bridges & Co., 1901), 55.

Figure 18. William Plumer, Jr. Etching from *The Granite Monthly: A New Hampshire Magazine*, Vol. 12, second series (Concord, NH: John N. McClintock, 1889), 76.

CHAPTER FIVE

The Power to Regulate the Territories

Christopher Childers

> **"The Congress shall have Power to dispose of and make all needful Rules and Regulations respecting the Territory or other Property belonging to the United States; and nothing in this Constitution shall be so construed as to Prejudice any Claims of the United States, or of any particular State."**
>
> [Article IV, Section 3, Clause 2]

WHEN NEW YORK congressman James Tallmadge introduced an amendment to the Missouri statehood bill prohibiting "the further introduction of slavery or involuntary servitude" and providing for the eventual manumission of slaves within the prospective state, he inaugurated the Missouri controversy and provoked a constitutional crisis over the boundaries of congressional authority.[1] On one level, Tallmadge's colleagues might well have questioned why the representative proposed to end slavery in a territory where it had existed since 1811. More significantly, Tallmadge's amendment transcended the issue of Missouri statehood because it spoke directly to Congress's authority to govern territories and dictate the terms of statehood. No one in Congress on February 13, 1819, the day Tallmadge sounded what Thomas Jefferson called the "fire bell in the night," could have missed the significance, and if they did, they would recognize it soon enough.[2] Northerners and Southerners alike realized that territorial administration and the process of state-making could be used to determine the boundaries of slavery. Thanks to James Tallmadge, the issue of permitting or prohibiting slavery in the territories became critically important to the future of the nation.

In constitutional terms, the issue centered on Article IV, Section 3, Clause 2 of the U.S. Constitution: "The Congress shall have Power to dispose of and make all needful Rules and Regulations respecting the Territory or other Property belonging to the United States."[3] This seemingly innocuous clause of the Constitution lay buried in the middle of the constitutional process of admitting new states to the Union. The section preceding it addresses how Congress can form new states; the section after it regulates the form of government permitted within new states. The Needful Rules and Regulations Clause, however, became a seminal part of the constitutional debates that stemmed from the Missouri controversy.

Though Jefferson professed shock and alarm at the Tallmadge Amendment, Congress had debated the right to extend slavery into the territories for thirty-five years preceding the Missouri crisis. One difference, however, distinguished the Missouri issue from previous debates. In prior cases, Congress had debated permitting or prohibiting slavery in the territories before a territory's application for statehood. The Northwest Ordinance of 1787, perhaps the most famous example of congressional prohibition of slavery in a territory, had occurred at the inception of a territory. Thereafter, Congress had essentially drawn a dividing line between slavery and freedom down the Ohio River. Created by Congress in June 1812, the Missouri Territory lay beyond the jurisdiction of the Northwest Ordinance. Faced with the issue of permitting or prohibiting slavery in the new territory, Congress was inclined to abide by the wishes of its resident settlers.

Approximately 10,000 slaves, or 15 percent of the total population, lived in the Missouri Territory on the eve of statehood. Slavery in Missouri differed markedly from the form it took in the emerging cotton South, but the territory's planter class did utilize slave labor in a significant hemp-growing market. Missouri's slaveholders knew their economy differed from that of the lower South, but they also intended to maintain slave-based agriculture in the long term.[4] Missourians wanted statehood as soon as possible. Four new states—Indiana, Illinois, Mississippi, and Alabama—had joined the Union in the 1810s, and Missouri aspired to become the fifth. Significantly, Congress had defeated a motion to prohibit slavery in the Mississippi Territory in 1798 but no one challenged its existence in the incoming states twenty years later. Missouri would prove different. On November 21, 1818, the Missouri territorial legislature applied for admission to the Union, citing a grossly inflated population of 100,000.[5]

Less than three months later, and almost seven years after Missouri's creation as a territory, Tallmadge proposed to reverse congressional policy on statehood by dictating an end to slavery as a condition of statehood. The Tallmadge Amendment sought to enable the federal government to end slavery in a place where it already had existed, a point that Southern slaveholders recognized instantly. The retired Jefferson framed the issue in constitutional terms by arguing that the Amendment violated the principle of state equality. The third president had worked harder than any other political leader of his time to ensure that new states entered the Union on equal grounds with the older states. And if Congress could end slavery in Missouri in 1819, where might it act against the South's peculiar institution in the future? For Southerners, Tallmadge had given renewed life to the Federalist idea of expansive federal power by declaring that the federal government had the authority to determine the conditions of statehood to a territory.[6]

Faced with an antislavery bloc in Congress led by Tallmadge and his colleague John W. Taylor, also a New York representative, Southern congressmen proposed their own reversal of precedent and policy. Having acquiesced in congressional prohibition of slavery in the territories in years past, proslavery congressmen during the Missouri controversy sought to deny the right of Congress to determine the status of slavery in a territory. Only the people who lived in a territory, they argued, had the authority to permit or prohibit slavery there. The Southerners' argument rested on an incredibly restrictive interpretation of the Needful Rules and Regulations Clause of the Constitution, one which became a staple of the most radical Southern defense of slavery from the Missouri crisis to the eve of the Civil War.

According to its opponents, the Tallmadge Amendment ignored the fact that slavery already existed in Missouri by virtue of its territorial enabling act. Based on that fact, Missourians had drafted a constitution that permitted slavery in the new state. Therefore, the restrictionists, those who supported the Tallmadge Amendment and its call to prohibit slavery in Missouri, were interfering with the right of Missourians to draft a constitution according to their own wishes. Congress had addressed the issue of slavery and westward expansion before, in particular the question of whether Congress or the people of a territory had the right to permit or prohibit slavery, but had averted the crisis that emerged in 1819 when slavery and westward expansion coalesced when Missouri sought statehood. Southerners questioned why the opponents of slavery had not acted back in 1812 if they had wished to bar slavery from the Territory of Missouri.[7]

In essence, Tallmadge and other antislavery Northerners had discovered a chink in the Southern proslavery constitutional armor. Prior to the Missouri crisis, Southerners had accepted congressional authority over slavery in the territories with only weak resistance. The Tallmadge Amendment changed that. Now Southerners began to question the wisdom of conceding federal authority over the territories under the Needful Rules and Regulations Clause because by 1819 it appeared that a growing bloc of congressmen, both Federalists and some Republicans, intended to use the clause to restrict the expansion of slavery to the territories.[8]

By 1820, the antislavery impulse had grown in the North as most states ended slavery within their borders. Some Northern politicians, Tallmadge included, harbored moral objections toward slavery. They also had political reasons for opposing the peculiar institution. Resentful of the outsized political influence of Southerners in the Jeffersonian political coalition, Northerners objected to the Constitution's infamous Three-Fifths Clause, which counted a slave as three-fifths of a human being for the purposes of apportionment, thereby enhancing the slaveholding section's power in the halls of Congress and the Electoral College. New England Federalists appeared the most likely restrictionists, so some political observers professed surprise when some of the most vocal opponents of slavery in Missouri came from the mid-Atlantic states of New York and Pennsylvania. Moreover, a significant number of Northern Republicans, including the New Yorkers Tallmadge and Taylor, joined the Federalists in opposition to the extension of slavery. In "probably the most candid discussion of slavery ever held in Congress," Northerners rallied behind the Tallmadge amendment, while Southerners fought what they saw as an attack on localism and states' rights.[9] The proslavery congressmen contended "that Congress had no right to prescribe to any State the details of its government, any further than that it should be republican in its form." Restrictionists responded by asserting that "Congress had the right to annex conditions to the admission of any new State" and that slavery "was incompatible with our Republican institutions."[10]

James Tallmadge may have inaugurated the Missouri crisis with his amendment, but his New York colleague John W. Taylor did the most to frame the terms of the constitutional debate. Taylor distilled the controversy into two questions. First, did Congress have the authority to demand that Missouri abolish slavery as a condition of statehood? Second, if Congress indeed had the power, should it use it?[11] Taylor answered both in the affirmative. While Southerners interpreted the Needful Rules and Regulations Clause narrowly, Taylor and the Northerners argued that Article IV, Section 3 of the Constitution granted "unlimited" authority to Congress over the territories, including the status of slavery. "It would be difficult to devise a more comprehensive grant of power," Taylor argued.[12]

The Missouri controversy blurred, if not temporarily dissolved, party lines because of the slavery question. Among the Jeffersonian Republicans, Northerners endorsed restriction while Southerners united in resistance to congressional authority over slavery in the territories. Sensing the danger to the Union, a small group of Northern and Southern nationalists sought to find a middle ground. Speaker of the House Henry Clay of Kentucky led the moderates. Though Clay insisted that Congress had "no right to prescribe any condition whatever to the newly organized States," he generally took a softer line on the question of restriction.[13] Clay's efforts notwithstanding, Northern Republicans had touched a raw nerve in the South, which intensified the tenor of the debate on Missouri. Southerners wanted to believe "that Federalists were the principal *provocateurs*," but the debates proved otherwise.[14] The Federalists, reeling from their party's demise after the fallout from the Hartford Convention, joined the Northern Republicans in favor of restriction. The Missouri crisis, and the constitutional issues underlying it, proved that the politics of slavery could divide the nation into sectional blocs.

The key to understanding proslavery opposition to restriction rests in their interpretation of the two clauses in Article IV, Section 3 of the Constitution—individually as well as in relation to one another. The first clause, "New States may be admitted by the Congress into this Union," provided for the admission of new states to the Union. The only condition, it seemed, was that Congress had to guarantee a "Republican Form of Government," as written in Section 4. The second clause of Section 3, the needful rules and regulations clause, applied to territories. The restrictionists during the Missouri crisis argued that in order to preserve a republican form of government in Missouri, Congress necessarily had to prohibit slavery. Proslavery congressmen flatly rejected that argument. They also created an inventive new interpretation of this Section 3, countering restrictionists by contending that the document forbade any infringement on the rights of the people in a territory to draft a state constitution. In other words, a sort of *proto-state* sovereignty extended to a territory drafting a constitution and seeking admission to the Union.[15]

Southerners like Philip P. Barbour of Virginia led the way in formulating the new Southern argument against federal authority in the territories. If Congress wanted to ban slavery in Missouri, he argued, it should have done so through territorial legislation. Barbour, a member of the Old Republican political faction in Virginia, articulated an early form of what would become the doctrine of popular sovereignty. Rather than usurping local control, Congress should consult the people of Missouri, "because [otherwise] we should be legislating directly against the wishes of a people who were competent to legislate for themselves."[16] Framed in these terms, the Southern constitutional argument becomes clear. Congress could not infringe on the people's right to draft their own state constitution as they saw fit, so long as it provided for a republican form of government.

The Missourians themselves embraced the Southern proslavery argument against restriction. Territorial delegate John Scott accused the restrictionists of reducing Missouri to a lesser among equals. Other than guaranteeing a republican form of government, he argued, all other decisions in the process of constitution making belonged to the people of the territory itself. "In no part of the Constitution was the power proposed to be exercised, of imposing conditions on a new State," Scott argued in Congress. Moreover, the Constitution gave the territories and new states the power "to regulate their own internal police, of admitting such citizens as they pleased, or of introducing any description of property, that they should consider as essential or necessary to their prosperity.[17] In spite of their protests, however, the opponents of restriction lost their first bid to defeat the Tallmadge amendment on constitutional grounds. Following an impassioned defense by its author on February 16, 1819, the House of Representatives passed the amendment on a strictly sectional vote.[18]

At the same time that the House of Representatives debated Missouri statehood, it also considered legislation creating Arkansas Territory. Carved from the southern portion of the old Missouri Territory, Arkansas Territory encompassed the present state as well as most of present-day Oklahoma. After the House passed the Missouri bill with the Tallmadge amendment, it opened debate on Arkansas. Attempting to assert congressional authority over slavery in the territories, John Taylor moved to insert a clause in the bill prohibiting slavery in Arkansas.[19] His motives were clear in light of the Southern attack on the restrictionists; this time, Taylor intended to test congressional authority over slavery in a territory from its inception.

Taylor almost certainly assumed that Southerners would object, and indeed they did, unsurprisingly arguing that the actual inhabitants of Arkansas should decide for themselves. Asserting that a ban on slavery in Arkansas Territory did not constitute a needful rule or regulation, Representative Felix Walker of North Carolina responded that Congress had "no legitimate power to legislate on the property of the citizens."[20] Walker and the proslavery Southern congressmen derived their argument from Thomas Jefferson's conception of state formation. To Jefferson, a new state could be equal with the existing states only "if it constituted itself, without outside interference, and if it was received into the union 'on an equal footing.'"[21] Walker took Jefferson's reading of the Constitution and extended it to the territorial phase by taking a narrow reading of the Needful Rules and Regulation Clause. "In organizing a territorial government, and forming a constitution," he argued, "they and they alone, have the right, and are the proper judges of that policy best adapted to their genius and interest, and it ought to be exclusively left to them."[22]

Restrictionists like Tallmadge and Taylor and anti-restrictionists like Barbour and Walker had staked out the extremes of constitutional interpretation in the issue of slavery in Missouri and Arkansas. Other congressmen began looking for middle ground. Moderates like Congressman Louis McLane of Delaware sought to avoid Walker's expansive definition of territorial sovereignty and narrow construction of congressional authority over the territories by looking to precedent. McLane proposed the "fixing of a line on the west of the Mississippi, north of which slavery should not be tolerated," which essentially extended the precedent set by the Northwest

Ordinance.[23] Other representatives soon followed, including John Taylor, who proposed banning slavery north of the line of north latitude thirty-six degrees, thirty minutes after his Arkansas amendment failed in the House. Taylor's more moderate form of restriction likewise failed when Southern congressmen united in favor of a stricter version of territorial sovereignty. The narrow interpretation of the Needful Rules and Regulations Clause had struck a nerve in the South, where slaveholders had become alarmed at any effort to restrict the peculiar institution. Though unfazed by restriction some thirty years earlier in the Northwest and Southwest Ordinances, Southerners now stood by their revised interpretation of the Constitution. Congress passed the Arkansas bill on July 4, 1819, implicitly leaving the matter of slavery to the territory. The Missouri Crisis, however, remained unsettled, as the 15th Congress adjourned without passing a bill for Missouri statehood.[24]

The Missourians would not, however, let go of their aspirations to statehood. Politicians in the territory assumed the arguments against restriction that had appeared in the congressional debate. Writing as "Hampden," Nathaniel Beverley Tucker derided restriction as an affront to the rights of the people of Missouri. A Virginia native who sympathized with the old Republicans, Tucker became a leading voice against restriction in St. Louis, taking aim at those who argued that the Needful Rules and Regulations Clause of the Constitution permitted restriction. Tucker offered his own interpretation of the clause, which borrowed from the congressional debate but expanded on it significantly. To Tucker, the Needful Rules and Regulations Clause referred only to federal property in the territories, not congressional power or oversight of local law. Here Tucker linked the territories clause with the Tenth Amendment and states' rights ideology. The prospective state of Missouri gained "none of its *powers* from Congress; all it needs from that quarter is the *means of organization*." Tucker spoke directly to the slavery issue as the crux of the debate. "Is it not insulting to our common sense, to be told that a constitution not only permitting, but partly based on domestic slavery" allowed for restriction, Tucker asked. The restrictionists, he affirmed, believed that Congress had the power "*to make laws to bind the territory in all cases whatsoever.*"[25] Other proslavery Missourians largely echoed Tucker's theories, emphasizing that the restrictionists sought, in the words of one observer, to "enforce a single restriction in direct opposition to the will of the people of this territory." Congress may have created the Missouri Territory, but the people themselves had created the federal government. "Shall the *creature* be permitted to assume an absolute sovereignty over his *creator,* and to stifle even an inquiry into his powers?" asked another correspondent.[26]

The restrictionists and anti-restrictionists had stumbled on a series of constitutional questions that had defied simple answers since the first effort to create a system for territorial government, the Ordinance of 1784 that Thomas Jefferson had drafted for the Confederation Congress. The national government clearly did not want to become a quasi-colonial power with a center governing a periphery. Yet the creation of territories implied a sort of intermediary phase on the way to statehood. Early Americans often referred to the territorial phase as a period of tutelage for future states. The Missourians, however, objected to the notion that they required any sort of supervision from the federal government. Moreover, questions arose regarding the power of a territory to draft a constitution free from congressional interference. Restrictionists argued that Congress indeed possessed the power to dictate terms to the territories, while the opponents of restriction argued that Congress only had the power to ensure that new states adopted a republican form of government.

Faced with rising antislavery sentiment from the North, the proslavery opponents of restriction sought to extend states' rights to the point at which a territory crafted a constitution and applied for statehood. The stakes were higher than Missouri alone, as Tucker made clear when he claimed that restriction would "establish a precedent that will sap the foundation of state authority and make this federal government a consolidated nation."[27] Southerners in 1819 believed that restriction in Missouri could and probably would lead to restriction elsewhere. Moreover, it could lead to a wider campaign for abolition. To protect the peculiar institution from antislavery attacks and to prevent the movement of an emboldened federal government against slavery elsewhere, the slaveholding class had to adopt a narrow definition of what constituted needful rules and regulations for the territories. Of course, that required ignoring precedent like the Northwest Ordinance, which is why Tucker and other Southerners argued that Congress could not restrict the right of a person to move to a territory with his personal property—including enslaved human beings.

Only when a territory prepared for statehood, could the people decide in a constitutional convention whether to permit or prohibit slavery. One can see in the Southern argument regarding Missouri the beginnings of the argument made thirty-seven years later by Roger Brooke Taney in *Dred Scott v. Sandford*, that slavery followed the flag and that Congress could not legislate against it within a territory.

The restrictionists rejected the proslavery idea that slavery in the territories lay beyond the purview of congressional authority. Their argument hinged on a broad definition of Congress's power to impose rules on territories and its discretion to create new states. Though the Constitution "admits all the *original* states to hold slaves as they please," a Northern observer wrote, the "*discretionary* power granted to admit new states into the union, by simply saying, 'new states may be admitted,' necessarily supposes a right in congress to designate the conditions of admission."[28] In addition to parsing the meaning of "new states may be admitted," Northerners rebutted the idea of states' rights as applying to a territory. An Illinois newspaper editor asked why a nation of six million people should allow "a few thousand the right of deciding a question of such vital importance, merely because the few, from pecuniary interest, wish for the future toleration of slavery?"[29]

The Sixteenth Congress would convene in December 1819 and everyone knew that Missouri would dominate the session. Against that backdrop, Northerners and Southerners increasingly debated Missouri statehood in constitutional terms. Citizens held political meetings throughout the nation to discuss the Missouri controversy. Numerous meetings in the Northeastern states focused on Congress's right—and duty—to reject an application for statehood if it deemed the prospective state's constitution "to be inconsistent or inimical to republican institutions."[30] Rallies in Trenton, New Jersey; New York City, Philadelphia, Boston, and other Northern cities all emphasized congressional authority over the territories and over state-making. Constitutional interpretation took center stage as a means of debating the future of slavery in the United States. The proceedings of these meetings suggest that sectional divisions over slavery had hardened over the course of the summer and fall of 1819 in anticipation of the renewed congressional debate over slavery in Missouri. Southern political committees demanded Missouri's admission "on an equal footing with the other states" and expressed resentment that the restrictionists had used slavery to deny Missouri admission to the Union.[31] "[E]very scheme to give us a fair participation in the benefits of the union, has been thwarted or defeated," argued a Kentucky anti-restrictionist.[32] In addition to citizens' committees, the legislatures of nine Northern states took to the old practice of instructing senators, who in the nineteenth century were elected by state legislatures, to vote in favor of restriction.[33]

As legislatures and citizens deliberated on the constitutionality of restriction, President James Monroe observed the debate and weighed his opinions. Monroe had remained silent on the Missouri issue during the last session of Congress, but by December he began taking a more active role in the crisis. "I indulge a strong hope that the restriction will not pass," Monroe wrote to his son-in-law and political advisor George Hay. Between December 1819 and March 1820, Monroe worked behind the scenes to shape policy toward slavery in Missouri.[34]

Monroe had a long history with the issue of slavery in the territories, having played a role in drafting what would become the Northwest Ordinance of 1787. Thirty years earlier, as a member of the Confederation Congress, Monroe had devised a structure for territorial governance that became part of the Northwest Ordinance and had prevailed in the intervening years. Monroe's record on congressional authority over the territories appears to have evolved over his career. He supported the Land Ordinance of 1784, though it is unclear whether he endorsed the proposed ban on slavery in the territories after the year 1800 that Jefferson had proposed. Three years later, the draft legislation he wrote to revise the Ordinance of 1784 did not restrict slavery. Only by the action of Monroe's political adversary Rufus King did the slavery prohibition become a part of the Northwest Ordinance.[35]

True to his roots as a Virginia slaveholder, Monroe by 1819 opposed restriction in Missouri and sought to sway the outcome in favor of proslavery interests. He questioned the constitutionality of the Northwest Ordinance's ban on slavery and sided with the South in Congress, which he argued could neither ban slavery in the territories nor impose conditions on a territory seeking admission to the Union.[36] Monroe stood firm against compromise on the issue of restriction until February 1820, when it appeared that failure to compromise could jeopardize the future of slavery in the West as well as his bid for a second term as president. Only then did he set aside his proslavery constitutional scruples and endorse what would become the Missouri Compromise.

The 16th Congress convened in December 1819, with Missouri foremost on its agenda. James Tallmadge, the congressman who had inaugurated the Missouri crisis, was a conspicuous absence; faced with poor health he had declined to run for another term. His amendment, however, loomed over the session. Three weeks later, the House of Representatives resumed debate on the Missouri statehood bill. Speaker of the House Henry Clay spoke from the floor, arguing that the restrictionists had overstepped the constitutional bounds of territorial administration. "When the population and extent of a territory had been such as to entitle a territory to the privilege of self-government, and the rank of a State," he argued, "the single question had presented itself to admit or reject it, without qualification."[37]

Clay's opening remarks, as well as the trajectory of the entire debate in Congress, suggest that constitutional interpretation of congressional authority over the territories and the power of Congress to admit states to the Union remained central to the Missouri controversy. Northern and Southern congressmen lined up to offer their versions of the restrictionist and anti-restrictionist arguments. The first round of deliberation over Missouri had played out in the House of Representatives, but in the Sixteenth Congress the Senate joined the debate. The lines of contention remained similar, though Southern senators in particular emphasized that the restrictionist interpretation of the Needful Rules and Regulations Clause deprived residents of the territories the right of self-government. Georgia senator Freeman Walker opposed congressional intervention, arguing that the Missourians "ought to be esteemed at least as capable of judging of this matter as those so far removed" from the issue. Walker framed the slavery issue as a matter of "internal police" that was beyond congressional purview. His argument resonated in the minds of those who objected to congressional interference with Missouri's right to draft a constitution of its own choosing. "Let us grant to them the boon of self-government without alloy," Walker concluded.[38] Nathaniel Macon, a senator from North Carolina, agreed. "A wise Legislature," he stated, "will always consider the character, condition, and feeling, of those to be legislated for." The Missourians clearly wished to permit slavery in their state; Congress should allow them that right.[39]

The proslavery contingent in Congress had developed a compelling argument about the right to territorial self-government based on a restrictive reading of the Constitution's clause on the territories. They linked restriction to a broader movement of consolidation of power in the hands of the federal government. The Missouri controversy represented a threat to state sovereignty and to the sovereignty of people in the territories because it placed the national government in the position of administering the territories as if they were colonies. The restrictionists' interpretation of the Constitution, Southerners argued, did not follow the original intent of the framers.

The proslavery argument about territorial self-government gained Southerners a few Northern allies. Henry Meigs, a first-term Republican congressman from New York, defended the right of the Missourians to create a government of their own choosing—with or without slavery. "We are attempting here to legislate for Missouri, without a due attention to the situation, the genius of the people, soil, climate, and all the matters which ought to constitute good law," he argued.[40] Like the Southern congressional delegation, Meigs took a narrow interpretation of the Needful Rules and Regulations Clause, but he advanced the anti-restrictionist argument in a way that no one else had anticipated. Meigs argued that Congress could not enact laws "contrary to the genius and will of a people" because they would resist such enactments anyway. "Such attempts will be mere absurdities," he continued, "violence will be committed upon the fundamental principles of all law, and can never be executed."[41] Perhaps Meigs drew his argument from the widespread evasion of the slavery prohibition in the Northwest Territory. Regardless of its inspiration, he had articulated a fundamental idea about slavery and the law. Settlers in Missouri and elsewhere would not tolerate what they considered excessive federal interference before they started evading the law. In other words, Congress neither had the power to prohibit slavery in Missouri nor did it want to do so lest it provoke resistance to the law. Thirty-five years later, Illinois senator Stephen A. Douglas made a similar point in a debate at Freeport, Illinois, with Abraham Lincoln—what became known as the Freeport Doctrine.

Meigs's opinions on the constitutionality of restriction certainly garnered support from his Southern colleagues. Some Northern Republicans also agreed. The Philadelphia printer Mathew Carey, likewise a Jeffersonian

Republican, warned of the cost to Congress if restrictionists were to "persist in shackling [Missouri] with restrictions." Carey opposed slavery, but he also believed the Southern argument against restriction as "sufficiently plausible." Both Carey and Meigs suggested that the restrictionists had waged a game of political opportunism by making a test case of Missouri for a broader campaign against slavery. One can see in their opinions on slavery and constitutional law hints of the coalition of planters and plain republicans that Martin Van Buren sought to make in the aftermath of the Missouri controversy.[42]

Some members of Congress looked for an escape from the heated debate over Missouri. For politicians like Meigs, that meant letting the settlers of Missouri decide the slavery question. For others, like Representative Samuel Augustus Foot of Connecticut, the judiciary provided a path out of the congressional impasse. Like Meigs, Foot wanted Congress to leave the question "to the good sense of the people of the States to be formed out of that Territory," but if Congress could not agree on the underlying constitutional issues, "it might be left for the proper tribunal, the Supreme Court" to determine the proper interpretation.[43] In other words, the Supreme Court via judicial review could determine the real meaning of the Needful Rules and Regulations Clause as well as the latitude of congressional power over state-making. How the Supreme Court would have ruled is anyone's guess. Under John Marshall's leadership as chief justice, the high court had taken a nationalist interpretation of the Constitution that might have suggested a victory for the restrictionists. On the other hand, the slaveowner Marshall also seemed to protect the interests of the slaveholding class. Foot's suggestion gained no support in Congress, but twenty-eight years later John Clayton, a Delaware Whig congressman, revived the notion during the debate over slavery in the Mexican Cession.[44]

Doctrinaire restrictionists and anti-restrictionists had set the polar ends of constitutional interpretation over slavery in the territories, but in the middle rested a number of congressmen who wanted a way out of the impasse over Missouri. Hints of a compromise had appeared in the previous session when Delaware congressman Louis McLane called for a dividing line between slave and free territory in the Louisiana Purchase. By January 1820, the conversation over compromise had resurfaced. On

February 3, 1820, Illinois senator Jesse Thomas proposed that Congress admit Missouri as a slave state but exclude it in the remaining territory that lay north of thirty-six degrees, thirty minutes north latitude—essentially Missouri's southern border. Southern senators had already successfully paired Missouri's admission as a slave state with the admission of Maine as a free state, thereby preserving the balance of free and slave states in the Union—and by extension, the balance of power in the U.S. Senate.[45]

The subsequent debate over statehood for Missouri and Maine as well as the Thomas plan tested the limits of the resolve among both the ardent restrictionists and anti-restrictionists. On the one hand, the effort to link the admission of Maine and Missouri "deeply alienated the North and stiffened the South."[46] The restrictionists, in particular, resented this element of the emerging compromise. On the other hand, the desire among many politicians to preserve national unity and end the crisis led to a softening of opinion regarding congressional authority over the territories. Louis McLane, for one, had to moderate his views on territorial restriction to placate constituents in Delaware. He maintained his opinion "that Congress does not possess the power to impose the contemplated restriction," but only because Congress had failed to restrict slavery when it created the Missouri Territory. When pressed about congressional authority in the territories, McLane wavered between defending the right of a territory to make its own laws on slavery and asserting that Congress "can give laws to a Territory." McLane, like other congressmen, concerned himself more with the right of a territory to draft a constitution without congressional interference rather than the more general question of federal oversight in the territories.[47]

Outside of Congress, the Old Republicans of Virginia remained the most unwavering defenders of a strict construction of congressional authority over the territories. "Can we compromise with the constitution of our country?" asked Thomas Ritchie, editor of the *Richmond Enquirer*, because according to him the Thomas compromise did just that.[48] The Old Republicans, according to Claiborne W. Gooch, a co-editor of the *Richmond Enquirer*, were "all in a ferment about this compromise spoke of in Washington." The proponents of compromise saw it as a way to save the Union, but Gooch believed precisely the opposite. "If the Southern people yield—the consequences will be serious—and unless the Northern people retrace their steps, the result will be equally so—the naked question will then be presented—war or disunion."[49]

Other Southerners took a less apocalyptic view of the negotiations even as they defended the right of the Missourians to write slavery into their constitution. For the sake of argument, Philip Barbour of Virginia conceded the point that Congress possessed authority over the territories. Nevertheless, the restrictionists had missed their opportunity because Congress had already delegated the authority over slavery to the Missouri territorial government by statute. "We have, by one of our own regulations, given it a legislative body; that we have extended to that body the whole power of legislation, subject only to the limitation that their laws shall not be inconsistent with the Constitution and laws of the United States," Barbour argued.[50] John Scott of Missouri, the territorial delegate to the House of Representatives, quickly agreed, noting that when Congress authorized a territorial government for Missouri it granted the territorial legislature "all legislative power without reserve."[51] In sum, the opponents of restriction argued that Congress had "already spoken on the slavery issue" when it established territorial governments for Louisiana, Missouri, and Arkansas, without legislating on the issue of slavery, yet the restrictionists sought to bend the Needful Rules and Regulations Clause of the Constitution to reverse precedent.[52]

The ambiguities of the Constitution's clause on territories remained, however, and some Southerners refused to yield on a question they feared could have a negative impact on the future of slavery. Specifically, the more radical anti-restrictionists saw that preventing slavery in a particular territory might ensure its eventual entry into the Union as a free state. "What is a territorial restriction to-day becomes a state restriction to-morrow," Thomas Ritchie opined.[53] A South Carolina congressman argued that "in making such regulations for the government of the territory, [Congress is] no more authorized to inhibit slavery in the territory, than they are in the State—for, if they should have the power, it would indirectly effect the same thing."[54] John Tyler, a Virginia congressman and future president, concurred with Ritchie and the Old Republicans by portraying the restrictionists in Congress as quasi-colonizers and framing the stakes involved in the language of the Revolution. "England denied to us the right to legislate, except by her special authority; nay, she proclaimed the very principle which you now proclaim as applicable to Missouri—the right to bind you by her own system of legislation."[55]

The restrictionists remained unpersuaded by the proslavery rhetoric on the territories clause. They flatly rejected the extent of territorial sovereignty proposed by the Old Republicans, but even more moderate formulations of the anti-restrictionist policy, such as the concept articulated by Louis McLane, failed to gain traction among the restrictionists. The "passing of one act prescribing the manner in which laws for the Territory shall be made," one Northern restrictionist argued, "does not commit Congress; they can change the mode at their pleasure." The restrictionists likewise had taken note of the differences of opinion on territorial power among the anti-restrictionists. "Even gentlemen on the opposite side of the question admit we may" legislate for the territories, argued a Northern congressman.[56] At the most extreme, some restrictionists remained convinced that Congress administered the territories on behalf of the nation and with unlimited authority. As a Massachusetts representative argued, "absolute sovereignty resides, not in minute portions or States, but in the whole people, whose will . . . is the law, and must be obeyed."[57]

By February 1820, however, a path toward compromise appeared despite speech after speech from congressmen who articulated rigid positions for and against restriction. Writing in early 1820, Mathew Carey called for compromise based on precedent—an "understanding" between the free and slave states as he put it—"that slavery should be tolerated within a certain line, and excluded beyond it."[58] The Thomas proviso extended the practice begun with the Northwest Ordinance using the Ohio River as a line between slave and free territory. By March, the House of Representatives had finally acceded to the principle of compromise and passage seemed imminent. Resistance certainly remained. Some Northerners objected to the compromise because it threatened to "establish different interests, and create the worst sort of parties that we can possibly have," that is, sectional parties based on the issue of slavery.[59] Southern conservatives, on the other hand, had tried to erase the precedent set by the Northwest Ordinance by taking a strong stance against federal authority over the territories and state-making. To the minds of Southern conservatives, the compromise yielded on the issue of congressional authority over slavery in the territories, a constitutional point that they believed their section could not afford to concede. "Why use this very expression which seems copied from the ordinance of '87," Thomas Ritchie asked in the *Richmond Enquirer,* "if it be not intended to pursue the precedent set in the N.W. territory?"[60] Even as Monroe warmed to the idea of compromise, he retained the skepticism of many of his fellow Virginians, fearing that the Thomas amendment's ban on slavery north of the compromise line "should apply to territories, after they become states as well as before."[61]

President Monroe feared that the South could do far worse if it held out against a modified form of restriction any longer. If the South rejected the compromise, the president realized, the restrictionists would stall Missouri's admission to the Union and work for a blanket prohibition of slavery in the western territories. That 1820 was an election year added urgency. What if the restrictionists gained control in Congress? What if Rufus King, Monroe's opponent in the 1816 election and a leader among the restrictionists, mounted a presidential campaign and won? The South, Monroe had become convinced, could not afford the risk.[62] Yet the president remained uncertain about the constitutionality of the Missouri Compromise and so in the days prior to its passage Monroe consulted with numerous colleagues on constitutional law. Former president James Madison responded to a letter from Monroe with a nuanced interpretation of the territorial clause of the Constitution. Madison recognized that the "ductile nature" of the Needful Rules and Regulations Clause left "much to legislative discretion." The territories required congressional oversight when initially created, but the "suspension of the great principle of self-government, ought not to be extended farther nor continued longer than the occasion might fairly require." For Madison, that meant that Thomas's proviso was unconstitutional.[63]

The Senate passed the compromise bill on February 17. Thanks to some clever maneuvering by Speaker of the House Henry Clay and campaigning by the president and his allies, the bill cleared the House on March 5. Monroe immediately summoned his cabinet for what was their first meeting on the Missouri crisis. The president asked them to submit written opinions on two questions: whether Congress had the right to prohibit slavery in the territories and whether the Missouri bill, which prohibited slavery north of the compromise line proposed by Thomas, applied only to territories or to states after their admission to the Union. Secretary of the Treasury William H. Crawford, Attorney General William Wirt, and Secretary of War John C. Calhoun—all slaveholders—responded that the federal government possessed the power to prohibit slavery in the territories, a peculiarity that Secretary of State John Quincy Adams, who concurred, noted afterward in his diary. "The progress of this discussion has so totally merged in passion all the reasoning faculties of the slave-holders," Adams wrote, "that these gentlemen, in the simplicity of their hearts, had come to a conclusion in direct opposition to their premises, without being aware of or conscious of inconsistency." Crawford, Wirt, and Calhoun, however, all believed that the slavery restriction in the bill applied only to the territories and could not bind a sovereign state. Adams disagreed on the second point, stating that the restriction was permanent, because "by its interdiction in the territory, the people, when they come to form a Constitution, would have no right to sanction slavery." Crawford disagreed strongly and the two men had a heated exchange in the meeting. Calhoun sought to make peace by asking the president to reword his second question to ask whether the word "forever" conflicted with the Constitution. All could agree on this equivocal question, and there the debate closed. On March 6, 1820, President Monroe signed the Missouri Compromise bill into law.[64]

In the end, moderates overcame those who took a more extreme view of congressional authority over the territories, though it had taken considerable effort by Speaker of the House Henry Clay to overcome Northern opposition to the compromise. By dividing the bill and voting separately on statehood and the territorial restriction, Clay succeeded at shepherding the compromise through his chamber. Southern moderates and the so-called Northern doughfaces as the eccentric Virginia Old Republican John Randolph called them, played a pivotal role in the compromise vote. Indeed, the "seventeen or eighteen doughfaces Randolph belittled made sectional peace possible in 1820."[65]

Some congressmen, especially the Northern doughfaces who supported the compromise, explained their votes to constituents after the session ended. Their explanations rested more on pragmatic politics than constitutional theory. Mark Langdon Hill, a congressman from the District of Maine, believed that the North had made a good deal for antislavery interests, exchanging slavery in Missouri for restriction "from a territory larger than all of the original thirteen United States, in exact conformity to the ordinance of 1787."[66] Representative John Holmes, also from Maine, justified the compromise by explaining that the Constitution itself was a "compromise of conflicting rights and interests" that required accommodating different interests and beliefs. That Maine gained admission to the Union as part of the new legislation likely swayed these two congressmen, but their points well explained the motivations of many moderates who voted in favor of compromise.[67]

Strict constructionists, such as the Old Republicans, however, regretted that Congress had conceded congressional authority over slavery in the territories and predicted that it would embolden antislavery interests in the future. In the context of 1820, though, most Southerners saw the compromise as merely an extension of precedent that a previous generation of slaveholders had accepted, however grudgingly. In the Missouri Compromise, Southerners saw a good deal and accepted the terms, believing that the compromise measures conceded little of significance. The roll call vote on the 36° 30′ territorial restriction indicates the limits of strict construction of the Constitution's territorial clause. Southerners in the House voted 39 to 37 in favor of the restriction. The Virginia delegation—twenty-two representatives in all—voted 18 to 4 against the compromise line. The rest of the South's representatives voted in favor, overwhelmingly so in the border states of Delaware, Kentucky, and Maryland.[68] Strict construction had its limits.

Some Southerners wishfully "doubted that Congress would actually impose the restriction when the region was organized into territories," recalling how the federal government had turned a deaf ear toward slaveholding in Indiana and Illinois, which was technically forbidden by the Northwest Ordinance.[69] Like the Southern members of James Monroe's cabinet, most Southerners maintained that the clause in the compromise that "forever prohibited" slavery north of the compromise line ceased to apply at the moment of statehood. Whereas some Old Republicans seemed to suggest that Congress should provide legal protection for the right of residents in the territories to determine the status of slavery, moderates instead focused on strengthening states' rights doctrine to counteract the antislavery restrictionists. For the moment, the moderates seemed to have taken the smart course. Thirty-five years later, however, when the fight over slavery in Bleeding Kansas raged and the Supreme Court issued its infamous decision in *Dred Scott v. Sandford*, Southerners would once again take up the idea of federal protection for slavery in the territories.

Predictably, the Old Republicans fulminated against the compromise. "A constitution warped from its legitimate bearings, and an immense region of territory closed for ever against the Southern and Western people—such is the 'sorry sight' which rises to *our* view," Thomas Ritchie wrote in his *Enquirer*.[70] Outside of Virginia, however, Southerners took a more sanguine view of the bill. From Washington, John C. Calhoun confided to Andrew Jackson that the "agitators" of the Missouri controversy "have, in my opinion, not only completely failed; but have destroyed to a great extent their future capacity for future mischief." A coalition of Southern Republicans, along with cooperative Northerners, had defeated the restrictionists. A majority of Southerners found the outcome acceptable.[71]

"Never has a Territory so young been called upon to act so great a part; for now is thrown into its hands the decision of a question upon which depends not only the liberties of the Missouri people and of their unborn posterity, but also the safety of the Republic and the preservation of the Union."[72] So wrote a correspondent to the *St. Louis Enquirer* several weeks after passage of the Missouri Compromise. The drama of the second Missouri Compromise was yet to unfold. As for the issue of congressional authority over the territories, the crisis had passed for the moment as proslavery Southerners conceded some power to Washington while the restrictions grudgingly accepted that federal authority had limits—if for nothing else than to preserve the Union. But the next generation of proslavery politicians who faced a crisis over slavery in the territories would not yield to federal power so easily. In the 1850s, they would renounce the moderate interpretation of needful rules and regulations in ways that finally fractured the Union.

NOTES

1. *Annals of Congress*, House, 15th Congress, 2d Session, 1170.
2. Thomas Jefferson to John Holmes, April 22, 1820, in Merrill D. Peterson, ed., *Thomas Jefferson: Writings* (New York: Library of America, 1984), 1434.
3. U.S. Constitution, Article IV, Section 3, Clause 2.
4. See Glover Moore, *The Missouri Controversy, 1819–1821* (Lexington: University of Kentucky Press, 1953), 31–32.

5. "Application of Missouri for Admission into the Union as a State," November 21, 1818, *American State Papers*: Miscellaneous, 28 vols. (Washington: Gales and Seaton, 1832-1861), 2: 557–58. The 1820 census lists Missouri as having a population of approximately 66,586.

6. See Peter Onuf, *Jefferson's Empire: The Language of American Nationhood* (Charlottesville: University of Virginia Press, 2000), 109–46; Robert Pierce Forbes, *The Missouri Compromise and Its Aftermath: Slavery and the Meaning of America* (Chapel Hill: University of North Carolina Press, 2007), 6–7.

7. See Forbes, *The Missouri Compromise and Its Aftermath*, 33–41; Matthew Mason, *Slavery and Politics in the Early American Republic* (Chapel Hill: University of North Carolina Press, 2007), 177–88.

8. See Mason, *Slavery and Politics in the Early American Republic*, 179–83; Forbes, *The Missouri Compromise and Its Aftermath*, 32–68; Shaw Livermore, Jr., *The Twilight of Federalism: The Disintegration of the Federalist Party, 1815–1830* (Princeton: Princeton University Press, 1962), 88–112.

9. Forbes, *The Missouri Compromise and Its Aftermath*, 36.

10. *Annals of Congress*, House, 15th Cong., 2d Sess., 1170.

11. *Annals of Congress*, House, 15th Cong., 2d Sess., 1170–71. On the alliance between Tallmadge and Taylor, see Forbes, *The Missouri Compromise and Its Aftermath*, 37–38; Moore, *Missouri Controversy*, 38–44.

12. *Annals of Congress*, House, 15th Cong., 2d Sess., 1171.

13. Remarks on the Tallmadge Amendment, February 15, 1819, in James F. Hopkins, et. al., eds., *The Papers of Henry Clay*, 11 vols. (Lexington: University of Kentucky Press, 1959–1992), II: 670. The House reporter did not transcribe Clay's speech (or many of his speeches from this session of Congress), so historians have reconstructed his argument from the context of other speeches and from statements in the press.

14. Livermore, *The Twilight of Federalism*, 90. For a discussion of the Federalist course in the Missouri debates, see pp. 88–112.

15. Forbes, *The Missouri Compromise and Its Aftermath*, 41; Sean Wilentz, *The Rise of American Democracy: Jefferson to Lincoln* (New York: W. W. Norton & Company, 2006), 227–28. The first scholar to make this distinction was Hermann von Holst, *The Constitutional and Political History of the United States*, 8 vols. (Chicago: Callaghan and Company, 1876–1892), I: 364–65.

16. *Annals of Congress*, House, 15th Cong., 2d Sess., 1191.

17. *Annals of Congress*, House, 15th Cong., 2d Sess., 1196–97.

18. For the vote, see *Annals of Congress*, House, 15th Cong., 2d Sess., 1214–15. For a sectional roll call analysis of the vote, see Moore, *Missouri Controversy*, 53.

19. *Annals of Congress*, House, 15th Cong., 2d Sess., 1222.

20. *Annals of Congress*, House, 15th Cong., 2d Sess., 1226.

21. Onuf, *Jefferson's Empire*, 144. For Jefferson's conception of territories and states, see pp. 118, 143–45.

22. *Annals of Congress*, House, 15th Cong., 2d Sess., 1227.

23. *Annals of Congress*, House, 15th Cong., 2d Sess., 1228.

24. See *Annals of Congress*, House, 15th Cong., 2d Sess., 1278–81, 1228, 1229, 1281. For the Arkansas bill, see Act of March 2, 1819, ch. XLIX, in Richard Peters, ed., *The Public Statutes at Large of the United States of* America, 7 vols. (Boston: Charles C. Little and James Brown, 1845), 3: 493–96. For the Senate's action on the Missouri bill, see *Annals of Congress*, Senate, 15th Cong., 2d Sess., 273, 279–80.

25. See Robert J. Brugger, *Beverley Tucker: Heart over Head in the Old South* (Baltimore: Johns Hopkins University Press, 1978), 49–57; *St. Louis Enquirer*, April 7, 1819.

26. *St. Louis Enquirer*, April 21, 1819. See also *Missouri Gazette*, April 7, 1819.

27. *St. Louis Enquirer*, April 28, 1819.

28. *Niles' Weekly Register*, August 14, 1819. Italics in the original.

29. *Niles' Weekly Register*, July 10, 1819.

30. Don E. Fehrenbacher discusses how the issue of slavery in the territories became increasingly "constitutionalized" in the antebellum era. See *The Dred Scott Case: Its Significance in American Law and Politics* (New York: Oxford University Press, 2001), 102–03, 135–51; *Niles' Weekly Register*, November 6, 1819. See also November 27, 1819.

31. *Niles' Weekly Register*, November 6, 1819.

32. *St. Louis Enquirer*, December 4, 1819.

33. See Herman V. Ames, ed., *State Documents on Federal Relations: The States and the United States* (1906; repr., New York: Da Capo Press, 1970), 196–203.

34. James Monroe to [George Hay], December 20, 1819, James Monroe Papers, 17881828.21, Mss2M7576a, Microfilm Reel C54, Virginia Historical Society, Richmond, VA.

35. Harry Ammon, *James Monroe: The Quest for National Identity* (New York: McGraw-Hill, 1971), 42, 54; Robert F. Berkhofer, Jr., "Jefferson, the Ordinance of 1784, and the American Territorial System," *William and Mary Quarterly* 29 (April 1972): 259–61.

36. See John Craig Hammond, "President, Planter, Politician: James Monroe, the Missouri Crisis, and the Politics of Slavery," *Journal of American History* 105 (March 2019): 1–25, for the latest and most compelling interpretation of Monroe's constitutional thought on Missouri.

37. *Annals of Congress*, House, 16th Cong., 1st Sess., 832.

38. *Annals of Congress*, Senate, 16th Cong., 1st Sess., 169–70, 175.

39. *Annals of Congress*, Senate, 16th Cong., 1st Sess., 222.

40. *Annals of Congress*, Senate, 16th Cong., 1st Sess., 944.

41. *Annals of Congress*, Senate, 16th Cong., 1st Sess., 946.

42. Mathew Carey, *Some Considerations on the Impropriety and Inexpediency of Renewing the Missouri Question* (Philadelphia: M. Carey & Son, 1820), 4, 38.

43. *Annals of Congress*, House, 16th Cong., 1st Sess., 949.

44. See Paul Finkelman, *Supreme Injustice: Slavery in the Nation's Highest Court* (Cambridge: Harvard University Press, 2018), 26–75, for Marshall's jurisprudence on slavery. For the Clayton compromise, see Fehrenbacher, *The Dred Scott Case*, 148–51.

45. *Annals of Congress*, House, 15th Cong., 2d Sess., 1228. For linking Maine and Missouri's statehood, see Moore, *The Missouri Controversy*, 86–90; for the motives behind the plan, see Forbes, *The Missouri Compromise and Its Aftermath*, 62–68.

46. Forbes, *The Missouri Compromise and Its Aftermath*, 68.

47. *Annals of Congress*, House, 16th Cong., 1st Sess., 1140, 1160.

48. *Richmond Enquirer*, February 10, 1820.

49. C. W. Gooch to David Campbell, February 16, 1820, Box 4, Campbell Family Papers, Rare Book, Manuscript, and Special Collections Library, Duke University, Durham, North Carolina.

50. *Annals of Congress*, House, 16th Cong., 1st Sess., 1237.

51. *Annals of Congress*, House, 16th Cong., 1st Sess., 1502.

52. *Annals of Congress*, House, 16th Cong., 1st Sess., 1320.

53. *Richmond Enquirer*, March 7, 1820.

54. *Annals of Congress*, House, 16th Cong., 1st Sess., 1327.

55. *Annals of Congress*, House, 16th Cong., 1st Sess., 1383. For Tyler's beliefs on states' rights during the Missouri controversy, see Dan Monroe, *The Republican Vision of John Tyler* (College Station: Texas A&M University Press, 2003), 24–47.

56. *Annals of Congress*, House, 16th Cong., 1st Sess., 1130, 1345.

57. *Annals of Congress*, House, 16th Cong., 1st Sess., 1294–95.

58. Carey, *Some Considerations on the Missouri Question*, 57.

59. *Niles' Weekly Register*, January 29, 1820.

60. *Richmond Enquirer*, February 26, 1820.

61. James Monroe to Thomas Jefferson, February 19, 1820, in Stanislaus Murray Hamilton, ed., *The Writings of James Monroe: Including a Collection of His Public and Private Papers and Correspondence Now for the First Time Printed*, 6 vols. (New York: G. P. Putnam's Sons, 1902), VI: 115–16.

62. See Hammond, "President, Planter, Politician," 19–25.

63. James Madison to James Monroe, February 23, 1820, *Letters and Other Writings of James Madison, Fourth President of the United States*, 4 vols. (Philadelphia: J. B. Lippincott & Co., 1865), III: 168.

64. Adams recalls the meeting in his diary. See entry for March 3, 1820, in Charles Francis Adams, ed., *Memoirs of John Quincy Adams, Comprising Portions of His Diary from 1795 to 1848*, 12 vols. (Philadelphia, PA: J. B. Lippincott & Co., 1874–1877), V: 4–11. See also Noble E. Cunningham, Jr., *The Presidency of James Monroe* (Lawrence: University Press of Kansas, 1996), 103–04; *Memoirs of John Quincy Adams*, V: 5. For the written responses of Crawford, Calhoun, and Wirt, see their letter to James Monroe, March 4, 1820, in Worthington Chauncey Ford, ed., *Writings of John Quincy Adams*, 7 vols. (New York: Macmillan, 1913–1917), VII: 1–2; *Memoirs of John Quincy Adams*, V: 6. Adams did not specify this in his written response to the president; see *Writings of John Quincy Adams*, VII: 1–2 for that letter. For the issue with the second question Monroe posed to the cabinet, see Ammon, *James Monroe*, 457.

65. Leonard L. Richards, *The Slave Power: The Free North and Southern Domination, 1780-1860* (Baton Rouge: Louisiana State University Press, 2000), 84. For the vote, see Forbes, *The Missouri Compromise and Its Aftermath*, 89–95; Hammond,

Slavery, Freedom, and Expansion in the Early American West (Charlottesville: University of Virginia Press, 2007), 161–68.

66. From Mark Langdon Hill, Massachusetts-District of Maine, March 31, 1820, in Noble E. Cunningham, Jr., ed., *Circular Letters of Congressmen to Their Constituents, 1789–1829*, 3 vols. (Chapel Hill: University of North Carolina Press, 1978), III: 1103.

67. From John Holmes, Massachusetts-District of Maine, in Cunningham, ed., *Circular Letters of Congressmen*, III: 1111.

68. John R. Van Atta, *Wolf by the Ears: The Missouri Crisis, 1819-1821* (Baltimore: Johns Hopkins University Press, 2015), 99. The border South states voted 16 to 2 for the line. The remaining Southern state representatives voted 19 t0 17 in favor.

69. Hammond, *Slavery, Freedom, and Expansion*, 167.

70. *Richmond Enquirer*, March 7, 1820.

71. John C. Calhoun to A[ndrew] Jackson, June 1, 1820, in Clyde N. Wilson, et. al., eds., *The Papers of John C. Calhoun*, 28 vols. (Columbia: University of South Carolina Press, 1959–2003), V: 164.

72. *St. Louis Enquirer*, March 25, 1820.

CHAPTER SIX

The Three-Fifths Clause

Brook Poston

> **"Representatives and direct Taxes shall be apportioned among the several States which may be included within this Union, according to their respective Numbers, which shall be determined by adding to the whole Number of free Persons, including those bound to Service for a Term of Years, and excluding Indians not taxed, three fifths of all other Persons."**
>
> [Article I, Section 2, Clause 3]

STANDING BEFORE HIS senatorial colleagues, Rufus King declared "Freedom and slavery are the parties which stand before the senate this day." The year was 1819, and the subject was Missouri, but it was not the first time that the New York senator and former Federalist presidential candidate had debated these matters. For King, the key issue in the Missouri controversy was one he had personally discussed more than 30 years earlier at the Constitutional Convention of 1787, namely the Three-Fifths Clause. During this speech, which became so popular that it was later published in a short pamphlet, King argued that by granting slaveholding states a "disproportionate number of representatives and electors" the Northern delegates to the Philadelphia convention had made a great "concession." Bitterly, King remarked that the years since had "proved" that the compromise over slave representation was the "greatest which was agreed to secure the adoption of the Constitution." King had watched, and stewed, for more than three decades as the North's "concession" on the Three-Fifths Clause seemed to loom larger with each passing year.[1]

Several issues divided Congress during the Missouri Controversy from 1819 to 1821, but for many Northerners it was the Three-Fifths Clause that rankled most. Unlike many of the other constitutional arguments debated during the Congressional debates during this period the Three-Fifths Clause had been a regular point of contention for Federalists like King since at least 1800. As slaveholding Virginia Republicans won election after election in the early nineteenth century the injustice of the Three-Fifths Clause, or the "federal ratio" as it was often called, became a rallying cry in the North. The debate over the clause reached its zenith during the Missouri debates, but the fight was long in the making. Originating with the nation's founding document itself, the Three-Fifths Clause became an increasingly divisive issue during the first two decades of the nineteenth century before exploding in the halls of Congress in 1819. In the end, the clause survived the debate over Missouri statehood in large measure because those who fought against it lacked the will and the support to alter fundamentally the constitutional compromises that gave it birth in 1787.

Though Rufus King emerged as perhaps the most prominent critic of the Three-Fifths Clause during the debates over the Missouri Compromise, he had not always been so vociferous in his attacks on the federal ratio. The three-fifths formula was originally proposed by James Wilson of Pennsylvania and Charles Pinckney of South Carolina (not to be confused with fellow delegate Charles Cotesworth Pinckney, also of South Carolina) during the early stages of the Constitutional Convention of 1787. Pinckney was, coincidentally, later a member of the House of Representatives in 1820, making him and King the only members of Congress who participated in the Missouri debates in 1820 to have attended the Philadelphia Convention. The Three-Fifths Clause was not, however, cut from whole cloth from the minds of Wilson and Pinckney. Though it had never been applied, the federal ratio had been debated and agreed to for purposes of taxation by the Confederation Congress during the early 1780s. Initially, there was little debate over the clause at the Philadelphia Convention because most saw it as part of the larger question of proportional representation that divided the delegates of the large and small states and, ultimately, led to the Great Compromise that created the modern House of Representatives and the Senate. When the delegates chose to create a chamber of Congress based on equal state representation it meant, at the time, that the superior population of the slave states counted for less than originally proposed in James Madison's famous Virginia Plan. This made some form of slave representation likely as a way to protect the interests of these larger slave states. The Convention accepted the Three-Fifths Clause in early June by a vote of nine to two. Even the "no" votes from New Jersey and Delaware did not represent opposition to the clause itself, so much as those two "small" states continuing in their opposition to proportional representation more broadly.[2]

King, future critic of the Three-Fifths Clause though he later became, was typical of most of the Northern delegates in Philadelphia in that he accepted that the South would require some kind of accounting for their property in slaves. During the debates he said that "he had always expected that as the Southern States are the richest, they would not league themselves with the Northn. [sic] unless some respect were paid to their superior wealth."[3] King's point here is important to understanding the Convention's general view of the clause. In the minds of most delegates the Three-Fifths Clause had little to do with the relative "humanity" of a slave, but was rather a way to measure the South's superior wealth. Eighteenth-century understandings of republicanism and political theory demanded that wealth be protected against the excesses of democracy. This was still, after all, an era during which most states had property qualifications for the franchise. The question boiled down to the percentage of slaves that ought to be counted. Historian George Van Cleve explains that because the Three-Fifths Clause had been "debated and widely approved" by the Confederation Congress as a means for measuring wealth for purposes of taxation in 1783, it was by far "the most likely compromise" at the time of the Constitutional Convention four years later. Congress had debated the relative merits of counting either three-fourths or one-half of slaves but had eventually settled on the three-fifths ratio as suggested by none other than Madison.[4] By the time of the Philadelphia Convention of 1787 there was virtually no support for counting either the free population only or the entire slave population for purposes of representation.[5] According to King, both sides had to "allow some advantages" to the other. He pointed out that "Eleven out of 13 of the States had agreed to consider Slaves in the apportionment of taxation; and taxation and Representation ought to go together."[6] Members of the Convention, North and South, therefore decided that three-fifths of slaves would be counted for purposes of both representation and taxation.

Years later, during the debates on Missouri, King claimed that the Northern delegates had been more or less hoodwinked into making this deal, not realizing how seldom direct taxes would be used at the federal level. Most historians who have analyzed the record at the Convention have concluded that this was not the case. In 1787, King and other Northerners likely understood that direct taxation would be used rarely. Most delegates, including King himself, saw it as a reasonable way to account for the wealth of the slave states, and perhaps most important, neither King nor any other delegate made a concerted case against the Three-Fifths Clause on the basis of morality or racial justice. The argument centered primarily on questions of wealth and power.[7]

The primary debate over the Three-Fifths Clause occurred when Southerners attempted to push their demands for representation even further. In July, Gouverneur Morris of Pennsylvania emerged as the harshest critic of the clause. He pointed out the inconsistency of counting slaves for purposes of representation when the convention refused to count other sources of property for the same purpose. "If slaves were to be considered as inhabitants, not as wealth," Morris declared, the Three-Fifths Clause made no sense and should be abandoned. But if they were counted "as wealth, then why is no other wealth but slaves included?" Hoping to keep the peace, King explained that while he saw "great force in the objections of Mr. Govr. Morris," he was prepared to "accede to the proposition for the sake of doing something." King was intent on securing Southern acceptance of the Constitution even at the cost of extra representation for the Southern states.[8]

Despite King's efforts at conciliation, Morris's attack on the three-fifths ratio opened the door for Southerners to demand that the entire slave population be counted for representation. Charles Pinckney explained the South's reasoning: "Blacks" he began, careful to avoid the term *slave*, should be the "equal to the whites in the ratio of representation." After all, he continued, "the blacks are the labourers, the peasants of the Southern States: they are as productive of pecuniary resources as those of the Northern States. They add equally to the wealth . . . and to the strength of the nation." Morris's criticism of the federal ratio, far from giving the Southern delegates pause, emboldened them to reach for even greater representation for the slaveholding states. Some of the Southern delegates even hinted that should the institution be left unprotected they might quit the Convention and the proposed union entirely.[9]

After some wrangling throughout July and August, the delegates eventually settled on Wilson and Pinckney's original three-fifths compromise, but during the debates King did foreshadow the role the clause would play in the years to come. "He must be short sighted indeed," King warned, "who does not foresee that whenever the Southern States shall be more numerous than the Northern, they can & will hold a language that will awe them into justice. If they threaten to separate now in case injury shall be done them, will their threats be less urgent or effectual, when force shall back their demands. Even in the intervening period there will be no point of time at which they will not be able to say, do us justice or we will separate." Notwithstanding his criticism, King and his Northern colleagues never put up a concerted opposition to the Three-Fifths Clause, and they certainly never made a moral case against it or slavery in general. For them, securing the constitution and the union was paramount.[10]

Over the intervening years, however, the Three-Fifths Clause took on a more sinister meaning for King and those who became Federalists. They eventually blamed it for the decline in their political fortunes after Thomas Jefferson's election in 1800, and it played a vital role in their near political suicide at the Hartford Convention. Though Northerners tamely acquiesced to slave representation in 1787 with minimal struggle, by the time Missouri applied for statehood in 1819, they were ready to revisit the, by-then infamous, Three-Fifths Clause.[11]

The Three-Fifths Clause existed with little controversy for the first decade of the nation's history. It made no difference in the Federalist victories from 1788 to 1796, but all that changed in 1800 with the election of Jefferson as president. Jefferson, a Virginia Democratic-Republican slaveholder, defeated Massachusetts Federalist John Adams by a 73–65 margin in the Electoral College. Some historians, and certainly most Federalists at the time, believed that Jefferson owed his victory to the Three-Fifths Clause.[12] One Federalist newspaper complained that Jefferson's victory stemmed from the "500,000 negro slaves in the United States . . . who have not more voice in the Election of President and Vice President . . . than 500,000 New England horses, hogs and oxen." Yet, despite this fact, the Federalists complained, "their masters for them choose 15 Electors."[13]

Federalists grew ever more vocal in their denunciations of the Three-Fifths Clause during Jefferson's presidency. James Callender's revelation in 1802 that Jefferson had a slave mistress named Sally Hemmings encouraged some Federalists to connect the salacious allegations to slave representation. One attack on Jefferson came in the form of the following poem accusing the president of having fathered his own electoral votes.

"A Southern Negro is you see, man,
Already three fifths of a freeman,
And when Virginia gets the staff,
He'll be a freeman and a half,

Great men can never lack supporters,
Who manufacture their own voters,
Besides 'tis plain as yonder steeple,
They will be *fathers* to the people."[14]

Jefferson's acquisition of Louisiana further stoked Federalist concerns. The expansion of slavery to these new western lands, bolstered by the Three-Fifths Clause, seemed to portend the perpetual dominance of the slaveholding Republican South over the Federalist North. In response, a Massachusetts congressman named William Ely drafted an amendment to eliminate the Three-Fifths Clause and in early 1804 sent it to several state legislatures, where it predictably failed to pass the necessary three-quarters of the various state houses. Nevertheless, Timothy Pickering, U.S. senator from Massachusetts and former Federalist secretary of state under George Washington and John Adams, introduced it in Congress in December of 1804, wherein the Republican majority tabled the motion and let it die.[15] Pickering, the quintessential arch-Federalist, even began contemplating New England's secession as an alternative to Republican dominance. It is perhaps illustrative of Federalist desperation that Pickering was even willing to court as unreliable an ally as Aaron Burr for this abortive secessionist movement.[16]

According to historian Matthew Mason, the "high water mark" of Federalist assault on the Three-Fifths Clause came during the War of 1812. During the war one Northerner called the federal ratio a limb of the

Constitution that required "amputation." This rhetoric culminated at the Hartford Convention.[17] In 1814, as the war with Great Britain dragged on, New England Federalists met in Hartford, Connecticut, and issued a list of demands in the form of proposed amendments to the Constitution. At the top of the list was the following revision of the Three-Fifths Clause: "Representatives and direct taxes shall be apportioned among the several States which may be included within this union, according to their respective numbers of free persons, including those bound to serve for a term of years, and excluding Indians not taxed, and all other persons."[18] This would have explicitly eliminated the Three-Fifths Clause from the U.S. Constitution. Unfortunately for Federalists, word of the Hartford Convention's demands was accompanied by the news that General Andrew Jackson had defeated the British at New Orleans and that the commissioners in Ghent had reached a peace settlement ending the War of 1812. The ill-timed convention thus dealt a blow to the Federalist Party from which it never recovered, but for many the true cause of the reversal in Federalist fortunes lay with the continued existence of the now despised Three-Fifths Clause.

The years immediately following the Hartford Convention were not kind to the Federalist Party. Rufus King himself stood as the nominal Federalist candidate in 1816, but was soundly defeated by James Monroe, another Virginia slaveholding Republican, who was then re-elected in 1820 during the height of the Missouri controversy. By that time, the Federalist Party was well on its way to extinction on a national level, with the president coming within one vote of a unanimous re-election. But the demise of the Federalist Party did not signal the end of the debate over the Three-Fifths Clause.

By 1819, a mixture of the last remaining Federalists, including King himself, who had been elected as a U.S. senator from New York as a result of a split in that state's Republican ticket, combined with disgruntled Northern Republicans to oppose Missouri's application for statehood. These Northern Republicans resented the South's, and particularly Virginia's, continued dominance over both their party and national politics generally. Party unity, such as it was during Monroe's "Era of Good Feelings," was insufficient to quell these fears. This new, very loose, and in the end very temporary, coalition of Federalists and Northern Republicans on the slavery issue in Missouri breathed new life into the debate over the Three-Fifths Clause.

Like the delegates at the Philadelphia Convention in 1787, many Northern members of Congress in 1819–1820 were not driven primarily by moral outrage over the Three-Fifths Clause or slavery itself, but rather by questions of sectional politics and power. Missouri statehood with slavery did not anger Northerners only because they had moral qualms about the institution, though, to be sure, many did and often expressed these arguments during the debates. Instead, for many it was the prospect of the continued expansion of slavery across the continent that motivated opposition to Missouri's entry into the Union as a slave state. Missouri would, many Northerners feared, set a precedent for slavery's spread into the rest of the Louisiana Territory, and with the signing of the Adams-Onís Treaty of 1819, slavery might, they feared, even extend all the way to the Pacific Ocean. Northerners might not have dreaded the idea of slavery's expansion were it not for the impact it would have on the sectional balance of power. In the minds of Missouri "restrictionists," every new slave state would bring two new proslavery senators, and if the Three-Fifths Clause were extended to include these new states—like Missouri, with its more than 15,000 slaves—it would mean extra representation in the House and the Electoral College as well. For Northerners, then, Missouri statehood meant Virginia and her Southern allies would continue to dominate national affairs indefinitely. The debate was first and foremost about power, and power was most closely linked to the infamous federal ratio that had vexed Federalists since Jefferson's election in 1800.

As the debate over Missouri began, the Federalist remnant found new allies in the fight over the Three-Fifths Clause when a New York Republican named James Tallmadge stood up in the House on February 13, 1819, and proposed "that the further introduction of slavery or involuntary servitude be prohibited . . . and that all children born within the said State, after the admission thereof into the Union, shall be free at the age of twenty-five years."[19] Three days later, as Congress first debated the amendment that bears his name, Tallmadge fired the first salvo against the Three-Fifths Clause.

While defending his amendment, Tallmadge acknowledged that the delegates to the Constitutional Convention had accepted the Three-Fifths

Clause "as one of the mutual sacrifices to the union." Perhaps in order to quell Southern fears, Tallmadge insisted he had no intention of undermining the application of the federal ratio to the slaveholding states. "On that subject," he assured Southerners, "I consider the faith of the Union pledged." A new state like Missouri was another matter. According to Tallmadge, new territories looking to become states had "no claims to such an unequal representation." The Three-Fifths Clause, he believed, should not apply to Missouri because it had not "borne a part of the Revolution." To extend the federal ratio to such a state would be "unjust in its operations . . . unequal in its results, and a violation of its original intention."[20] In other words, Northerners may have had to put up with the Three-Fifths Clause for the slaveholding members of the original thirteen states, but nothing justified extending this boon to new states.

Predictably, Tallmadge's amendment sent the proslavery members of Congress into a frenzy, and the debate was fierce during this initial clash over the issue in the last days of the 15th Congress in February 1819. Critics warned the New York Congressman to "beware the fate of Caesar." Tallmadge responded with equanimity. "Language of this sort," he assured his opponents "has no effect on me." He explained that "setting bounds" to slavery was "a great and glorious cause." Likewise, Southern threats of disunion did not concern him. If his amendment led to a "dissolution" of the Union, he told his colleagues "let it be so," and if civil war then, "let it come." Unfortunately for Tallmadge, his part in the "great and glorious cause" was nearing its end.[21] The House voted in favor of the Tallmadge Amendment, but the Senate rejected it, and Congress adjourned with the two houses at an impasse over Missouri's statehood. In the interim between the 15th and 16th Congresses, many Northerners took up the cause of restriction in Missouri and made blistering attacks on the Three-Fifths Clause. Despite the popular support for his amendment in the North, Tallmadge himself failed to win re-election, and in December of 1819 Congress again took up the debate without the New York Congressman who had started the fight earlier that year.[22]

With Tallmadge gone, Missouri restrictionists in Congress were led primarily by longtime opponent of the Three-Fifths Clause Senator Rufus King. King had participated in the first round of debates in early 1819, and his arguments were so well received that he published a pamphlet containing the text of those speeches. King focused much of his argument on the Three-Fifths Clause. Historian Glover Moore called the clause the issue "closest" to King's heart. King explicitly focused not on the injustices associated with the institution of slavery itself but on the political interests of the various regions. The Three-Fifths Clause, he argued, gave whites in the South far more political power than those in the North, who had received nothing in return. Southerners were supposed to have paid more in taxes in exchange for the extra representation the three-fifths ratio provided. King claimed that at the Constitutional Convention "no one anticipated the fact that the whole of revenue on the United States would be derived from indirect taxes" which were left untouched by the federal ratio. Instead, "it was believed that a part of the contribution to the common treasury would be apportioned among the states by the rule for the apportionment of representatives." Whether King misremembered, misinterpreted, or misrepresented the facts is unclear. But this was not the sentiment among the delegates in 1787, himself included. Nevertheless, he claimed that this was why the non-slaveholding states "acquiesced in the disproportionate number of representatives and electors that was secured to the slaveholding states." King accepted that he and his Northern colleagues had to live with the bargain they made in 1787, but to now extend it would be "unjust and odious." It was King and Tallmadge who set the parameters of the debate, and as other Northern congressmen took up the fight over Missouri, they weaved interconnected criticisms of the federal ratio through their arguments, centering on the clause's fundamental unfairness to the North's interests.[23]

Apart from Tallmadge, who began the fight, and King, who had the gravitas and clout to carry the banner in the Senate, perhaps the next most important critic of the Three-Fifths Clause was Congressman John Taylor of New York, who, like Tallmadge, was a disgruntled Northern Republican. Taylor ultimately repeated many of Tallmadge's and King's critiques of the famous Clause during the debates in the House in late 1819 and early 1820, assuring his Southern colleagues that he had no "wish to alter the basis of compromise on which the Federal Constitution was founded." He and his Northern allies yielded "without grudging, to the slaveholding states all the political advantages they have a right to demand." This was, of course, not entirely true. As we have seen there was considerable "grudging" when it came to the application of the Three-Fifths Clause to the original slaveholding states. But Taylor limited his criticisms to preventing what he saw as "new and unreasonable burdens" in extending the benefits of the clause to new states. He then referred to the problems underlying the equity of the three-fifths compromise. Echoing King's arguments concerning the relationship between taxes and representation, Taylor argued that the Constitutional Convention's application of the Three-Fifths Clause to both representation and direct taxes was supposed to have been a compromise to ensure that while the South was granted greater representation, it would also be taxed on three-fifths of its slaves. The problem, according to Taylor, was that direct taxation had rarely been used at the federal level. Instead, "nearly the whole amount has been levied by duties on importation," which tended to affect the North at least as much as the South and were in no way tied to slaves, three-fifths or otherwise. Further, "We have no reason to believe that the present revenue system will soon be superseded by that of direct taxation; and while it continues, our contribution to the public treasury will ever remain greatly disproportionate to our political power in the federal government." So, what had seemed an equitable bargain between North and South in 1787 had turned out to significantly favor the Southern states. The idea of extending this unjust settlement to new states appalled Taylor and his fellow Northerners.[24]

Most of the rest of the Northern critics of the Three-Fifths Clause focused on these same issues throughout the debate. Joshua Cushman, a Massachusetts Republican congressman, put a fine point on the question of Southern taxation and slave representation by asking his fellow members, "How is a black slave to be considered . . . as property, or a human being?" He then deftly summarized the Southern position, and the inherent injustice of the arrangement, in a single elegant sentence, "When gain is concerned the black slave is considered as property; but when power is in question he is dignified with three-fifths the attributes of a man."[25] Like the other critics of the clause, Cushman lamented the very existence of the compromise dating back to the Philadelphia Convention, but some Northerners cast their gaze into the future and predicted dire consequences for both the North and the nation as a whole should slavery and the Three-Fifths Clause be extended to Missouri.

Senator James Burrill, a Federalist from Rhode Island, was one of the harshest critics of the clause. He predicted that the union itself was threatened by Missouri statehood. The various compromises between North and South had, he argued, created "equilibrium" and "reciprocity" within the union. But extending the Three-Fifths Clause "beyond the Mississippi" was something entirely different. If Congress were to allow it, "I need not state to you the result in twenty years." It was obvious to Burrill that the results would be dire, particularly for his region. "The eastern section of this country" he warned "would be cypherized[26] in both branches of the government." Because the East continued to receive no "equivalent," according to Burrill extending the federal ratio across the continent would eventually extinguish their remaining political power. The future for the non-slaveholding states looked bleak in Burrill's mind. "If we proceed far, as we are going on," he warned, "in a short period the slave representation will have a very controlling influence in government." Burrill also made it perfectly clear that his concerns were for the political power of white Northerners alone, not the slaves. The original principle of the Union must be that the "free citizens or their representatives, are to rule the country," he insisted. For Burrill and many of his Northern colleagues this was not primarily a question of equality, but one of power. Burrill made this point plain when he told his colleagues that he did not want to see the Missouri Territory "blackened." He was as "averse" to a black population residing in Missouri as he was a slave one.[27]

Southerners, of course, chafed at these assaults on the Three-Fifths Clause, and their counterattack was fierce. Southerners, and several of their Northern allies, cited textual evidence, the intent of the clause's framers, and even charged the Federalists of engaging in a partisan conspiracy. Throughout, the Southerners were able to poke holes in most of the North's criticisms of the federal ratio. Missouri's own John Scott, the Territory's lone non-voting representative in the House, was one of the first to take aim at the Tallmadge Amendment, and he took pains to defend the Three-Fifths Clause. Scott, citing the Constitution's text, argued that the clause was not limited to the original thirteen colonies but all those that "might be included within this union." This, according to Scott, meant that the delegates at the convention had clearly contemplated "the admission of new states" in the three-fifths calculus. As proof Scott pointed to states such as Kentucky, Louisiana, and Mississippi, none of which were part of the original thirteen, and all of which had been admitted with slavery and the full benefits of the federal ratio.[28]

Somewhat ironically, it was a Massachusetts congressman named John Holmes who made perhaps the most comprehensive defense of the Three-Fifths Clause. Holmes was a Republican and eventually wrote a pamphlet defending the compromise to the citizens of Maine, where he would later be elected a U.S. senator. Jefferson himself praised this pamphlet in a letter to Holmes, and it was here where the former president wrote his famous line that the Missouri controversy had awakened him like a "fire bell in the night."[29] During the debates in Congress, Holmes touched on most of the Southerners' major criticisms of the North's interpretation of the Three-Fifths Clause. First, like Scott, he pointed specifically to the section of the Constitution that read "as may be included within this Union" to explain that the framers had clearly expected the clause to be extended to new states. He then went on the offensive, pointing out that the compromise of 1787 was made between counting all the slaves or counting merely three-fifths of their number, and had little bearing on the question of taxation. He called direct taxation itself "odious" and claimed that those at the Convention knew the United States would rarely resort to such measures. Finally, he questioned the motives of his opponents. The entire crisis, he claimed, was a plot driven by "ambitious, desperate men" hoping to produce "a geographical division of party and rise to power under its banners." In other words, Holmes believed that the Missouri controversy had been manufactured by disgruntled Federalists like Rufus King, who hoped to use the crisis to create a new political party. Holmes even reminded his colleagues of the Hartford Convention and hinted that this crisis over Missouri had been manufactured by the treacherous behavior of these same Northern Federalists.[30]

Throughout the debate Southern defenders of the Three-Fifths Clause focused on many of the same themes to which Holmes referred. Congressman Benjamin Hardin of Kentucky agreed with Holmes that this smacked of a Northern Federalist plot. He accused Federalists of using slavery and emancipation as a "rallying point" upon which to rebuild their faction. He believed their plan was to block Missouri in order to "give the union a majority of non-slaveholding states." Then, he claimed, the

Federalist remnant would be in a position to facilitate the rise of "a new party." On the subject of the Three-Fifths Clause itself, Hardin claimed that the North's attacks on it were hopelessly contradictory. If they were really "humanitarians" who desired "emancipation" for the oppressed slave population how could these Northern critics possibly oppose the Three-Fifths Clause? After all, with emancipation eventually five-fifths of blacks would be counted for representation. He argued, more or less, that the entire controversy had little to do with concerns over the morality of slavery, but was nothing more than a political maneuver by Northern politicians hoping to shift the balance of power away from the slave states by rallying opposition to Missouri statehood. While Hardin attacked the Federalist authors of this crisis, other Southerners looked back to the Convention to defend the federal ratio. Here they found ample fodder for dismantling the Northern position, by threatening dire consequences should the Three-Fifths Clause be discarded.[31]

Many Southern delegates, and even some of their Northern allies, consistently referred to the intent of the Constitution's framers to defend the Three-Fifths Clause. Senator William Smith of South Carolina claimed that it was the "northerners" and "easterners" at the convention who had originally proposed the three-fifths compromise, noting that they had accepted it with little debate when direct taxes had been applied during the conflict with France in the 1790s and during the War of 1812. Smith's claims on these points were at best half true. Though they may have ignored the Three-Fifths Clause during the 1790s, by 1812 most Northern Federalists had come to loathe the federal ratio. But opponents of slavery's restriction also pointed out that discarding one part of the Constitution might have implications for other sections of the country's founding document.[32] In other words, if the clause was not applied to new states, then other sections of the constitution might be in jeopardy. Senator Ninian Edwards of Illinois expressed his concern that this debate would not end with the elimination of the Three-Fifths Clause only. He feared that "popular excitement" might lead to the elimination of the "Great Compromise" that had birthed the Senate as a chamber with equal representation for each state.[33] Philip Barbour, Congressman from Virginia, agreed. "There were other subjects besides slavery adjusted by compromise" he pointed out. If the Three-Fifths Clause was not to be applied to the new states neither should the other compromises. Why, he asked, should Indiana, small as it was, receive the same representation in the Senate as his much larger home state of Virginia?[34] Francis Jones of Tennessee took the argument a step further. Reading further down the same section that contained the Three-Fifths Clause, Jones said that if the federal ratio did not apply to new states neither should the clause that outlines the taking of the U.S. census. Along with these textual arguments in favor of the federal ratio, Southerners also went beyond the Constitution to defend the clause.[35]

Congressman Alexander Smyth of Virginia was one such figure. Smyth tied the debate over the Three-Fifths Clause to the concept of diffusion, one of the South's favored arguments for extending slavery across the continent. Southerners claimed that spreading slavery to Western states would spread the slave population wider and make for a more humane institution. Northerners, most of whom thought diffusion a fantasy, feared that the number of slaves would grow if the institution were extended west. Smyth argued that allowing slavery in Missouri would not add to the total number of slaves, and thus slave representation, but would simply move the same number of slaves around the country. But Smyth went even further. States like his home one of Virginia should, he argued, "exercise power" and "bear a share of public burdens" based on the state's "ability." Ability should be based on labor. Yet, he lamented, unproductive men and children were counted fully even though "five negro men, productive laborers, are only counted three." Thus, he argued, it was the South who made the concession at the Constitutional Convention by not counting all of these "productive" slaves.[36] Senator Richard M. Johnson of Kentucky agreed, saying that it was only right to count slaves because women and minors were counted despite their inability to vote.[37] Representative Charles Pinckney of South Carolina, who like King had been a member of the Constitutional Convention when it debated the Three-Fifths Clause, claimed to be "astonished" by the claim that the North had made a "great concession" to the South "in granting them a representation of three-fifths of their slaves." Instead things were quite the opposite. It was the South who had suffered from the Three-Fifths Clause, who had conceded on the issue of slave representation. While the Northern and Eastern sections of the country remained "as fully represented as they ought to be" the South was "unjustly deprived of any representation for a large and important part of our population," which he believed were "more valuable to the union . . . than any equal number if inhabitants in the Northern and Eastern states." As was true during the Convention three decades earlier, many Southerners like Pinckney were not in a compromising mood when it came to the clause.[38]

James Barbour, Republican Senator from Virginia, agreed with his fellow Southerners, claiming that it was the slave states who made the sacrifice according to "the principles of those who hold all men equal" because they had given up two-fifths of the black population for representation. In other words, if the Northerners truly believed in equality and emancipation they ought to be arguing for all the slaves to be counted for representation.[39] Barbour, in his role as president pro tempore of the Senate, was instrumental in helping push through the Thomas Amendment which linked Missouri statehood to that of Maine. This new compromise headed off the controversy by allowing slavery to exist in Missouri but limiting slavery's existence beyond that to territory north of the 36° 30′ parallel. The Missouri Compromise also ultimately resulted in preserving the Three-Fifths Clause for the next forty years.

As the dust cleared from the debate over Missouri, King and Pinckney, the two members with the longest history of debating the Three-Fifths Clause, surveyed the compromise and came to nearly the same conclusion. Pinckney was jubilant. The compromise represented "a great triumph" for the South, he told one South Carolina newspaper.[40] King agreed, telling a correspondent that the North had not only lost on Missouri but that this compromise would eventually mean the spread of slavery across the continent. Slavery's restriction above the 36° 30′ would last only "until our masters the slave states are pleased to order otherwise." He believed that there was now an "avowed understanding that whenever Congress choose they may make the same or any part thereof a slave Region, and . . . that whenever any new State shall be formed there, that it must and will be free to establish slavery."[41] For both men this was a clear victory for the South and for the defenders of the Three-Fifths Clause.

During the height of the debate in 1820 William Plumer, a New Hampshire congressman who opposed slavery's extension to Missouri, complained in a letter to his father that "the great speakers are almost all in the other side of the House." At least on the issue of the Three-Fifths

Clause, one major reason for this is undoubtedly that the Southern representatives in both the House and Senate had the better constitutional arguments upon which the debate over the clause was fought. The Northern opponents of the Three-Fifths Clause could not win the arguments on constitutional grounds because the U.S. Constitution was more or less on the Southerners' side. It was clear from the text and the debates in Philadelphia that the delegates had contemplated the extension of the clause to new states, and that direct taxation was not seen as something that would be used at the federal level with any kind of regularity. Furthermore, the Southerners were right that if Congress refused to apply the Three-Fifths Clause to Missouri in this instance it could set a precedent for omitting other sections of the Constitution for new states. Finally, former Federalists like King did in fact hope to use Missouri, and particularly the three-fifths issue, as a means to build a new regional political party.[42] In other words, the Southerners were right on all the issues that animated the debate in Congress. The modern student of the debate over the clause during the Missouri crisis may be struck by the inherent contradictions of this fact. After all, the Southerners were arguing in favor of the infamous Three-Fifths Clause and defending slavery generally, two morally indefensible positions. But this was not the grounds upon which the battle was waged. It was fought on political and constitutional grounds. The clause, along with other protections for slavery, had been included in the nation's founding document with relatively little controversy. From 1787 to 1820 much had changed, but the changes in attitudes concerning the clause were mostly of the political variety, those related to power, partisan politics, and sectional interests. Northerners tried to win the fight over the Three-Fifths Clause on these issues, but they lacked the political will and the popular support to reckon with the protections for slavery found in the constitution itself.

One Southern defender of the Three-Fifths Clause's arguments drove this point home. During the debates Benjamin Hardin of Kentucky claimed if the Northern critics were really "humanitarians" who desired "emancipation" they should want to count five-fifths of the slaves. Hardin's point, albeit circuitous, is that a truly emancipationist argument against the Three-Fifths Clause would be to count all slaves as a precursor to abolition and the incorporation of the former slaves into the body politic.

If Northerners were serious about eliminating the clause, they needed to tackle the question of slavery and emancipation head-on. Northern critics of the Three-Fifths Clause such as King were reluctant to make this argument. It was left to later generations to accomplish this task. Interestingly, Hardin's grandson and namesake was a Confederate general named Benjamin Hardin Helm, who died some forty years later during the Civil War, and was brother-in-law to none other than Abraham Lincoln. The elder Hardin touched on an indelible truth about the North's position on the Three-Fifths Clause. The only method of attack that could have been successful for Northern politicians was the argument that the clause had been a mistake and that the Convention had erred by placing political expediency and union over justice and equality. Of course, as Americans discovered, that path might have led to civil war in 1820 just as it did in 1861, during which Hardin's grandson died on the battlefield even as his brother-in-law Lincoln pushed through both the Emancipation Proclamation and the 13th Amendment, which finally won the fight over the Three-Fifths Clause for the North by abolishing it and slavery forever.

NOTES

1. Rufus King, *The Substance of Two Speeches Delivered in the Senate of the United States, on the Subject of the Missouri Bill* (Philadelphia: Clark and Raser Printers, 1819), 1–8.

2. Richard Beeman, *Plain Honest Men: The Making of the American Constitution* (New York: Random House, 2009), 152–54.

3. Max Farrand, ed. *The Records of the Federal Convention of 1787,* 3 vols. (New Haven: Yale University Press, 1911), 1: 562–63.

4. Gary Wills, *Negro President: Thomas Jefferson and the Slave Power* (Boston: Houghton Mifflin, 2005), 53.

5. George Van Cleve, *A Slaveholders' Union: Slavery Politics and the Constitution in the Early American Republic* (Chicago: University of Chicago Press, 2010), 119–20.

6. Farrand, ed., *The Records of the Federal Convention of 1787,* 1: 562–63.

7. Van Cleve makes this case throughout his chapter on the Convention, and Matthew Mason says much the same in his work, claiming that the Three-Fifths Clause was a secondary issue at the Convention and slavery itself was primarily used by delegates as a weapon to utilize in the defense of what they saw as more important causes. See, Van Cleve, *A Slaveholders' Union,* 117, 135–42 and Matthew Mason, *Slavery and Politics in the Early American Republic* (Chapel Hill: University of North Carolina Press, 2008), 32.

8. Farrand, ed., *The Records of the Federal Convention of 1787,* 1: 581–83.

9. Farrand, ed., *The Records of the Federal Convention of 1787,* 1: 596–97; for a short discussion of the argument over the Three-Fifths Clause at the convention see, Beeman, *Plain Honest Men,* 204–15.

10. Farrand, ed., *The Records of the Federal Convention of 1787,* 1: 595–96.

11. Farrand, ed., *The Records of the Federal Convention of 1787,* 1: 595–96.

12. Gary Wills, *Negro President: Thomas Jefferson and the Slave Power* (New York: Houghton Mifflin Harcourt, 2005), 2, 234; For the opposing view that the Three-Fifths Clause did not account for Jefferson's electoral victory see Van Cleve, *A Slaveholders' Union,* 140–42.

13. *Washington Federalist (Gazette of the United States)* Jan. 14, 1801 in Linda Kerber, *Federalists in Dissent: Imagery and Ideology in Jeffersonian America* (Ithaca: Cornell University Press, 1970), 36.

14. Thomas Green Fessenden, *Democracy Unveiled* (New York: I. Riley and Co, 1806), 18–19, 21, 25, found in Kerber, *Federalists in Dissent,* 52.

15. Kerber, *Federalists in Dissent,* 36–39.

16. See generally, Gerard Clarfield, *Timothy Pickering and the American Republic* (Pittsburgh: University of Pittsburgh Press, 1980), 219–28.

17. Matthew Mason, *Slavery and Politics in the Early American Republic,* 51–63, 72–73.

18. *The proceedings of a convention of delegates, from the states of Massachusetts, Connecticut, and Rhode-Island; the counties of Cheshire and Grafton, in the state of New-Hampshire; and the county of Windham, in the state of Vermont—convened at Hartford, in the state of Connecticut* (Hartford: Andrus and Starr, 1815), 26. (Emphasis added)

19. *Annals of Congress,* 15th Cong., 2d Sess., 1170.

20. *Annals of Congress,* 15th Cong., 2d Sess., 1213–14.

21. *Annals of Congress,* 15th Cong, 2d Sess., 1204.

22. John R. Van Atta, *Wolf by the Ears: The Missouri Crisis, 1819–1821* (Baltimore: Johns Hopkins University Press, 2015), 78–89.

23. Glover Moore, *The Missouri Controversy: 1819–1821* (Lexington: University of Kentucky Press, 1953), 58–59; Rufus King, *The Substance of Two Speeches Delivered in the Senate,* 5–6; King's speech was not recorded but he published it later in this pamphlet; Van Cleve explains "There is no substantial evidence that the three-fifths clause was a result of the convention's agreement to use the federal ratio for direct taxation." Though the two were linked it was not a bargain in any real sense of the term. See Van Cleve, *A Slaveholders' Union,* 117.

24. *Annals of Congress,* House, 16th Cong., 1st Sess., 952, 964.

25. *Annals of Congress,* House, 16th Cong., 1st Sess., 1300–01.

26. Cypherized here meaning "a person or quantity of no influence."

27. *Annals of Congress,* House, 16th Cong., 1st Sess., 217–18.

28. *Annals of Congress,* 15th Cong., 2nd Sess., 1198.

29. Thomas Jefferson to John Holmes, 22 April 1820, *Founders Online,* National Archives, accessed April 11, 2019, https://founders.archives.gov/documents/Jefferson/98-01-02-1234.

30. *Annals of Congress*, House, 16th Cong., 1st Sess., 987–88.
31. *Annals of Congress*, House, 16th Cong., 1st Sess., 1089–90.
32. *Annals of Congress*, House, 16th Cong., 1st Sess., 265–66.
33. *Annals of Congress*, Senate, 16th Cong., 1st Sess., 190.
34. *Annals of Congress*, House, 16th Cong., 1st Sess., 1231–32.
35. *Annals of Congress*, 16th Cong., 1st Sess., 1462.
36. *Annals of Congress*, 16th Cong., 1st Sess., 995–96.
37. *Annals of Congress*, Senate, 16th Cong., 1st Sess., 357–58.
38. *Annals of Congress*, 16th Cong., 1st Sess., 1311.
39. *Annals of Congress*, Senate, 16th Cong., 1st Sess., 331–32.
40. Van Cleve, *A Slaveholders' Union*, 241.
41. Van Cleve, *A Slaveholders' Union*, 241.
42. William Plumer Jr. to William Plumer Sr., Jan 30, 1820 in *The Missouri Compromise and Presidential Politics, 1820–1825*, ed. Everett Somerville Brown (St. Louis: Missouri Historical Society, 1926), 5; Robert Ernst, *Rufus King: American Federalist* (Chapel Hill: University of North Carolina Press, 1968), 373.

CHAPTER SEVEN

The Migration and Importation Clause

William S. Belko

> "The Migration or Importation of such Persons as any of the States now existing shall think proper to admit, shall not be prohibited by the Congress prior to the Year one thousand eight hundred and eight, but a Tax or duty may be imposed on such Importation, not exceeding ten dollars for each Person."
>
> [Article I, Section 9, Clause 1]

AMID THE CONTENTIOUS congressional debates over Missouri's admission into the Union, a perplexed former president James Madison wrote the sitting President James Monroe. "I have been truly astonished at some of the doctrines and deliberations to which the Missouri question has led," declared the Father of the Constitution, "and particularly so as the interpretations put on the terms 'migration or importation &c.'" Indeed, Article I, Section 9, Clause 1—the Migration and Importation Clause—stood with Article IV as the most debated section of the U.S. Constitution, leading to considerable confusion as to its meaning and producing myriad conflicting and novel interpretations. Congressmen for and against slavery restriction in Missouri could not have agreed more with Madison. "Sir, plain as this section really is, different constructions have been attempted," recognized Clifton Clagett, the restrictionist representative from New Hampshire. The proslavery senator from North Carolina, William Smith, noted that the clause "has received a different construction by different gentlemen, on both sides of the question." Fellow anti-restrictionist senator from Georgia, Freeman Walker, concurred. "It is much to be regretted that any section of this inimitable instrument [Constitution] should have been so constructed as to admit even of doubtful interpretation." But it did, and it did so with broad befuddlement as to what the clause even meant.[1]

One of the most prominent advocates for slavery restriction in Missouri—one of the more recognized and ardent proponents of the Tallmadge Amendment in the halls of Congress—New York's John Taylor, noted that the clause "has given great trouble to the opponents of restriction on slavery," and pointed out the "extraordinary construction" to which they had resorted. Fellow staunch restrictionist from Pennsylvania, John Sergeant, likewise assailed opponents of the Tallmadge Amendment for their seeming confusion and contradictory construction of the clause. "Various interpretations of this clause of the Constitution have been attempted by those who are opposed to the amendment, but none of them, I think, consistent with the fair import of the terms or the manifest spirit of the Constitution." Opponents of slavery restriction countered as consistently, constantly charging restrictionists with the same inconsistencies and incongruities in their interpretations. Maine congressman John Holmes, as one example among many, believed that the clause proved highly "troublesome to the advocates of restriction, so troublesome that, I trust, they might much better have let it alone." After several years of debate, and the consequent admission of Missouri, Congress failed miserably in providing any clarity over the meaning and intent of the clause. If anything, the Missouri debates merely heightened the confusion. A bloody civil war would ultimately resolve the question, but only because the clause no longer applied with the end of slavery.[2]

The Migration and Importation Clause first appeared during the Constitutional Convention, when the Committee of Detail proposed in early August of 1787 that the national legislature could neither prohibit nor levy a tax or duty on the "emigration or Importation of such Persons as the several States shall think proper to admit." The Committee of the Whole upheld the proposed prohibitory clause. Whether or not the delegates deemed the term "emigration" as meaning the voluntary arrival of free foreigners from abroad and "Importation" as referring only to the involuntary arrival of African slaves, no evidence exists. The definition of the words themselves seemingly defend such a construction; that both terms connote arrival from foreign jurisdiction, and do not apply to internal migration of persons within the same jurisdiction, appears obvious.[3]

Still, opposition to this clause arose, mainly from Rufus King and Gouverneur Morris. They sought repeal for economic, political, and security reasons—that the South could import slaves, but the products of slave labor for export could not be taxed, thus limiting the economic benefits to the Northern states; that unlimited importation merely increased the political power of the slave states in the national government due to the Three-Fifths Clause; and, that Northern states were bound to come to the protection of the Southern states in the case of slave insurrection, which increased accordingly with the unlimited increase in African slaves. Of course, both delegates deemed slavery a "nefarious institution" overall, aside from the economic, political, and safety considerations.[4]

To address these concerns, Luther Martin proposed that the Constitution allow the national legislature "a prohibition or tax on the importation of slaves." Debate ensued. Some, like Charles Dickinson and John Langdon, argued that the question of slave importation be left to the national government and not to the states engaged in the traffic. Others, like Roger Sherman and Elbridge Gerry, felt that they had nothing to do with the conduct of the slave states at all, while most desired to seek a compromise in order to keep South Carolina and Georgia in a union of states or to provide an equal advantage to Northern interests. Finally, on August 24, William Livingston, representing the eleven-member committee tasked with devising the language, proposed a new clause: "The migration or importation of such persons as the several States now existing shall think proper to admit, shall not be prohibited by the Legislature prior to the year 1800, but a tax or duty may be imposed on such migration or importation at a rate not exceeding the average of the duties laid on imports." Note that "migration" had replaced "emigration." What the delegates thought of the change was never recorded. In any case they, by a vote of seven states to four, adopted Charles Pinckney's amendment to extend the deadline to 1808.[5]

But debate over the Migration and Importation Clause only addressed the arrival of slaves from foreign parts and the consequent increase of that population in the Southern states currently existing; no discussion addressed the potential *spread* of slavery *within* the United States, whether into other states or into the territories thereof. Only Virginia's George Mason hinted at this latter facet. "The Western people are already calling out for slaves for their new lands," he surmised in his opposition to the "infernal traffic" in slaves, "and will fill that Country with slaves if they can be got thro' [sic] S. Carolina & Georgia." He held it "essential in every point of view," therefore, "that the Genl. Govt. should have power to prevent the increase of slavery." Whether he intended to accomplish this feat via the prohibition of slave importation or by halting the internal spread of slavery, he never explicated.[6]

On that note, one thing seems certain from the debates over the clause, and that is the delegates felt slavery would eventually disappear from the United States. Roger Sherman, for example, observed that "the abolition of slavery seemed to be going on in the U. S. & that the good sense of the several States would probably by degrees compleat [sic] it." Oliver Ellsworth concurred, declaring that slavery "in time will not be a speck in our country." Georgia's Abraham Baldwin commented that if his state be left alone regarding slavery, "she may probably put a stop to the evil." The South Carolinian slaveholder Pinckney seemingly agreed. If left alone as well on this subject, his state would also "probably of themselves stop importations," and he as a citizen of South Carolina would "vote for it." Maryland and Virginia had already done such, leaving only South Carolina and Georgia as slave importers; North Carolina still imported slaves, but had laid various restrictions on that importation. Still, Pinckney maintained that his state and Georgia "cannot do without slaves," and the importation of slaves economically benefitted the entire union, for the more the slaves produced, the more consumption and the greater the carrying trade of the Northern states, and a consequent increase in revenue for the common treasury.[7]

In addition, the debates indicate that the delegates entertained only the introduction of *slaves* and no other category of population, namely, free white foreign immigrants. Some delegates desired to refrain from using the term "slaves" and "slavery" in the Constitution, hence the term finally employed of "such Persons," which would only muddy the waters during the Missouri debates. Some delegates chided at laying a duty on the importation of "such Persons," as it "acknowledged men to be property, and thus characterizing them as slaves." Morris then raised an issue that would haunt Congress during the Missouri crisis—as the clause now stood, he argued, "it implies that the Legislature may tax freemen imported." In response, Mason argued that the provision proved necessary "for the case of Convicts in order to prevent the introduction of them." The question remained of what the delegates meant by "migration," and if the clause may be applied to voluntary arrival from foreign jurisdictions of free white persons, or providing Congress the authority to halt the migration within U.S. jurisdiction after 1808.[8]

The ratification debates did little to clarify the meaning of the Migration and Importation Clause. Although no one ever *explicitly* employed the term "migration" as a congressional tool to regulate the domestic slave trade, from one state to another state or territory, most Northerners felt the clause would eventually eradicate slavery in the United States. Many agreed with Pennsylvania's Thomas McKean, that the clause "puts within the reach of the federal government" the power to eliminate slavery. Fellow Pennsylvanian James Wilson likewise hoped that the spread of slavery within the United States would soon be prohibited. He declared at the Pennsylvania convention that the "new states which are to be formed" would be under the "control of congress in this particular, and slaves will never be introduced amongst them." A delegate at the Massachusetts ratifying convention claimed the same, declaring that migration or importation "is confined to the states now *existing only*" and that new states "cannot claim it." Proponents of slavery restriction in Missouri would regularly make this argument. But Southern slave owners—Antifederalists particularly—said little about the clause during the ratification debates, giving the appearance that they did not see it as a potential threat of Congress one day interfering with the domestic slave trade or the existence of slavery at all. Virginians mentioned it casually and South Carolinians never mentioned it at all.[9]

Some Antifederalists feared that the clause could apply to whites arriving voluntarily from Europe, claiming that the duty would fall on this class as well as on slaves. Federalists contended otherwise, however, arguing that the clause applied only to slaves. According to Centinel, one of the anonymous Antifederalists, the "objects of this article, are slaves," and that the clause was merely a compromise with the slave states to secure two decades more of the introduction of slaves from abroad. Other Antifederalist tracts concurred. *A Friend to the Rights of the People* suggested that "by the importation of the persons above-mentioned is doubtless meant the Guinea trade, by which thousands and millions of poor negroes have been wrested from their native country, their friends and all that is dear to them, and brought into a state of the most abject slavery and wretchedness." But James Iredell, at the North Carolina ratification convention, drew a distinction between "migration" and "importation." The former term, he claimed, "will extend to persons who come into this country as free people," while the latter term "extends to slaves only." The term migration "refers to free persons," but the word importation "refers to slaves, because free people cannot said to be imported." The tax, moreover, "is only to be laid on slaves who are imported, and not on free persons who migrate." To Iredell, both terms meant arrival from foreign territory into the United States, of two different classes of people, free and slave, but migration did not mean the movement of these classes *within* U.S. jurisdiction. Opponents of slavery restriction in Missouri consistently defended Iredell's interpretation during the Missouri debates.[10]

The ratification debates, much like the Convention debates, therefore, never settled the actual meaning of the Migration and Importation Clause. The clause fostered considerable confusion as to its intent—questions regarding the meaning of "such Persons," "migration," "states now existing," and "admit." Even the phrase about congressional authority to levy a tax on "such Persons" caused considerable misunderstanding about what the clause really concerned. Illinois congressmen Daniel Cook may have best summed it up when, during the Missouri debates, he recognized that "some say they [terms "migration" and "importation"] apply exclusively to slaves, but contend they were used as synonymous terms. Others say that the power to prohibit migration is given in aid of the power to prohibit importation. And others contend that it is given to prohibit the migration of free white persons, when the public security may require it." Subsequent congressional debates involving the clause during the Federalist period proved no better.[11]

In February of 1790, Congress entertained a memorial presented by a Quaker abolitionist group calling for an end to the slave trade. Congressmen recognized that all they could do at this juncture was impose a duty of ten dollars on the importation of slaves, due to the constitutional restriction during the period prior to 1808 preventing them from touching the slave trade altogether. Debate focused overwhelmingly on the importation of slaves, and, as declared by New Jersey Federalist congressman Elias Boudinot, the "importation of such persons" clearly extended solely to "negro slaves." In fact, a report of a special House committee declared firmly that "the General Government is expressly restrained from prohibiting the importation of such persons" until 1808. Then, a committee of the whole House amended this section by simply adding the term "migration" before importation. Interestingly, the only time that migration came under scrutiny was when Madison admitted they could not implement any measures abolishing the slave trade, yet he immediately hinted that there existed "a variety of ways" whereby Congress could "countenance the abolition" through regulations that "might be made in relation to the introduction of [slaves] into the new States to be formed out of the Western Territory," and he thought that object was "well worthy of consideration." Just how to accomplish this objective, Madison never pursued. Neither did Congress, for that matter, which never considered Madison's comment.[12]

Congress addressed the slave trade on several occasions during the 1790s, but only the *foreign* slave trade. In 1794, it banned the carrying of slaves *from* the United States *to* foreign countries and from one foreign jurisdiction to another on vessels fitted out in the United States. In 1800, Congress enacted penalties for any U.S. citizen who had any interest, direct or indirect, in vessels conducting the slave trade, including serving on such vessels, and it commissioned ships to enforce these regulations and gave the federal courts prosecutorial jurisdiction. Three years later, Congress passed a law prohibiting and penalizing the importation of "any negro, mulatto, or other person of colour" into the port of any state which had already terminated the importation of such persons via state statute. At the time of their passage, none of these enactments produced intense or lingering debate about congressional authority to halt the importation of slaves into states that had allowed it prior to the twenty-year period, all of which had banned it anyway by 1803; nor was there any concern that such legislation would hinder the domestic slave trade, including the carrying of slaves from one U.S. jurisdiction to another where slavery was allowed.[13]

During the 1798 debates over the Alien and Sedition Acts, particularly in reference to the Alien Bill, Congress revisited the clause, specifically as to whether it applied to whites coming from a foreign jurisdiction. Georgia congressman Abraham Baldwin—a delegate at the Constitutional Convention—argued that the clause stood in direct opposition to the principle of the Alien Bill, implying that the clause entertained white immigrants as much as slaves, and he recognized that some congressmen in the current debates believed the clause "would extend to other persons besides slaves, which was not denied, but this did not produce any alteration of it." He insisted that the clause, when adopted at the Constitutional Convention, was never confined "entirely to the subject of slaves." Baldwin also warned that if the Alien Bill passed, then "advocates for abolition of slavery" would use the measure to request that the president of the United States send slaves out of the country. Federalist congressman from Connecticut, Samuel Dana, disputed Baldwin's assumption. The purpose of the clause was to secure to the South their property in slaves, but that reason did not apply in the case of the Alien Bill, "which does not say the States shall not admit the migration of foreigners," but that "where persons have not attained the right of citizenship they shall be removed" if the president deemed them dangerous. Another Federalist congressman from Connecticut, John Allen, also disagreed with Baldwin's contention that the clause applied to persons other than slaves. It was "pretty evident" to him that the provision applied only to slaves, for if it had "related to emigrants," there would have been no limitation of time whereby Congress could act. "If Africans, or slaves, had been inserted by name," he concluded, "the thing could not, in his opinion, have been more clear." The Federalist speaker of the house, Jonathan Dayton, agreed, arguing that the clause applied only to the introduction of slaves and never extended to "the importation or introduction of citizens from foreign countries." But Baldwin, a Jeffersonian Republican, was not alone in his contentions. Other statesmen of this political creed thought the clause included white immigrants. Thomas Jefferson, in his draft of the Kentucky Resolutions in 1798, implied as much. He applied the clause to the migration of white aliens into Virginia, which that state thought proper to admit, and thus the Alien Bill, "prohibiting their migration" is unconstitutional, "that to remove them when migrated, is equivalent to a prohibition of their migration." Obviously, the 1798 debate over the interpretation of the clause fell along partisan lines, as it would during the Missouri admission debates.[14]

As the constitutionally mandated twenty-year prohibitory period approached its end, Congress revisited the slave-trade issue, specifically, to inquire as to what, if any, additional provisions were necessary "to prevent the importation of slaves into the Territories of the United States." In February 1806, a House committee, chaired by North Carolina's David Williams, reported back that, in regard to the territories of Mississippi

(1798) and Louisiana and Orleans (1804), the citizens thereof could not lawfully import slaves from abroad, but they all retained the right "to import slaves from any place within the limits of the United States." In short, those settling these territories could bring slaves with them if they carried them from another slave jurisdiction within the country. But it was no secret to anyone that slaves recently imported into Southern ports, such as Charleston, were whisked into the Orleans Territory, and Congress recognized that this practice would continue "to a very great extent" if it did not pass a law to forbid it. The committee deemed it expedient, then, "to prohibit any slave or slaves, who may be hereafter imported into the United States, from being carried into any of the Territories thereof," and so recommended a resolution making it unlawful for "any person or persons to import or bring into any of the Territories of the United States any slave or slaves that may hereafter be imported into the United States" as of December 31, 1807.[15]

During the lengthy debates, all—even Southern congressmen—declared publicly their intentions to terminate once and for all the "detestable traffic,"—that is, the importation of slaves, which Congress expanded to include to any person of color brought into the United States. Not until the very end of the debates, however, even after the House voted 113 to 5 to pass the Senate's version of the legislation, did the concern over congressional power to prevent the migration of slaves within U.S. territory become an apparent concern. Some Southern congressmen, such as David Williams, feared that the bill as it stood "would provide that no negroes shall be transported from one State to another to be sold or held in service." He desired greater assurances that the act could not be interpreted so. The irascible Virginia congressman John Randolph took it further, arguing that if the House version of the bill, which contained such assurances, failed, then Southerners "would set the law at defiance." He, for one, would defiantly take his slaves from Virginia to another slave state, just to assert the rights of slaveholders. The next step, he continued, "would be to forbid the slaveholder himself going from one State to another." The problem, specifically, was a recommendation inserted by a conference committee restricting the transportation of slaves along the U.S. coastline to be sold elsewhere in the country. For that matter, as the legislation stood, Georgia congressman Peter Early suggested that it would not forbid the introduction of slaves from Spanish Florida. Rep. William Findley of Pennsylvania was the only congressman raising the question of white aliens. Congress, he declared, possessed the right by the law of nations to expel aliens, and that the Migration and Importation Clause "clearly implies, that were it not for the restraining clause, we should now have the right of preventing any aliens coming to this country." The House and Senate made modifications appeasing such fears. On March 2, 1807, President Jefferson signed the legislation into law. After January 1, 1808, it was unlawful "to import or bring into" the United States or any of its territories, "from any foreign kingdom, place or country," any "negro, mulatto, or person of colour" bound to be sold into servitude.[16]

The 1807 act offered, however, plenty of safeguards assuring the continuance of the domestic slave trade and preventing congressional interference with the transportation of slaves from one U.S. slave jurisdiction to another. The act consistently explicated the importation of persons of color from any of the coasts or kingdoms of Africa, or from any other foreign jurisdiction, including a section levying penalties for slaves being brought into the United States from any adjoining foreign territory, i.e., Spanish Florida. Although the law prohibited the transportation of slaves on vessels under forty tons, which would include travel along the U.S. coastline, nothing in this section would prohibit "the taking on board or transporting on any river, or inland bay of the sea, within the jurisdiction of the United States, any negro, mulatto, or person of colour, (not imported contrary to the provisions of this act) in any vessel or species of craft whatever." For vessels weighing above forty tons plying the American coastline from one U.S. port to another and transporting persons of color bound for involuntary servitude, the captain and/or master simply needed to provide a list of the names of the slaves to be sold and to swear none had been imported into the United States after January 1, 1808. Nothing in the law pertained to any overt or covert congressional authority, implicit or explicit, to touch the internal migration, via land, from one slave jurisdiction in the United States to another, whether a state or a territory, the latter of course allowing slavery—the Louisiana (and hence Missouri) Territory included. Seemingly, then, Congress had defined more clearly what "migration or importation" meant. The Missouri crisis soon demonstrated otherwise.

Initially, the Migration and Importation Clause went unnoticed as the debates over Missouri's admission commenced in earnest in January of 1819. Massachusetts congressman Timothy Fuller was the only individual to broach it during the first debates in the 15th Congress. No one in the Senate addressed it at this time. That all changed during the debates consuming the 16th Congress, when Maryland Congressman Samuel Smith cited the clause immediately in the first speech of the Missouri debates, where it received regular attention, in both chambers of Congress.

One thing proved certain—there was no debate over the meaning of *importation*. All congressmen agreed that it applied to slaves coming into the United States, whether into states or territories, from abroad. All understood, for that matter, that importation was no longer a concern. By 1803, the states themselves had enacted legislation prohibiting the slave trade into their respective lands, and Congress followed suit in 1807, terminating the slave trade for good—well before the Missouri admission debates. When Missouri sought entry into the Union, therefore, antislavery congressmen apparently needed a new and novel argument in their quest to halt the spread of slavery, and, hence, the focus on the meaning of "migration"—and not of "importation"—of expansion of slavery overland, not by water, and from one state to another under the same jurisdiction, and not from foreign lands. The term *migration* and what it actually meant quickly emerged as the most controversial component of the clause. Many congressmen commiserated with Virginia's James Johnson when he complained about how often his colleagues dwelled incessantly on the terms *migration* and *importation*, "which have been so often repeated, during this debate, as to cause them to grate on the ear as harshly and disagreeably as the chains of a convict."[17]

Proponents of slavery restriction in Missouri argued that the framers of the Constitution desired to limit the expansion of slavery, and, to achieve this objective, the delegates inserted the term "migration" into the clause, with the intent of prohibiting the movement of slaves into new states and territories. "Hitherto it has been found necessary for Congress to prohibit migration or transportation from State to State," argued Fuller. "But now it becomes the right and duty of Congress to guard against the further extension of the intolerable evil and the crying enormity of slavery." The Tallmadge Amendment, he contended, was necessary, as the opening of an extensive slave market in the territory west of the Mississippi River would merely "tempt the cupidity of those who otherwise perhaps might gradually emancipate their slaves." In order to "check an evil which produced so much difficulty in settling the principles of the Constitution," Illinois's Cook declared that the "right was understood and intended to be vested in Congress, to prevent the migration of slaves into the new States, from the time of the adoption of the Constitution, and even in the old states, after the year 1808." As such, restrictionists argued consistently that, in the words of Clagett, importation entailed no other meaning than bringing in slaves from abroad, with the intention of preventing the further introduction of slaves, and that migration concerned the "act of moving from place to place," and that "can only mean from State to State." Taylor defined importation as the "bringing into this country from abroad, either by land or by water," while migration meant "moving within it from one State or Territory to another." The power of Congress to prohibit the internal movement of slaves, therefore, was never denied, and had been exercised prior to 1808 in numerous instances with the admission of new states in the decades following ratification. Restrictionists in Congress frequently resorted to the history of the admission of new states as proof of their contention, claiming that Congress had on previous occasions placed restrictions regarding slavery as a condition to enter the Union.[18]

Free state legislatures ardently supported the arguments made by their representatives in Washington, consistently claiming that Congress possessed the power to prevent extension of slavery into new territories and states. The Pennsylvania state legislature declared that the clause "expressly recognized" congressional authority "to prohibit the migration of servile persons" after 1808, meaning the movement of slaves from one state to another state or territory. The state legislature of New Jersey argued that the clause, "by necessary implication," admits the "general power of Congress over the subject of slavery" and conceded to that body "the right to regulate and restrain such migration and importation" after 1808 "into the existing or any newly to be created state." Vermont agreed. By the clause in question, Congress had the right "to inhibit any further introduction or extension of slavery" as a condition for entering the Union.[19]

Massachusetts's Fuller argued that the terms *migration* and *importation* were, therefore, *not* synonymous, simply because the framers would not have needed to employ the former term if the two meant the same thing. Restrictionists stood unanimous on this claim. Some congressmen, such as Pennsylvania's Sergeant, pointed to the application of a duty for importation of slaves as proof that the clause applied to the internal movement of slaves. The Constitution's restriction preventing Congress from levying duties on exports from any of the states "strongly supports this interpretation." These two clauses inserted in the same article of the Constitution, he surmised, suggested that Congress cannot prohibit importation of slaves until after 1808, but, in the meantime, it could impose a duty upon such importation; during this same period, moreover, Congress cannot prohibit migration, but it could not likewise impose a duty, because migration applied to the transfer of slaves from state to state, thereby constitutionally prohibiting the levying of a duty. "That migration and importation do not mean the same things is evident, because a tax may be imposed on the latter, but not on the former," Taylor concurred.[20]

Restrictionists in Congress bolstered their claims by focusing on the clause's phrase "states now existing," an argument their Northern predecessors had emphasized during the ratification debates. Fuller, the first to raise the issue of the Migration and Importation Clause during the debates, insisted that the clause recognized the right of the states "at the time of the framing of the Constitution" to allow slavery until such time as they deemed fit to "meliorate their condition." States allowing slavery at the time of ratification were thus permitted "from the necessity of the case" and "for the sake of union" to keep slaves "until they should think it proper or safe to conform to the pure principle [of republicanism] by abolishing slavery." The clause, he continued, "cannot, without violence, be applied to any other States than those in which slavery was allowed at the formation of the Constitution."[21]

Northern congressmen opposed to slavery extension immediately adopted this line of reasoning. The framers had intended "to arrest the progress and prevent the further extension of involuntary servitude," argued Rhode Island Senator David Morril, so they adopted a compromise clause affecting only "states now existing," thus providing Congress the right to prohibit importation of slaves and their migration into any state or territory "except those within the jurisdiction of the original States." Congress could not halt the migration or importation of slaves until after 1808, but was "at liberty to make such prohibition as to any new State which might, in the meantime, be established." Even after 1808, Congress was authorized "to make such prohibition as to all of the States, whether, new or old." Fellow Rhode Island Senator James Burrill concurred, claiming that congressional power to prevent migration and importation of slaves after 1808 only pertained to the states existing at the time, but such authority was "not even temporarily restrained" regarding states subsequently admitted to the Union. As for territories and news states, "as to States not then existing," the power of Congress "was unfettered—was supreme." Sergeant believed that the clause "plainly intimates a design to give a control to Congress over the introduction of slavery into the States to be formed," and the framers provided such power to Congress immediately, with no prohibition prior to 1808. Ohio Senator Benjamin Ruggles asserted that Congress was "left free and untrammeled with regard to the territories" of the United States "or any State that might be created out of them before the year 1808." The clause applied, therefore, only "to the States then existing, not to any that were afterwards to exist." The framers, he concluded, desired to confine slavery to states where it existed and thus "forever to prohibit it in the territories or States that might be formed out of them."[22]

Opponents of slavery restriction countered, of course, but in contesting restrictionist claims that migration merely meant the movement of slaves from one state to another state or territory, and thus the terms *migration* and *importation* were not synonymous, they adopted an assortment of apparently incongruous arguments—a fact that restrictionists regularly raised to incriminate their opponents with inconsistency. "In this debate it seems generally to be admitted, by gentlemen on the opposite side, that these two words are not synonymous; but what their meaning is, they are not so well agreed," insinuated Pennsylvania's Walter Lowrie. "These constructions cannot both be right."[23]

A plethora of anti-restrictionists in Congress indeed argued that the terms *migration* and *importation* were *not* synonymous, claiming that importation applied only to slaves and migration concerned only free whites, both coming from abroad. Congressmen from the Mid Atlantic to the Upper South, and from the Lower South to the Old Southwest, opposed to slavery restriction in Missouri, espoused this position. "The term, or word, migration," declared Pinckney, "applies wholly to free whites," and in its "Constitutional sense, as intended by the Convention, it means 'voluntary change of servitude', from one country to another." According to Johnson of Virginia, migration applied "to all persons of whatever color or description, who should voluntarily remove to the United States, or any particular State," and importation "to all persons who should be brought, by the will of others, into any of the States." Missouri's John Scott defined importation "as solely intended to provide against the further introduction, from abroad, of the unhappy sons and daughters of Africa, and not to give to Congress the power to regulate the distribution of those that were here." Migration, on the other hand, "indicated an exercise of free will, the exercise of which was not to be attributed to slaves," and thus the clause authorized Congress to prohibit after 1808 "that great influx of the rabble from foreign countries" who might "endanger the Constitution and the Union." Migration, declared Virginia congressman Philip Pendleton Barbour, "implies to *freemen*, not *slaves*." Migration "intended to refer to free foreigners coming into this country," argued Philip's elder brother, James, in the U.S. Senate, while importation "intended to apply to slaves from abroad." The framers designed the clause, alleged Mississippi congressman Christopher Rankin, so as to enable Congress "to prohibit the influx or migration of foreigners to our country, after a limited period," and thus "intended to apply to emigration from Europe."[24]

Anti-restrictionists considered Scott's allusion to free will quite apropos, and made this distinction the philosophical foundation for their argument that migration addressed white emigration. "The terms migration and importation are not synonymous," surmised Georgia Senator John Elliot. "Migration implies volition, choice, self-direction—but these being not to a slave," for a slave "may be carried or imported, or he may abscond, but he can never *migrate*." Delaware Senator Nicholas Van Dyke stated that migration "implies free agency, and the exercise of will, in the persons migrating, which cannot be predicated of a slave." Delaware Representative Louis McLane concurred, assuming migration "cannot apply to the forcible or involuntary removal of a slave from any State, foreign or domestic," that migration was "the voluntary act of a free agent" and a slave "has no such will, and is no such agent." Migration meant "the coming of free foreigners to the States," argued Mississippi congressman Walter Leake, that is, "the voluntary coming of a free person, acting according to his own volition."

Rankin supported his colleague from Mississippi, stating that migration included "such persons as have volition, and can migrate," while importation included "such as have no volition, but are imported carried along by the will of the master." "*Importation* means property," concluded North Carolina Senator Nathaniel Macon, "*migration* does not." John Holmes of the Maine District claimed that "such Persons" meant slaves when applied to importation and free persons when applied to migration. "The former implies constraint, and excludes volition," while the latter "implies volition, and excludes constraint." Importation involved introducing by either land or water, he continued, while migration was "a voluntary going from one jurisdiction or sovereignty to another."[25]

The idea that migration necessarily entailed the movement from one foreign jurisdiction to another also proved a popular argument for opponents of restriction. Migration and importation "must be taken to refer to a foreign country or territory, as the *terminus a quo*," argued Van Dyke. McLane deemed migration "has relation to the government which it is to be controlled," and thus the true meaning was that "of quitting their own country, and of removing beyond the jurisdiction of the Government." As long as an individual remained under the jurisdiction of the United States, therefore, his change of residence could not be considered migration, whether within a state or from one state to another. He was still in the same country, still a citizen, subject to the same laws and enjoying the same rights.[26]

In their assertion that migration applied only to free white persons, some congressmen claimed that the framers designed the Migration and Importation Clause to appease the Northern states. McLane argued that the year 1808 was a compromise between the slaveholding and non-slaveholding states regarding the increase in population of either freemen or slaves from abroad. Because of the Three-Fifths Clause, the argument ran, the slaveholding states would increase their political power by way of importation of slaves from abroad, so the framers placed a limit on the period of that importation. At the same time, this concession "could not have been made without a similar license to the emigration of free persons in favor of the Northern and non-slaveholding States, and thus the affair was adjusted by allowing the same period to each." The framers adopted the Migration and Importation Clause, moreover, in order to prevent the "premature ascendency" in the South of an "undue increase" in its slave population, "an object which would have been as effectually promoted by the dispersion of the slaves among other States, as by inhibiting their introduction from abroad, for, in case of their diffusion," the Northern states would acquire their "share of the numbers," and so "the representation would be equalized." Virginia's Barbour brothers made similar claims. James thought the clause was so designed as to prevent Congress from interdicting the migration of freemen to populate the Northern states during the twenty-year prohibitory period. Philip felt it "fair to conclude" that the framers agreed that Congress should not have the power to prohibit the importation of slaves prior to 1808, whereby the importation of slaves would increase the representation of the slaveholding states in the meantime, while the "jealousy" of the non-slaveholding states required "an offset to this," so that the migration of free persons to these states would not be prohibited as well.[27]

Another reason for restraining congressional power "to prevent migration hither" for twenty years, according to Pinckney, centered on the fact that the United States possessed "immense and almost immeasurable territory," and thus the need to encourage emigration of "able, skilful [sic], and industrious Europeans." The "portals of the only temple of true freedom now existing on earth," he waxed eloquently, "should be thrown open to all mankind." By 1808, the Union would be sufficiently settled, and Congress could then halt "further accession of foreigners" and rely on the progress of "our own stock." The clause sought, therefore, to equalize the influx of slaves in the South with the influx of Europeans in the North.[28]

Some congressmen turned to semantics to make their claim that migration referred only to free whites coming from abroad. Philip Barbour suggested that the word *admit* in the clause proved "incontestably" that the term *migration* meant emigrating from foreign regions, for if the persons were already in the United States, they could not logically be admitted. "Sir, it would be a solecism in language," he deduced, "to talk of admitting a man into a house, who was already in it." Rankin also believed the phrase "shall think proper to admit" strongly proved an "admission from abroad," rather than "a change of residence within" the United States. Congressmen likewise looked to the application of the tax on importation, and not on migration, as further evidence of their claims. By not including a duty on the migration of persons, James Barbour "fairly inferred" that the framers believed that migration applied to freemen.[29]

A few congressmen cited the Declaration of Independence as further proof that migration applied only to the emigration of white Europeans. The document contained an indictment against King George III for preventing "the population of these States; for that purpose obstructing the Laws for Naturalization of Foreigners; refusing to pass others to encourage their migrations hither, and raising the conditions of new Appropriations of Lands." Since this was the only state paper employing the term *migration* until the Constitution, some thought this indicated a desire to increase the population of the nation by migration from Europe. A few others mentioned the 1798 Alien Law in defense of congressional power to prohibit the migration of foreign freemen under particular circumstances. Pinckney, as one example, claimed the purpose of inserting migration into the clause was to provide Congress the power to regulate the arrival of foreigners for reasons of national security, to protect against potential spies and alien enemies. As such, the clause, in its design to protect the public interest after 1808, was "a *negative pregnant,* restraining for twenty years and giving the power after."[30]

Of course, this line of debate brought a whole other part of the clause into question—the meaning of "such Persons." Restricionists to a man cited the desire of the framers to avoid placing the term *slave* or *slavery* into the Constitution. According to Cook, it was "apparent to every candid mind" that the delegates at the Convention "meant slaves and slaves only," that "whenever slaves are meant, the word persons is invariably used in describing them." If the clause meant to include white persons, Cook queried, then why confine it to states "now existing," especially if the purpose was to populate new states? "Although the words, slave, slaves, or slavery, are not in the Constitution, yet it is inferred," proclaimed Pennsylvania's Thomas Forrest, "and servitude is confined to the then United States, and not extended to the territory." Fellow Pennsylvanian Sergeant argued that the clause was a restraint upon Congress demanded by South Carolina and Georgia as grounds for their approval of a union of states. "This is familiarly known to every person who has any acquaintance with the history of the Constitution," he chided the House. "That slaves are the persons here intended, and none others," Rhode Island's Morril reproached the Senate, "seems to be too clear to admit a doubt." Opponents of restriction, to the contrary, claimed that the term *persons* was, in the words of Mississippi's Rankin, "a generic term, embracing every description of human beings, no matter of what complexion."[31]

Yet, in their challenge to counter restrictionist claims that migration pertained only to the internal movement of slaves, some anti-restrictionist congressmen insisted that the two terms, *migration* and *importation*, *were* synonymous, and applied to the *same* class of people, that is, slaves brought from abroad into U.S. jurisdiction. The term *migration* applied to "slaves imported," claimed Senator Smith, and "it had no reference whatever to the native born slaves." The framers, he surmised, introduced the term in order "to permit slaves, imported into [Charleston], to be passed, without molestation, into Georgia and North Carolina." Migration involved, therefore, no other reference "to any other than slaves imported" and "none whatever to native born slaves." Migration and importation, therefore, referred only "to such slaves as the existing States may admit to be imported during the given time, and to none other."[32]

Many a Southern slaveholder agreed that *migration* and *importation* were the same. "A removal from district to district, within the same jurisdiction, is never denominated a *migration* of persons," argued the other senator from Maryland, William Pinkney, for "it should seem certain that human beings do not *migrate*, in the sense of the Constitution, simply because they transplant themselves from one place, to which the Constitution extends, to another which it equally covers." Both importation and migration, therefore, meant the same thing, the coming to the United States from foreign areas. Migration indicated "a coming," while importation connoted "a bringing," both from abroad. South Carolina's Pinckney concurred. Migration, he maintained, merely meant the "change of residence from one country or climate to another," and not the movement from one jurisdiction to another *within* the same country. How was it possible, he asked, "to migrate from one part of a country to another part of the same country?" The term "admit," argued Kentucky's Benjamin Hardin—reiterating the argument made by Philip Barbour—applied equally to migration and importation, and demonstrated unequivocally that "the persons there intended were not then in the United States," for if they were, "the word 'admit' could not be used in relation to persons in [the country] already."[33]

So why, if the two terms meant the same thing, would the framers have purposely used them both? According to the opponents of restriction, the delegates to the Constitutional Convention, in their determination to end slavery, sought every means possible to secure such a desired end. All agreed that *importation* implied "bringing into our ports from foreign countries," Hardin continued, but the founders found it expedient to insert *migration* as added security. Migration, according to the Kentuckian, meant "bringing [slaves] into the United States, not through regular channels of our commerce, by entering them at the custom-house, but in any and every other way by which they could be introduced into the United States." By inhibiting the migration of Africans after 1808, concurred Georgia's Robert Reid, the framers sought "to more effectually" prevent "evasions of the laws interdicting the importation of slaves" in the quest "to prevent the accumulation of this species of property." According to Reid, the founders believed that once the slave trade ended, slavers would resort to "every artifice which ingenuity and avarice could devise" for violating the law, such as introducing slaves onto adjacent foreign soil (e.g., Spanish Florida) and smuggling them overland. "May it not have been to guard against such frauds, shifts and artifices, that the word 'migration' was inserted in the Constitution?" Although migration and importation "have distinct meanings," and are not necessarily synonymous, enjoined fellow Georgian, Senator Freeman Walker, each term was to be "employed in the performance of a particular office." Importation "looks abroad" and "intended to embrace slaves into this country from Africa and elsewhere by water." Migration "intended to embrace such as should be brought into the United States by land, from foreign contiguous territory belonging to foreign powers." By giving such a construction to the Migration and Importation Clause, "you satisfy the full meaning of both words." Virginia's James Pindall believed the framers inserted the word migration "from abundant caution, lest the word *importation* should not imply a full and effectual authority sought to be invested in Congress to prohibit the bringing in of slaves from foreign countries, under all circumstances." He pointed to the fact that nearly every act of congress since ratification to regulate the foreign slave trade "used terms of prohibition additional to, and rather broader than, simple *Importation*." In addition, these congressmen believed that "such Persons" meant slaves only.[34]

As further proof of the convoluted and complicated nature of the debate over the Migration and Importation Clause, this school of anti-restrictionists received support from a very unlikely source—Massachusetts Senator Harrison Gray Otis. He believed that the scope of the clause "embraced the mischief (and that only) of bringing slaves into the United States from foreign countries," and that importation alluded "to the bringing in by water" and migration "to the introduction by land." Furthermore, Otis claimed that the clause "was never contemplated to prevent a proprietor of slaves from taking them from one of the old States into another." But anti-restrictionist congressmen touting this line could not rejoice for long, for one of their own, North Carolina Senator Nathaniel Macon, declared at the same time that migration was "not intended for slaves brought into the United States by land."[35]

Adding to the argument that migration did not apply to the internal movement of slaves, anti-restrictionists also directed attention to the fact that slavery restriction, that is, the Tallmadge Amendment, applied only to Missouri. If the clause indeed meant to prevent slaves from passing from state to state, wondered Philip Barbour, then why does the restriction operate solely on Missouri? Legislation to this effect, concluded the Virginia congressman, should be general and apply equally to all states. The representatives of the two territories seeking admission—Missouri and Maine—seized upon this irregularity immediately. If Congress possessed the power to use the clause to prohibit the migration of slaves from one state to another, asked Holmes, then legislate it outright, rather than attaching a stipulation to a bill affecting only Missouri. "If you can by this clause of the Constitution shut up slaves in the States, let your legislation be general, and exercise upon all the slaveholding States," he demanded. "Why make Missouri the scape-goat [sic]?" Missouri's delegate, John Scott, countered restrictionists that if their interpretation of "migration" be correct, then the "power to prohibit the migration [of slaves] had reference alone to the States where the slaves were, and not to Missouri."[36]

In their quest to prove or disprove congressional authority to regulate the migration of slaves within the United States, congressmen also debated rather extensively as to the authoritative nature of the clause itself—that is, was it a grant of power or a restriction thereof? Restrictionists considered the clause to be a *negative pregnant*, essentially giving Congress a power to regulate, restrict, or prohibit the migration of slaves from one state to another state or territory. Cook argued that "the restriction upon any power necessarily presupposes the existence of that power." Although the clause did not contain an *express* delegation of power, it did by "a necessary and universal rule of construction" admit the existence of a power. It was, in "technical language," he asserted, "a negative pregnant," that is, "negating the power of Congress for a given period, and affirming it after that period." Congress possessed the power to prohibit the importation of slaves because it could construe the clause "as a negative pregnant negativing [sic] the power of Congress to prohibit such importation until 1808, and after that period affirming that power."[37]

Fellow Northerners supporting congressional power to restrict slavery in Missouri supported the negative pregnant argument. Sergeant argued that the clause was "an exception or restraint for a limited time, of the exercise of a power," and such an exception proved to be "conclusive evidence of a grant," for if no power was granted, then there could be "no exception from, or restraint upon, its exercise." Thus, the clause was equivalent to "a grant of the power, after the expiration of the time." Other restrictionists suggested that, although not a delegated grant of power, other powers expressly granted—namely the Commerce Power—provided Congress a power under the Migration and Importation Clause. Ruggles deemed the clause to be "a negative in its character, and confers no power whatever," rather it served as "a prohibition, for a limited time, of the exercise of other powers, with which Congress are invested by the Constitution," and that was through its powers to regulate commerce. Morril added that "it follows from this restriction, that, if it had not been inserted [in the Constitution], Congress would have had power to prohibit the commerce [in slaves], under the general powers of Congress, aided by the power to regulate commerce." Had not this "prohibition been inserted restricting the commerce of slaves," he concluded, Congress might have enacted legislation suppressing the migration or importation of slaves prior to 1808.[38]

To no one's surprise, opponents of restriction denied such claims of congressional power, arguing adamantly to the contrary that the clause was a restriction on power—period. Thus, Congress had no authority to touch the internal movement of slaves. "There is not one word in that clause which contains a delegation of power," declared Kentucky's Hardin. Rather, the clause was "from beginning to end, a restriction and limitation upon power already granted." A limitation of power was not, therefore, a grant of power. Congress "can lay no duty, impose no restriction, upon any article of trade or commerce" carried on from one state to another; Congress had no power to prevent a person from taking his property from one state to another. The intention of the clause, Hardin believed, was actually to prevent *states* from trammeling upon each other's trade and commerce with other states. Virginia's Pindall argued that the clause never conferred any power on Congress, as it merely prohibited that body from exercising a power prior to 1808, and to support his contention, he cited a clause from New York's ratifying convention: "that those clauses in the said Constitution which declare the Congress shall not have or exercise certain powers, do not imply that Congress is entitled to any powers not given by the said Constitution; but such clauses are to be construed either as exceptions to certain specified powers, or as inserted merely for greater caution." Mississippi's Rankin asserted there was no negative pregnant, that no implied power existed at all, and that the clause was simply added to the Constitution as "abundant caution" to avoid any appearance of an implied power, considering the extreme jealousy of the states against the usurpation of centralized power at the time of the founding. Fellow Mississippian Leake concurred. The clause "makes no grant of power, nor does it enlarge any power before granted, but on the contrary, it restricts them." Leake argued that the clause clearly restrained Congress from prohibiting the migration or importation of such persons as any state then existing might think proper to admit until a given period, and, as the restraint operated no longer than 1808, it "expired by its own limitation, and having performed its offices, becomes *functus officio*." The power of Congress to impose any restriction on Missouri, therefore, "cannot be derived from that clause." Any attempt "to infer so important a power from this prohibitory clause," providing Congress the power to prevent the internal migration of slaves, concluded Delaware's Van Dyke, "is novel, unprecedented, and dangerous."[39]

To bolster their various interpretations of the Migration and Importation Clause, congressmen on both sides of the aisle regularly referred to the original intent of the framers of the Constitution. Some, like Illinois's Cook, offered extensive renditions of their own version of the adoption of the clause at the Constitutional Convention, while others, such as

Pennsylvania's Lowrie, discussed their own account of how the Founding Fathers—namely, Madison and Wilson—viewed the clause during the ratification debates and in subsequent public pronouncements during the preceding three decades. But, as expected, these references did little to provide any clarity or agreement. Disagreement over the meaning of the clause proved the order of the day.[40]

Yet, living founders indeed discussed the clause while the debates in Congress raged in 1819 and 1820. John Adams and Thomas Jefferson remarked on the Missouri crisis in their regular exchange of letters, and two who had written under the penname Publius commented as well. In fact, John Jay and James Madison directly addressed the Migration and Importation Clause during the Missouri debates, each giving contradictory interpretations to the origins and the meaning of the clause, and assisting no one in clarifying the issue. In November of 1819, in a letter to a colleague, Jay argued that the clause provided constitutional authority to prohibit the introduction of slaves into new states. "I understand the sense and meaning of this clause to be, that the power of Congress," he avowed, "was not to be exercised with respect to the *then existing* States (and them only) until the year 1808; but that the Congress were at liberty to make such prohibition as to any new State; which might, in the mean time, be established." Thus, the author of the fewest of the *Federalist Papers* unsurprisingly sided with his fellow Northerners; the other living Publius, however, disagreed.[41]

Madison offered the most testimony on the origins and intention of the clause, establishing what one scholar of the subject deemed to be the traditional interpretation. In the same month of Jay's missive, the Father of the Constitution also wrote a friend providing his perspective regarding the "intention of the framers of the Constitution." As to the terms "migration" and "persons," it was most certain that the terms referred "exclusively to a migration or importation from other countries into the U. States," and not "to a removal, voluntary or involuntary, of slaves or freemen, from one to another part of the U. States. Nothing appears or is recollected that warrants this latter intention. Nothing in the proceedings of the State conventions indicates such a construction thereto." Neither was there any indication, Madison continued, that Congress "have heretofore considered themselves as deriving from this Clause a power over the migration or removal of individuals, whether freemen or slaves, from one State to another, whether new or old," and that every indication "is against such a construction by Congress of their constitutional powers." Although the "great object of the Convention seemed to be to prohibit the increase by the *importation* of slaves," Madison opined, he never recollected anything that "denoted a view to control the distribution of those within the Country." The framers, therefore, "forebore [sic] to extend the prohibition to the introduction of slaves from other parts of the Union."[42]

In February of 1820, Madison confirmed this view to Monroe:

> "Judging from my own impressions I shd. deem it impossible that the memory of any one who was a member of the Genl. Convention, could favor an opinion that the terms did not *exclusively* refer to Migration & importation *into the U. S.* Had they been understood in that Body in the sense now put on them, it is easy to conceive the alienation they would have there created in certain States; And no one can decide better than yourself the effect they would have had in the State Conventions, if such a meaning had been avowed by the Advocates of the Constitution. If a suspicion had existed of such a construction, it wd. at least have made a conspicuous figure among the amendments proposed to the Instrument."

Still, in his November of 1819 correspondence, Madison hinted that Congress had the power to prevent the spread of slavery into U.S. territories. Congress, he wrote, could not interfere with the slave trade until 1808, but "with an implication, that after that date, they might prohibit the importation of slaves into the States then existing, & previous thereto, into the States not then existing." He had implied such in the 1790s debates over the regulation of the slave trade.[43]

Madison also indicated that the framers did not apply the clause exclusively to slaves. He admitted that, at the Convention, some states did not want the term *slaves* inserted in the Constitution, hence the descriptive phrase of "migration and importation of persons." Yet, it was "possible tho' not recollected" that some of the delegates "might have had an eye to the case of freed blacks, as well as malefactors"—that is, white "foreign malefactors." Decades earlier, in *Federalist* No. 42, Madison had recognized

Antifederalist attempts to "pervert this clause into an objection against the Constitution, by representing it on one side as a criminal toleration of an illicit practice, and on another as calculated to prevent voluntary and beneficial emigrations from Europe to America." Reference to this tract resurfaced during the Missouri debates, and to confirm his original statement made as Publius, Madison, in January of 1820 confirmed his original position as consistent with his recollections of the Convention, by focusing on the "discriminating term" of "beneficial" added to "voluntary emigrations from Europe to America." During the Missouri debates, both supporters and opponents of slavery restriction in Missouri interpreted Madison's statements—whether made in 1787, 1790, or 1819—in order to endorse their respective views on the origins and meaning of the Migration and Importation Clause.[44]

On March 6, 1820, Missouri officially entered the Union, or seemingly so. During the summer of that year, the "state" adopted its first constitution and sent it off to Congress for approval. But a clause in the new state's constitution, empowering the state legislature "to prevent free Negroes and mulattos from coming to and settling in this State, upon any pretext whatsoever," spurred another round of intense debate in Congress. While it would seem on the surface that this stipulation involved, at the very least, the question of migration of "such persons" other than slaves or free white persons from one state to another, and thus whether the Supremacy Clause empowered Congress to weigh in on the issue because of the Migration and Importation Clause after 1808, not a single congressman broached the idea. The clause never again resurfaced in the final round of the Missouri debates.[45]

Yet debate over the interpretation of the Migration and Importation Clause continued in the decades after Missouri's admission until the Civil War terminated the question altogether. Within a few years of Missouri statehood, during the 1820s, two of the nation's preeminent antebellum jurists—John Marshall and Joseph Story—apparently confirmed the Southern version of the definition of migration. In his renowned *Commentaries on the Constitution,* Story declared that migration "seems appropriately to apply to voluntary arrivals, as importation does to involuntary arrivals." He had made a similar declaration in a charge to a grand jury during the 1820 May term in the U.S. Circuit Court. Although he proudly declared the 1807 congressional statute as a "general prohibition of the traffic as well in our domestic as foreign trade," he never explicated what he meant by "domestic" trade. In fact, he proceeded to give a detailed explanation of the 1807 law, and cited only the bringing in from foreign countries any person intended to be a slave anywhere in the nation. He never mentioned anything about preventing the migration of slaves from one U.S. jurisdiction to another. In one of the most famous of the Commerce Clause cases before the U.S. Supreme Court, *Gibbons v. Ogden*, Chief Justice Marshall argued that migration "applies as appropriately to voluntary, as importation does to involuntary, arrivals."[46]

Even Roger Taney weighed in on the meaning of the clause, albeit indirectly. In the *Dred Scott* case, the Chief Justice declared that the clause indicated beyond doubt that the Constitution considered "the negro race" as a "separate class of persons," and thusly not considered citizens. Importation applied to this very class, of slaves particularly, while "no one of that race had ever migrated to the United States voluntarily," thus seemingly indicating that the former term implied involuntary entry into the United States from abroad, while the former implied voluntary entry into the same.[47]

From Missouri's admission to the eve of Civil War, antislavery advocates continued to cite the clause as a legitimate tool for congressional authority to halt the spread of slavery into U.S. territories. In 1841, G. W. F. Mellen quoted a letter of James Birney, who wrote that the Constitution gave Congress the authority "to prevent the transfer of slaves, as articles of commerce, from one State to another, and the introduction of slavery into the Territories." In 1844, William Goodell argued that migration and importation of such persons applied to slaves only, and only then to the states then existing at ratification. The clause did not extend, therefore, to Kentucky, Tennessee, Louisiana, Alabama, Mississippi, Missouri, Arkansas, and Florida, as none of these states were party to the compromises adopted at the Constitutional Convention. In 1856, William Duer defined "such Persons" as slaves only and "migration" as the interstate movement of slaves, which gave Congress power under the Commerce Clause to prohibit the interstate trade in slaves. On the eve of the Civil War, Luther Marsh quoted Alvan Stewart: "The word 'migration' employed in the first clause of the ninth section of the first article, is significant indeed, and means nothing more nor less than going from one State to another, not from one part of a State to another; not coming from a foreign country beyond sea." Also in 1860, Lysander Spooner wrote that migration "applies only to those who were to *go out from* one of our own States or Territories into another." Migration "is the act of *going out* from a state or country; and differs from immigration in this, that immigration is the act of *coming into* a state or country. It is obvious, therefore, that the '*migration,*' which Congress are here forbidden to prohibit, is simply the *going out of* persons from one of our own States or Territories into another . . . and that it has no reference to persons *coming in* from foreign countries to our own." Such references proved sporadic, however, from 1821 to 1861.[48]

The Civil War and the consequent end of slavery terminated any debate once and for all; the clause meant nothing afterwards. Ironically, it appears no one after 1865 ever employed the clause to address the spike in immigration to the United States in the late nineteenth century—specifically as to the emigration to and migration within the United States of free whites or other immigrants deemed undesirable to many "old stock" Americans. Missouri's admission, arguably, had settled the question of the clause once and for all, and it did so without ever arriving at any agreement as to its meaning and intent.

NOTES

1. James Madison to James Monroe, February 10, 1820, *James Monroe Papers*, Library of Congress, https://www.loc.gov/item/mjm018701; *Annals of Congress*, U.S. House of Representatives, 16th Congress, 1st Session, 1038; *Annals of Congress*, U.S. Senate, 16th Congress, 1st Session, 259.

2. *Annals of Congress*, House, 16th Cong., 1st Sess., 959, 972, 979.

3. Max Farrand, ed., *The Records of the Federal Convention of 1787*, Rev. Ed., 4 vols. (New Haven: Yale University Press, 1937), 2: 168–69.

4. Farrand, ed., *The Records of the Federal Convention of 1787*, 2: 220–23.

5. Farrand, ed., *The Records of the Federal Convention of 1787*, 2: 364–65, 369–75, 400, 414–16.

6. Farrand, ed., *The Records of the Federal Convention of 1787*, 2: 364–65, 369–75.

7. Farrand, ed., *The Records of the Federal Convention of 1787*, 2: 364–65, 369–75. Later in this debate, Pinckney "thought himself bound to declare candidly" that South Carolina would not stop importation of slaves in "any short time," but "only stop them occasionally as she now does." Rutledge immediately concurred, declaring that the people of the slave states "will never be such fools as to give up so important an interest."

8. Farrand, ed., *The Records of the Federal Convention of* 1787, 2: 415–17. Rutledge feared that the Constitution's amending power could allow the free states to alter the

Migration and Importation Clause and thus avoid the twenty-year prohibitory period, so the delegates inserted the caveat that no amendments to the Constitution could ever alter that particular clause.

9. Walter Berns, "The Constitution and the Migration of slaves," *Yale Law Journal* 78, no. 2(1968): 203–04, 205–07; "James Wilson on the Slave Trade Clause," December 3, 1787, in Bernard Bailyn, ed., *The Debate on the Constitution: Federalist and Antifederalist Speeches, Articles, and Letters During the Struggle Over Ratification*, 2 vols. (New York: Library Classics of the United States, 1993), 1: 830; G. W. F. Mellen, *An Argument on the Unconstitutionality of Slavery, Embracing an Abstract of the Proceedings of the National and State Conventions on This Subject* (Boston: Saxton & Peirce, 1841), 157.

10. "Centinel, No. 3," November 5, 1787, in Herbert Storing, ed., *The Complete Antifederalist*, 7 vols. (Chicago: University of Chicago Press, 1981), 2.7.76; "A Friend to the Rights of the People: Anti-Foederalist No. 1," *Exeter Freeman's Oracle*, February 8, 1788, in Storing, ed., *The Complete* Antifederalist, 4.23.3; James Iredell, "Debate in North Carolina Ratifying Convention," July 26, 1788, in Philip B. Kurland and Ralph Lerner, eds., *The Founders' Constitution*, 5 vols. (Chicago: University of Chicago Press, 1987, revised Indianapolis: Liberty Press), 3: 295. Wilson also argued that the tax could only be levied on persons imported and not migrating.

11. *Annals of Congress*, House, 16th Cong., 1st Sess., 1094.

12. *Annals of Congress*, House, 16th Cong., 1st Sess., 1246; *Annals of Congress*, House, 16th Cong., 2d Sess., 1517, 1524. For the entire debate, see *Annals of Congress*, House, 16th Cong., 1st Sess., 1224–33, 1239–47, and *Annals of Congress*, House, 16th Cong., 2nd Sess., 1465–66, 1500–25.

13. *Statutes at Large*, U.S. House of Representatives, 3rd Cong., 1st Sess., 11: 347–49, 6th Cong., 1st Sess., 51: 70–71, 7th Cong., 2nd Sess., 10: 205–06. Congress tightened the 1807 law in 1818, only months after the first petitions for Missouri statehood had reached Congress. *Statutes at Large*, 15th Cong., 1st Sess., 91: 450–53. loc.gov/law/help/statutes-at-large/.

14. *Annals of Congress*, House, 5th Cong., 2d Sess., 1968–69, 1991, 1993, 2003, 2004.

15. *Annals of Congress*, House, 9th Cong., 1st Sess., 472–73, 522–23. In his Sixth Annual Message to Congress, in December of 1806, President Jefferson gleefully looked forward to the period when Congress could act constitutionally to end the slave trade permanently, and, although no laws passed to this end could take effect until January 1, 1808, the president suggested that the "intervening period" was not too long "to prevent by timely notice expeditions which can not be completed before that day." James D. Richardson, ed., *A Compilation of the Messages and Papers of the Presidents, 1789–1897*, 10 vols. (Washington, D.C.: Government Printing Office, 1896), 1: 408.

16. *Annals of Congress*, House, 9th Cong., 2d Sess., 226, 527, 528, 626; *Statutes at Large*, 9th Cong., 2nd Sess., 22: 426.

17. St. George Tucker, *Blackstone's Commentaries*, 1:App.290, 1803, in Kurland and Lerner, eds., *Founders' Constitution*, 3: 297; *Annals of Congress*, House, 16th Cong., 1st Sess., 1365.

18. *Annals of Congress*, House, 15th Cong., 2d Sess., 1184, 16/1, 959, 960, 1096.

19. "Resolutions of Pennsylvania," in Herman Ames, ed., *State Documents on Federal Relations* (Philadelphia: University of Pennsylvania, 1911), 199; "Resolutions of New Jersey," in Ames, ed., *State Documents on Federal Relations*, 200; "Resolutions of Vermont," in Ames, ed., *State Documents on Federal Relations*, 202.

20. *Annals of Congress*, House, 15th. Cong., 2d Sess., 1183, 1197.

21. *Annals of Congress*, House, 15th Cong., 2d Sess., 1181–82.

22. *Annals of Congress*, Senate, 16th Cong., 1st Sess., 137, 138, 139, 211, 281; *Annals of Congress*, House, 16th Cong., 1st Sess., 1195.

23. *Annals of Congress*, Senate, 16th Cong., 1st Sess., 202.

24. *Annals of Congress*, House, 16th Cong., 1st Sess., 1316, 1335, 1365, 1501; *Annals of Congress*, Senate, 16th Cong., 1st Sess., 318.

25. *Annals of Congress*, House, 16th Cong., 1st Sess., 973, 1164, 1335; *Annals*, Senate, 16th Cong., 1st Sess., 130, 198, 231, 306.

26. *Annals of Congress*, House, 16th Cong., 1st Sess., 1165; *Annals of Congress*, Senate, 16th Cong., 1st Sess., 306.

27. *Annals of Congress*, House, 16th Cong., 1st Sess., 1165, 1166, 1238; *Annals of Congress*, Senate, 16th Cong., 1st Sess., 318.

28. *Annals of Congress*, House, 16th Cong., 1st Sess., 1316–17.

29. *Annals of Congress* House, 16th Cong., 1st Sess., 973, 1238–39, 1335; *Annals of Congress*, Senate, 16th Cong., 1st Sess., 130–31, 318.

30. *Annals of Congress*, House, 16th Cong., 1st Sess., 941, 1165, 1316, 1372; *Annals of Congress*, Senate, 16th Cong., 1st Sess., 261, 306, 318–19.

31. *Annals of Congress*, House, 16th Cong., 1st Sess., 1094, 1128, 1129, 1198–99, 1335, 1560; *Annals of Congress*, Senate, 16th Cong., 1st Sess., 139.

32. *Annals of Congress*, Senate, 16th Cong., 1st Sess., 941.

33. *Annals of Congress*, House, 16th Cong., 1st Sess., 1097, 1317; *Annals of Congress*, Senate, 16th Cong., 1st Sess., 415, 416, 417.

34. *Annals of Congress*, House, 16th Cong., 1st Sess., 1026, 1027, 1078, 1272; *Annals of Congress*, Senate, 16th Cong. 1st Sess., 167. There is some precedence for this viewpoint. To prevent the practice of slavery and the importation of slaves into the Virginia, Thomas Jefferson pushed for a state law declaring "all persons" imported forthwith into Virginia "by Sea or by Land" to be freed. Thomas Jefferson, "Bill to Prevent the Importation of Slaves," June 16 1777, in Kurland and Lerner, eds., *Founders' Constitution*, 3: 278.

35. *Annals of Congress*, Senate, 16th Cong., 1st Sess., 230, 246.

36. *Annals of Congress*, House, 16th Cong., 1st Sess., 973, 1238, 1501.

37. *Annals of Congress*, House, 16th Cong., 1st Sess., 1094, 1098.

38. *Annals of Congress*, House, 16th Cong., 1st Sess., 1199; *Annals of Congress*, Senate, 16th Cong., 1st Sess., 281, 295.

39. *Annals of Congress*, House, 16th Cong., 1st Sess., 1079, 12, 73, 1334; *Annals of Congress*, Senate, 16th Cong., 1st Sess., 198, 305. Anti-restrictionists offered several other approaches to the authoritative nature of the clause. "That this clause had no sort of reference to a power to prevent the removal of slaves from State to State is

further evident," suggested Delaware's McLane, "from the important consideration that, previous to the adoption of the Constitution, each State itself possessed the undoubted authority to prohibit the bringing of slaves from any other States." It was extremely improbable, then, that the North, even with all of its hostility regarding this subject, would call upon the central government to accomplish what they could already do. Anderson of Kentucky argued that the clause gave Congress a legislative power, and thus any action to restrict slavery must be done by a direct act of Congress, and not through any compact with Missouri as proposed by the Talmadge Amendment. Virginia's Pindall agreed with this assertion. *Annals of Congress*, House, 16th Cong., 1st Sess., 1166, 1255, 1271.

40. For Cook's and Lowrie's interpretation of original intent, see, respectively, *Annals of Congress*, Senate, 16th Cong., 1st Sess., 202–03, and *Annals of Congress*, House, 16th Cong., 1st Sess., 1095–96, 1097.

41. John Jay to Elias Boudinot, November 17, 1819, in Kurland and Lerner, eds., *Founders' Constitution*, 3: 297–98.

42. James Madison to Robert Walsh, November 27, 1819, in Kurland and Lerner, eds., *Founders' Constitution*, 3: 298-300. According to Walter Berns, Madison and the framers concocted the traditional interpretation of the clause, that congress possessed power to prohibit the slave trade after 1808, but had no authority to regulate the internal trade.

43. Madison to Walsh, November 27, 1819, in Kurland and Lerner, eds., *Founders' Constitution*, 3: 298–300.

44. Madison to Walsh, November 27, 1819, in Kurland and Lerner, eds., *Founders' Constitution*, 3: 298–300; *Federalist* No. 42, in Kurland and Lerner, eds., *Founders' Constitution*, 3: 281–82; James Madison to Robert Walsh, January 11, 1820, in *The Papers of James Madison*, Retirement Series, Vol. 1, *4 March 1817–31 January 1820*, eds. David B. Mattern, J. C. A. Stagg, Mary Parke Johnson, and Anne Mandeville Colony (Charlottesville: University of Virginia Press, 2009), 1: 584–85.

45. Virginia congressman Alexander Smyth made vague reference to the clause during the debates covering Missouri's constitution: "The right of a State to close its doors against migration is, I conceive, acknowledged by the Constitution to be in the States. [Here Mr. S. read part of section 9 of article 1.]" *Annals*, House, 16th Cong., 2d Sess., 559.

46. Joseph Story, *Commentaries on the Constitution*, 3: 1327–31, in Kurland and Lerner, eds., *Founders' Constitution*, 3: 308; "Slavery & the Slave Trade, from Judge Story's Charge to the Grand Jury of the U.S. Circuit Court, in Portsmouth, N. H.—May Term 1820," 2–3; 22 U.S. (9 Wheat.) 1 (1824), 216.

47. *Dred Scott v.* Sandford, 60 U.S. 393 (1857), 411.

48. William Goodell, *Views of American Constitutional Law, in Its Bearing upon American Slavery* (Utica, NY: Jackson & Chaplin, 1844), 28–30; G. W. F. Mellen, *An Argument on the Unconstitutionality of Slavery, Embracing an Abstract of the Proceedings of the National and State Conventions on This Subject* (Boston: Saxton & Pierce, 1841), 21, 22, 157, 276; William A. Duer, *A Course of Lectures on the Constitutional Jurisprudence of the United States Delivered Annually in Columbia College, New York* (NY:

Harper, 1856), 209; Luther R. Marsh, ed., *Writings and Speeches of Alvan Stewart on Slavery* (New York: A. B. Burdick, 1860), 106; Lysander Spooner, *The Unconstitutionality of Slavery* (Boston: Bela Marsh, 1860), 55–56.

CHAPTER EIGHT

The Treaty-Making Powers

William S. Belko

> **"[The President] shall have Power, by and with the Advice and Consent of the Senate, to make Treaties, provided two thirds of the Senators present concur; . . . ."**
>
> [Article II, Section 2, Clause 2]

ON THE LAST day of April 1803, American and French commissioners signed the Louisiana Purchase Treaty in Paris, France. The president and the U.S. Senate ratified the treaty several months later, in October of that same year. In the interim, between the signing and the ratification, the president of the United States, Thomas Jefferson, proposed a constitutional amendment to ease qualms about acquiring foreign territory, an action nowhere stipulated in the U.S. Constitution, at least not explicitly. The amendment proposed to make the Louisiana Territory "a part of the U.S.," whereby the "white inhabitants" of the region "shall be citizens, and stand, as to their rights & obligations, on the same footing with other citizens of the U.S. in analogous situations." Obviously, the proposed amendment to the Constitution went nowhere. Although the written record remains silent, Jefferson may have been somewhat dissatisfied at the time, but sixteen years later he may have been outright disconcerted. For had the proposed amendment passed, the 1803 Treaty specifically—and the treaty-making power in general—may not have been one of the more divisive, often contended, subjects in the congressional debates over the admission of Missouri.[1]

The sole portion of the 1803 treaty that caused considerable consternation in 1819 and 1820 was Article III—"The inhabitants of the ceded territory shall be incorporated in the Union of the United States and admitted as soon as possible according to the principles of the federal Constitution to the enjoyment of all these rights, advantages and immunities of citizens of the United States, and in the mean time they shall be maintained and protected in the free enjoyment of their liberty, property and the Religion which they profess." This article in particular, President Jefferson wrote his secretary of state, James Madison, in 1804 "has been worded with remarkable caution on the part of our negociators [sic]." Yet nothing could have been farther from Jefferson's assumption. What appeared to be a rather straightforward clause quickly turned into a penetrating forensic, syllogistic debate, whereby congressmen dissected every phrase—even concentrating at times on the supposed meaning of a single word—in order to support or reject slavery restriction in Missouri. Congress also examined, and often questioned, the treaty-making power itself, especially as it concerned the constitutional powers of the House of Representatives.[2]

Opponents of slavery restriction in Missouri used the 1803 treaty, Article 3 specifically, to argue that Missouri required immediate admission to the Union, and without any conditions attached to its entrance. They founded their argument on the premise that treaties became the supreme law of the land, per the Supremacy Clause of the Constitution. "By your Constitution, a treaty is the supreme law of the land, and paramount to the constitution which you propose to force Missouri to adopt," Virginia congressman Alexander Smyth berated supporters of the Tallmadge Amendment. "Treaties are in part the supreme law of the land, and paramount to the constitution of any State; yet you propose to violate the treaty with France by means of a State constitution, which is of inferior obligation to a treaty." Other Southerners agreed. "The treaty of 1803 is the supreme law of the land, and must be obeyed," demanded Georgia congressman Robert Reid. Alluding to Vattel, South Carolina's Charles Pinckney held that treaties were "most holy and sacred among nations"; for the nations of the world, treaties "determine the most important affairs, give rules to their pretensions, and secure their most precious interests." The 1803 treaty with France "has become a part of the supreme law of the land," concluded fellow South Carolinian, U.S. Senator William Smith. "It is made so by the Constitution itself, and is as obligatory as the Constitution can be," and, as such, the 1803 treaty was "absolutely binding to the fullest extent of its stipulations."[3]

According to anti-restrictionists, a treaty bound the United States to meet the stipulations to which the parties agreed. "If I receive a deed on condition, I am bound to perform the condition," lectured Smyth of Virginia. "Every engagement in a treaty is a condition, the breach of which releases the other party from his engagement." Citing Grotius, Smyth noted that the United States had "received a deed of trust of this territory," and if Congress failed to "perform the trust," then it had no title at all. Although the treaty-making power cannot compel Congress to perform any act, reasoned Kentucky congressman Benjamin Hardin, a treaty can still "constitutionally stipulate for an act to be done by Congress," and, in this case, admit Missouri as a state, and, "if not done, the national honor and faith will be violated." Quite simply, the U.S. government was bound by the 1803 treaty to fulfill the obligations contained in the document, and Article III mandated that Congress take action to meet the treaty requirements—namely, admit Missouri as a state without any conditions.[4]

The most obvious stipulations of Article III demanding Missouri's immediate admission as a state, argued opponents of slavery restriction, were the sequential clauses "shall be incorporated in the Union of the United States" and "admitted as soon as possible." Missouri's Territorial Delegate to Congress, John Scott, understood the term *incorporated* as nothing else than the expectation that his territory would form "a constituent part of this Republic," that Missouri would become "joint partners in the character and councils of the country," and participate fully in the "national losses and gains," and this could only be achieved as a state, not as a territory. From his understanding of the phrase "admitted as soon as possible," moreover, this could only mean admission as a state once the territory had met the requisite stipulations for seeking admission, and he reiterated that Missouri had the necessary number of residents to do so. So, then, Article III of the 1803 treaty clearly dictated immediate statehood. These two specific clauses of Article III, argued Delaware's Louis McLane, demonstrated beyond doubt that Missouri's incorporation into the Union "meant more than a Territorial form of government." The United States was a Union of states, not territories; Missouri, therefore, can only be incorporated into the Union as a state. All the friends of Missouri's admission *sans* conditions concurred with Georgia Senator Reid when he summed up that "no other construction to the words of the treaty," that "incorporated in the Union of the United States," means anything else than admitting the territory as a state. That Article III gave Missouri "an unconditional admission into the Union," declared fellow Georgia senator John Elliott, could not be more obvious "by a bare recital of this section." Article III of the 1803 treaty, concluded Virginia congressman James Pindall, therefore imposed "an express obligation on this Government to admit the inhabitants of the ceded country into the Federal Union as soon as possible," and do so without conditions.[5]

Failure to enforce these two obligatory clauses of the treaty violated other sections of Article III as well, according to the opponents of restriction in Missouri. If Congress denied admission, then that body denied to the people of Missouri the expressly stipulated "enjoyment of all these rights, advantages and immunities of citizens of the United States." Scott had already argued that, as a territory, Missouri was not an essential part of the government of the United States, and, therefore, as residents of a territory, Missourians "had not all of the rights, advantages and immunities of citizens of the United States." He noted his lack of a vote in Congress as additional proof. The people of Missouri, Scott contended, had a right to call for admission, without conditions placed on them, but if Congress imposed such restrictions, then it denied Missourians the "solemn treaty stipulation" of allowing them the enjoyment of all the rights, advantages, and immunities enjoyed by other citizens of the Union. The people of a territory are not citizens of the United States, he continued, and thus have no share in government while in a territorial status, a condition which abrogated Article III.[6]

At the heart of such rights, advantages, and immunities beat the privilege of self-government, the very lifeblood of the American Republic. "Sir, the rights, advantages, and immunities, of citizens of the United States," confirmed Delaware's McLane, "and which are the proudest boast, are the rights of self-government—first, in their State constitutions, and secondly, in the Government of the Union, in which they have equal participation." Georgia's Elliott considered "all the rights, advantages, and immunities" of citizens of the United States to be "a phrase of the most extensive latitude," which necessarily included the "momentous and inalienable right of self-government, which appertains to all the States." What are people entitled to when admitted into the Union, queried Mississippi's Christopher

Rankin? They were entitled to "the enjoyment of all the 'rights, advantages and immunities of citizens of the United States'." Yet, restrictionists denied the people of Missouri "one of the most essential and dearest rights," that is, the "right to form their own constitution, and shape their own municipal regulations." If the citizens of the "old States" were entitled "to an exemption from the interference of the Government, saving only as to the powers derived from the Constitution," concluded Virginia's Pindall, and if the residents of Missouri were likewise guaranteed the same immunities via Article III, then "they must be entitled to govern themselves as an American State."[7]

Continuing with their dissection of Article III, in order to promote Missouri's immediate admission as a state without any prescribed conditions, anti-restrictionists cited another clause in Article III, that the citizens of the Louisiana Territory (i.e., Missouri in this instance) "shall be maintained and protected in the free enjoyment of their liberty, property and the Religion which they profess." The key to this clause was the protection of property, and as "a part of this property, for which the United States stand thus solemnly pledged," claimed Elliot of Georgia, "was, unquestionably, slaves." Fellow Georgians, Thomas Cobb, Freeman Walker, and Reid ardently agreed. By the treaty with France, Cobb surmised, "the people of that territory [Louisiana] were secured in the enjoyment of the property which they held in their slaves." The Tallmadge Amendment, therefore, was "an infraction" of this treaty. "Slaves were property at the time of ratification of the treaty, and therefore within its meaning," Reid followed, "and their right to possess this species of property is guarantied [sic] by the treaty." "It has been admitted, or, at any rate, it has not been denied, that slaves constituted a part of the property of the inhabitants of the ceded territory," Walker added, "and of which the United States guarantied [sic] the free enjoyment; thus recognizing the existence of slavery in the territory in question." A concord of Southern voices chimed in to support this crucial chorus of their argument that Article III of the 1803 treaty mandated Missouri's admission without restriction on slavery. Slaves, they adamantly avowed, were a species of property, which was acknowledged by England, France, Spain, and all of the signatories to the 1803 treaty, to be held by the inhabitants of the Louisiana Territory, and, therefore, the treaty of cession explicitly protected such property rights.

Even Maine's delegate, John Holmes, supported beleaguered Missourians in this cause, maintaining that at the cession of the Louisiana Territory, the people thereof held property in slaves, and the 1803 treaty secured them this right when acquired by the United States. For opponents of restriction in Missouri, then, Article III of the 1803 treaty clearly made the Tallmadge Amendment, in the words of Missouri's Scott, "unconstitutional and unwarrantable."[8]

Friends of slavery restriction in Missouri quickly and categorically countered their opponents' numerous arguments by first asserting their constitutional authority to admit new states under Article IV of the Constitution. The treaty-making power, they argued consistently, could never restrict in any way the powers exclusively and explicitly granted by the Constitution to the House of Representatives. All underscored, in the words of Illinois congressman Daniel Pope Cook, "the inability of the treaty-making powers to control Congress in the admission of States into the Union." The very author of the notorious slavery restriction amendment, New York congressman James Tallmadge, Jr., asserted that the "Senate, or the treaty-making power of our Government, have neither the right nor the power to stipulate, by a treaty, the terms upon which a people shall be admitted into the Union." After Tallmadge, one of the most prominent proponents of restriction in Missouri, fellow New York congressman John W. Taylor, fully agreed. The 1803 treaty "made no provision for the erection of new States in the ceded territory." The framers of the treaty, he presumed, "well knew that the President and Senate could not bind Congress to admit new States into the Union." Surely no one could contend that the House was bound by the treaty to admit Missouri, declared New Hampshire congressman Arthur Livermore, since the "treaty-making power does not extend so far." Another New Hampshire congressman, Clifton Clagett, declared the Constitution to be paramount to any treaty, and "any stipulation inconsistent with the Constitution would be, *ipso facto* void." The Constitution created the treaty-making power, Indiana's congressman William Hendricks postulated, "and the moment the treaty-making power passes the boundaries of the Constitution, that moment its powers become annihilated." Hendricks represented the great body of congressmen who objected to any construction of the treaty-making power "unknown to and unauthorized by the Constitution" and that ignored the express discretion of Congress in carrying out its constitutionally assigned powers, in this case, the admission of new states under Article IV.[9]

The 1803 treaty was the first treaty in American history that acquired foreign territory, and this fact concerned supporters of the Tallmadge Amendment and colored their interpretation of the treaty-making power. Massachusetts congressman Timothy Fuller deemed it obvious that the president and the Senate—the treaty-making powers—"cannot make a stipulation with any foreign nation in derogation of the Constitutional powers and duties of this House, by making it imperative on us to admit the new territory according to the literal tenor of the phrase" contained in Article III. The "additional phrase" of "according to the principles of the Constitution," Fuller continued, "put it beyond all doubt that no such compulsory admission was intended" by the framers of the treaty. Any concession to the contention that "the Executive and Senate can make a treaty which shall devolve on Congress a moral obligation to admit new States into this Confederacy," was comparable to declaring that the treaty-making authorities could arguably annex all of the Western Hemisphere, thereby leaving no check in Congress "to ambition or imbecility of the co-ordinate branches of the Government." The treaty-making power entailed, according to Fuller, the "same great checks which constitute the safety of a free government" and thusly cannot "annex foreign territories without limit." Notwithstanding the "remote possibility" of treachery in making treaties, the admission of states into the Union was a power "distinctly intrusted [sic]" to Congress, therefore making it evident that no treaty can be made in derogation of that power. For that matter, the admission of a new state by one Congress, Fuller concluded, could never bind a subsequent Congress to admit any other state.[10]

Friends of restriction in Missouri also contested claims that Article III required Missouri's immediate admission to the Union as a state. Congressman Cook of Illinois, as one example, argued that Article III of the treaty related only to the ceded territory in its territorial status; the article in question never stated explicitly that the inhabitants be admitted as a state, which must be accomplished only according to the principles of the Constitution. The phrase "as soon as possible," moreover, meant "nothing more than as soon as Congress should deem it fit and proper," and it must be acknowledged by all, Cook concluded, "that they did not mean immediately."[11]

Anti-restrictionists attempted a rebuttal to their opponents' new assertions of the authority assigned to Congress by Section 3 of Article IV. Reasserting the claim that a treaty was the supreme law of the land, but also recognizing the constitutional right to admit new states as one of the delegated powers of Congress, Delaware's McLane suggested that the exercise of admitting new states "may be regulated and controlled by the treaty-making power," which was the "extraordinary and supreme power of the same Government." This "extraordinary power" of making treaties, therefore, could stipulate regarding the exercise of any of the executive, legislative, and judicial powers, and these potential stipulations were binding, "because they render the exercise of power necessary." No treaty could be deemed unconstitutional, McLane reasoned, which stipulated for the performance of any duty within the power of the government to perform. A treaty was only unconstitutional when it stipulated "for the exercise of powers, or the surrender of rights, which never have been given to the General Government, but belong to the States and the people." The powers to regulate commerce with foreign nations, and to appropriate funds to raise armies, for example, clearly belonged to Congress, but the treaty-making power "may make stipulations in regard to either, and for the exercise of either, and the Congress and the nation would be bound by them." The interposition of Congress "might, in some instances, be necessary to carry the stipulations into effect," and it would be the duty of Congress "in good faith to yield it." If Congress refused to do so, it would violate the "national faith," but the treaty would still be valid. In referring to the supremacy of treaties and the congressional power to admit new states, Mississippi congressman Rankin summed it up best by asserting that "your 'may' in the Constitution is converted into 'shall' in the treaty."[12]

Opponents of the Tallmadge Amendment could find some solace from Publius that their contention of treaties being the supreme law of the land had obtained the full assent of the framers. "The treaties of the United States to have any force at all, must be considered as part of the law of the land," Hamilton wrote in *Federalist* No. 22. "Their true import as far as respects individuals, must, like all other laws, be ascertained by judicial determinations. To produce uniformity in these determinations, they ought to be submitted in the last resort, to one SUPREME TRIBUNAL." James Wilson, at the Pennsylvania ratification convention, proclaimed beyond doubt that "under this constitution, treaties will become the supreme law of the land."[13]

Yet, while the framers of the Constitution never foresaw this particular disagreement between the treaty-making power (President and Senate) and the power to admit new states (House), both expressly granted in the U.S. Constitution, the Ratification debates revealed some discontent among the founding generation about the exclusion of the House from the treaty-making process and the potential of treaties conflicting with congressional statutes. One of George Mason's objections to the proposed Constitution was that, by declaring all treaties the supreme law of the land, the president and the Senate possessed "an exclusive power of legislation," which "might have been avoided by the proper distinctions with respect to treaties, and requiring the assent of the House of Representatives, where it could be done with safety." In its dissent from Pennsylvania's ratification of the U.S. Constitution, Antifederalists at the state's ratifying convention demanded that the Constitution be so amended as to prevent conflict between a treaty and a law of Congress. A treaty that contradicted the U.S. Constitution (or any of the state constitutions), they argued, shall be invalid. North Carolina Antifederalists agreed. They, too, requested changes in the Constitution, whereby "no treaties shall be directly opposed to the existing laws of the United States in Congress assembled" and no treaty shall be valid "which is contradictory to the Constitution of the United States." Supporters of slavery restriction in Missouri may have found solace in these assertions, as they defended congressional power to admit new states against anti-restrictionists' assaults promoting the supremacy of the 1803 treaty with France.[14]

Following President George Washington's Neutrality Proclamation in 1793 and the consequent *Pacificus-Helvidius* exchange between James Madison and Alexander Hamilton in 1793 and 1794, debate arose in Congress about whether the House of Representatives does, or should have, a role in the treaty-making process. But the concern at hand in the early 1790s centered on the war powers—Article I, Section 8, Clause 11—and not the power to admit new states—Article IV, Section 3, Clause 1—as during the Missouri admission crisis. If Congress, the House included, possessed the sole authority to declare war, then why was it excluded from the power to declare peace (via a treaty with a foreign power)? Although this specific debate never reached a resolution, opponents of restriction contending for the supremacy of treaties and thus using the 1803 treaty to justify Missouri's admission without restriction, could turn to another of Madison's writings, this time under the pseudonym of Helvidius. In Helvidius No. 1, Madison contended that treaties, "when formed according to the constitutional mode," have the "force and operation of *laws*," and thus "are to be a rule for the courts in controversies between man and man, as much as any *other laws*." Treaties are, then, "emphatically declared by the constitution to be 'the supreme law of the land'." Hamilton as Publius fully concurred.[15]

Following the ratification of the Jay Treaty in 1795, the House of Representatives formally took up the question of the treaty-making power. Madison delivered a lengthy speech in the House exploring the "Constitutional rights of Congress, and of the House or Representatives, on the subject of treaties," and correctly noted near the end of his address that "this was the first time the Treaty-making power had come under formal and accurate discussion." Congress revisited the issue, albeit with less depth and intensity, in 1803 with the Louisiana Purchase treaty, but the question of the treaty-making power resurfaced with a vengeance during the Missouri admission crisis, resulting in a more divisive "formal and accurate discussion." Some supporters of the Tallmadge Amendment hinted, as did congressmen in the wake of the Jay Treaty, that the House need not execute the 1803 treaty under its appropriations power. Other restrictionists recoiled at such a thought. Fuller of Massachusetts, for example, deemed a treaty made according to the Constitution to be "morally binding" on Congress and the nation overall. He considered any notion that Congress may decide on the merits of a treaty by either granting or withholding appropriations necessary for the treaty's execution to be a "dangerous and absurd doctrine." If Congress assumed the power to annul a treaty made constitutionally, even to the point that Congress may virtually rescind it under its appropriation powers at any subsequent period, Fuller argued, then no treaty ever made was obligatory on Congress.[16]

While Jefferson sought constitutional sanction for the Louisiana Purchase by way of amending the Constitution, the noted American jurist

St. George Tucker actually broached the potential conflict between the treaty-making power and the grants of power to Congress under Article IV. Under the U.S. Constitution, Tucker wrote in *Blackstone's Commentaries*, "there is no restriction as to the subjects of treaties, unless perhaps the guarantee of a republican form of government, and of protection from invasion, contained in the fourth article, may be construed to impose such a restriction." Although he never listed among these restrictions the power to admit new states into the Union, Tucker did query what the effect would be of a treaty "made by the president and senate," where some of the articles "may contain stipulations on legislative objects, or such as expressly vested in congress by the constitution, until congress shall make a law carrying them into effect." The Missouri debates had renewed another constitutional and political struggle between Article II (the power to make treaties) and Article IV, this time, with the latter Article's express grant of power to admit new states. As with the previous debate over Jay's Treaty in the mid-1790s between the executive and Senate on the one hand and the House on the other, Congress again could not come to agreement.[17]

In countering anti-restrictionist claims that the 1803 treaty required Missouri's admission into the Union without conditions, restrictionists also cited various clauses in Article III of the 1803 treaty in order to justify congressional authority to restrict slavery as a condition for Missouri's admission. Supporters of the Tallmadge Amendment challenged their opponents' interpretation of the clause in Article III protecting the liberty, property, and religion of the inhabitants of the Missouri Territory, precisely the anti-restrictionist argument that property included slaves. Some restrictionists, following the lead of New York's Taylor, asserted outright that *property* did not mean *slavery*, and thus the latter institution received no protection under the treaty, leaving Congress free to regulate it. As Pennsylvania Senator Walter Lowrie declared categorically, "*slaves* and *property* are not convertible terms."[18]

Yet Lowrie introduced another line of approach challenging the claim that Article III put slavery beyond the reach of Congress. Admitting for a moment that slaves were property, the clause in question only protected slaveowners at the date of the treaty; slavery introduced by Americans thereafter received no such protection. Therefore, the Tallmadge Amendment did not touch the inhabitants who were the parties to the treaty. Other senators likewise claimed that the Tallmadge Amendment did not interfere with holding slaves in Missouri, rather, as Ohio Senator William Trimble assumed, the legislation affected only the further introduction of slavery in the territory, and thus the 1803 treaty stipulation guaranteeing slavery as property had not been violated. There was nothing at all in the last clause of Article III, opined the other Ohio Senator, Benjamin Ruggles, "to prevent any regulation Congress might think proper to make, as to the future acquisition of such property." Massachusetts Senator Harrison Gray Otis concurred, claiming that the Tallmadge Amendment "touches not the property in slaves already introduced, but regards the future augmentation of their numbers."[19]

Restrictionist congressmen also challenged the anti-restrictionist interpretation of the clause guaranteeing the enjoyment of the rights, privileges, and immunities of citizens of the United States as securing slavery in Missouri. Ruggles suggested the Louisiana Territory had been transferred with the understanding by the contracting parties that the inhabitants of the territory had no more rights, privileges, and immunities than those possessed by the residents of the Northwest Territory, which was the standard formula at the time the treaty was made. Otis, too, referred to the Northwest Ordinance as the benchmark for territorial status and the future of slavery as the Union expanded. "There is no rule more certain in the interpretation of treaties, than that which prescribes a regard to be had to the condition of the parties, and subject-matter of the negotiation at the epoch of its conclusion," he reasoned. The Northwest Ordinance provided the foundation for all U.S. territory during the negotiation of the 1803 treaty, Otis claimed, and thus Congress had restricted the expansion of slavery into the nation's territories, and that defined the meaning of the Union thereafter. He deemed it inconceivable that the U.S. ministers in 1803 "should lose sight either of an ordinance, or of the practice under it, which contained the fundamental principles that had been recognized and adopted in every former instance of the admission of a 'territorial' State." It followed uncontestably that Congress, by incorporating the people of Missouri into the Union, upon identical principles and with similar restrictions as those at the time of the treaty, which had been "moulded [sic] into the constitution of Ohio" and which were "promulgated and established as fundamental for the future States to be erected in the Northwestern Territory" would execute the treaty "not only in the spirit, but to the very letter." To these contentions, anti-restrictionists responded with the blanket assertion that the 1803 treaty trumped the Northwest Ordinance.[20]

Other proponents of restriction in Congress assumed that slavery could not be considered among the federal rights stipulated in the 1803 treaty, as New Hampshire's Clagett maintained, for the domestic institution found no guarantee under the U.S. Constitution. Another New Hampshire congressman argued the same. William Plumer, Jr., deemed slavery a *state* authorized institution, while the 1803 treaty conferred only *federal* rights, so no conflict existed with placing restrictions on the expansion of slavery into Missouri or other regions of the Louisiana Territory. The power to hold slaves, he outlined, "is fortunately not one of these rights, advantages, or immunities" as stipulated in the treaty. "No man can hold another in perpetual bondage by any authority derived from the Constitution of the United States," Plumer concluded. No man could own slaves in the free states, because the rights, advantages, and immunities of U.S. citizens provided by the Constitution were the same in every part of the Union.[21]

To bolster this argument, restrictionists focused on a clause of Article III of the 1803 treaty that anti-restrictionists apparently ignored, that is, the phrase "according to the principles of the federal Constitution," which immediately preceded the clause "to the enjoyment of all these rights, advantages and immunities of citizens of the United States." The "principles of the Federal Constitution" were "Federal principles" that extended to *all* citizens of the United States, "with the same influence, and in the same degree," New Hampshire senator David Morril deduced. "All the rights they possess, as such, are derived from the Constitution, and these are Federal rights, enjoyed by every citizen, in every State of the Union." Any citizen enjoying a right denied to another citizen acquired that right from another source than the U.S. Constitution, and the right to hold slaves, Morril concluded, was not a right of a citizen of the United States. Thus, the Tallmadge Amendment, according to Plumer, was not inconsistent with the 1803 treaty, because if Congress possessed the right to impose restrictions, then the people of Missouri, under the stipulations of the treaty, would be admitted in accordance with the principles of the "Federal

Constitution." New York's Taylor likewise denied the power to hold slaves as a right, advantage, or immunity arising from U.S. citizenship. "Whatever those rights are, they must be uniform," and slavery was undeniably a state right—confirmed by the anti-restrictionists themselves—and thus "not a right of United States citizenship, and consequently was not guarantied [sic] to the inhabitants of the territory by the treaty."[22]

Opponents of restriction attempted to dispute such interpretations. Senator James Barbour of Virginia countered the claim that rights under the "Federal Constitution" differed from those of the states. A citizen of the United States must be a citizen of a state, and thus "entitled to every right or privilege secured by the Federal or State government." If there existed any right pertaining to U.S. citizens, then it was creating government according to their "own will and pleasure," and the 1803 treaty, Barbour claimed, gave this right to the citizens of the Louisiana Territory. The phrase "according to the principles of the Federal Constitution," in the estimation of Delaware congressman McLane, "obviously apply to the extent of the population, or the obligations incurred in virtue of admission." This simply made it obligatory upon Congress, therefore, to admit Missouri "as soon as they have the power to admit them under the Constitution," and Congress had such power as soon as the population of Missouri stood "sufficiently numerous, according to the established ratio of representation, to entitle the State to one Representative."[23]

Supporters of the Tallmadge Amendment then turned their attention to the "incorporation" clause of Article III of the 1803 treaty, counterarguing that the phrase did not mandate statehood. In their estimation, that stipulation of the treaty had already been, in the words of New York's John W. Taylor, "faithfully fulfilled" in 1804, when Congress enacted legislation guaranteeing to the inhabitants of the Louisiana Territory protection under the Constitution, thereby meeting the terms of incorporation into the Union. Taylor claimed that this clause extended to all the inhabitants immediately with no contingency, for without this action, the inhabitants of the Louisiana Territory stood in the condition of aliens, as if it were a conquered territory. So, when Congress erected the Louisiana Territory into two territories in 1804, and provided them a territorial government, they were then officially incorporated into the Union, and "became a part of the American family."[24]

Restriction opponents capitalized on this approach, contending that precedent for admitting states without restriction had been established by congressional action following the ratification of the 1803 treaty. Treaties were the supreme law of the land, Mississippi congressman Rankin repeated, and the proper authorities, the president and the Senate, confirmed the treaty, and the House of Representatives "repeatedly sanctioned its provisions." Since 1803, he concluded, every successive Congress had recognized in various legislative capacities the validity of the treaty with France. Because of the admission of the state of Louisiana in 1812, Missouri's Scott declared, Congress was now obligated to admit other states from the Louisiana Territory. Some restrictionists seemed to validate this argument. Massachusetts congressman Fuller recognized that, despite any sentiments expressed in 1803 against admitting into the Union a foreign province beyond the 1783 original limits of the United States, the admission of Louisiana in 1812 was a "compact mutually binding," and thus Louisiana could not be disenfranchised by subsequent action of Congress. Still, Fuller asserted, this did not set precedent. The Louisiana Purchase Treaty, "being made by competent authority, derived no additional obligation from the acts of Congress at that time, or at any subsequent period." Congress was always at liberty, he asserted, "to interpret for ourselves," and if it found that "it does not require the making of States in the ceded province," then it could refuse to admit anymore.[25]

Tallmadge Amendment proponents also directed attention to the phrase "in the mean time" in Article III. A few supporters of slavery restriction used this phrase to counter anti-restrictionist claims that the 1803 treaty mandated immediate admission of Missouri as a state. "In the mean time" meant the period of time from the ratification of the treaty to the moment when Congress extended laws over the Territory, to ensure that the residents still possessed rights, advantages, and immunities held by U.S. citizens elsewhere in the Union. President Jefferson arguably had supported this claim in 1804. Under Article III, he wrote Madison:

> the inhabitants shall be admitted as soon as possible, according to the principles of our Constn. [sic], to the enjoyment of all the rights of citizens, and, *in the mean time, en* attendant, shall be maintained in their liberty, property & religion. That is that they shall continue under the

> protection of the treaty, until the principles of our constitution can be extended to them, when the protection of the treaty is to cease, and that our own principles to take it's [sic] place.

Of course, Jefferson also confirmed that Congress had already commenced that "by extending about 20 particular laws by their titles, to Louisiana."[26]

The question of citizenship, as it pertained to the inhabitants of the Louisiana Territory, the Missouri Territory included, came under scrutiny as well. While anti-restrictionists indirectly maintained that the incorporation clause automatically conferred citizenship through admission as a state, restrictionists argued that citizenship could only be accorded constitutionally by way of a naturalization law. Many agreed with Pennsylvania's John Sergeant when he declared that a treaty "cannot confer the privilege of citizenship." Until they became citizens of the United States, the inhabitants were protected in their enjoyment of liberty, property, and religion by Article III of the 1803 treaty. Until they are incorporated into the Union, therefore, they are aliens, "but are not to be prejudiced by their alienage." Illinois's Cook presumed that the clause protecting liberty, property, and religion of the territory's inhabitants was actually to give them the rights of citizenship "without going through the tedious and regular process of naturalization."[27]

Debate over the definition of citizenship necessarily bought the term *inhabitants* into question, as both sides of the Missouri admission crisis sought to decipher the meaning of that single word. In their attempt to confine the scope of the 1803 treaty, supporters of the Tallmadge Amendment, such as Connecticut congressman Henry Edwards, claimed that the treaty merely "respects only the inhabitants of the ceded territory, at the time the treaty was made," which embraced only a minute portion of the Louisiana Territory. The present application for statehood, however, was not submitted by these original "inhabitants," but rather by "a very different body of inhabitants." As such, the "present applicants" could not make a claim for admission according to the 1803 treaty. Edwards was not alone in this contention. Otis of Massachusetts concurred, maintaining that "those who had migrated thither [into Missouri]" from other parts of the United States "could claim no rights in Missouri under the treaty," as they were not in the same situation as the inhabitants represented by Napoleon. Fellow New Englander, Rhode Island Senator James Burrill, likewise argued that the "provision extends only to those who were inhabitants," as that was, in his estimation, "common provision when territory is ceded either after a conquest, or otherwise." Congress could not, therefore, refer to individuals "already citizens of the United States who buy land and remove thither," as such persons received "no aid from the treaty."[28]

In the end, the congressional debate over the meaning and interpretation of Article III of the 1803 Louisiana Purchase Treaty ironically exposed an ideological flip by both the contending parties, restrictionist and anti-restrictionist, as to how to interpret the Constitution, that is, whether through a broad or strict construction. On just about all other arguments involving constitutional authority and powers during the Missouri debates, opponents of restriction usually employed a strict interpretation of the Constitution, while the proponents of restriction often assumed a more liberal interpretation. But not so when it came to debating Article III. When interpreting the various phrases, terms, and words of this article, foes of slavery restriction tended to take a liberal approach; friends of slavery restriction, on the other hand, applied a far more literal translation to the article's contents. The "words of the treaty itself are sufficiently comprehensive for all the purposes of the argument," proclaimed Georgia Senator Walker. "They are broad and latitudinary [sic] in their extent." The words and phrases of Article III, agreed Virginia Senator Barbour, were "entitled to the most liberal interpretation of the treaty." The strange, absolutely literal, definition of "inhabitants" made by the pro-restrictionist Connecticut congressman Edwards certainly proved to be the superlative strict construction of the 1803 treaty, but he was most definitely not alone among his restrictionist colleagues in applying some very unique definitions to Article III.

The congressional debates over the admission of Missouri epitomized arguably the mantra that the end justifies the means, for congressmen appeared to employ any strategy, take any tactic, make any argument that justified or refuted congressional power to place restrictions on the admission of new states. That the restriction in this instance involved the subject of slavery not only added heightened emotion to the debates, but likewise seemed to invite every means necessary to decide once and for all the future course of the nation's most controversial domestic institution. In the end, Congress failed in this endeavor, and Missouri entered the Union without restriction.[29]

NOTES

1. The amendment reserved a substantial portion of the Louisiana Territory to American Indians, "in exchange for equivalent portions of land occupied by them," where no state could be established or grants of land made without further amendment to the Constitution; the amendment also provided for the acquisition of Florida "whenever it may be rightfully obtained," that part of Florida being the region east of the Mississippi River (excluding New Orleans) to the Perdido River, and south of the Mississippi Territory, which American and French officials believed was included in the Louisiana Territory. The proposed amendment is in *The Works of Thomas Jefferson,* collected and edited by Paul L. Ford, 12 vols. (New York: G. P. Putnam's Sons, 1904–1905), 10: 3.

2. *Statutes at Large,* in *A Century of Lawmaking for a New Nation: U.S. Congressional Documents and Debates, 1774–1875,* 8: 200, memory.loc.gov/ammem/amlaw/lwstdo.html.; Jefferson to Madison, 14 July 1804, in Paul L. Ford, ed., *The Works of Thomas Jefferson,* 12 vols. (New York: G. P. Putnam's Sons, 1904–1905), 10: 91–92.

3. *Annals of Congress,* U.S. House of Representatives, 16th Congress, 1st Session, 1006, 1007, 1031, 1321; *Annals of Congress,* U.S. Senate, 16th Congress, 1st Session, 87–88, 1038.

4. *Annals of Congress,* House, 16th Cong., 1st Sess., 1007, 1073.

5. *Annals of Congress,* House, 15th Cong., 2d Sess., 1200; *Annals of Congress,* House, 16th Cong., 1st Sess., 1145, 1275; *Annals of Congress,* Senate, 16th Cong., 1st Sess., 131–32, 1031.

6. *Annals of Congress,* House, 15th Cong., 2d Sess., 1200.

7. *Annals of Congress,* House, 16th Cong., 1st Sess., 1032, 1146, 1276, 1341; *Annals of Congress,* Senate, 16th Cong., 1st Sess., 1038, 131–32, 171.

8. *Annals of Congress,* House, 15th Cong., 2d Sess., 1199, 1436; *Annals of Congress,* House, 16th Cong., 1st Sess., 985, 1461–62; *Annals of Congress,* Senate, 16th Cong., 1st Sess., 131–32.

9. *Annals of Congress,* House, 15th Cong., 2d Sess., 1127, 1184, 1193, 1208–09, 1772; *Annals of Congress,* House, 16th Cong., 1st Sess., 1040, 1346.

10. *Annals of Congress,* House, 16th Cong., 1st Sess., 1478, 1479.

11. *Annals of Congress,* House, 16th Cong., 1st Sess., 1125–27.

12. *Annals of Congress,* House, 16th Cong., 1st Sess., 1143–44, 1340.

13. *Federalist* No. 22, guides.loc.gov/federalist-papers/full-text-21-30.; "James Wilson's Summation and Final Rebuttal," in Bernard Bailyn, ed., *The Debate on the Constitution: Federalist and Antifederalist Speeches, Articles, and Letters During the Struggle over Ratification,* 2 vols. (New York: Literary Classics of the United States, Inc., 1993), 1: 844.

14. George Mason, "Objections to the Constitution," in Bailyn, ed., *Debate*, 1: 348; "Dissent of the Minority of the Pennsylvania Convention," in Bailyn, ed., *Debate*, 1: 534; "Resolutions of North Carolina," in Bailyn, ed., *Debate*, 2: 571–72. Federalists, like James Wilson and Publius, argued during the ratification debates that the necessity of secrecy necessitated the exclusion of the House from the treaty-making process. See "Wilson's Rebuttal," Bailyn, ed., *Debate*, 1: 844; *Federalist* No. 75.

15. "Helvidius No. 1," 24 August 1793, in Morton J. Frisch, ed., *The Pacificus-Helvidius Debates of 1793–1794* (Indianapolis: Liberty Fund, Inc., 2007), 61; Speech of James Madison, in *The Writings of James Madison*, ed. Gaillard Hunt, 9 vols. (New York: G. P. Putnam's Sons, 1900–1910), 6: 263–79.

16. *Annals of Congress*, House, 16th Cong., 1st Sess., 1478.

17. St. George Tucker, *Blackstone's Commentaries: With Notes of Reference to the Constitution and Laws of the Federal Government of the United States and of the Commonwealth of Virginia*, 5 vols., (Philadelphia, 1803; Reprint, South Hackensack, NJ: Rothman Reprints, 1969), 4: 86. Tucker also raised the same concerns that Madison had in Helvidius a decade earlier, suggesting that the treaty-making power "appears to be somewhat extraordinary," as the House of Representatives, "who are by the constitution required to concur, in a declaration of war, . . . should be wholly precluded from voting at all, upon a question of peace," and he believed that the "safety of the nation" required the "final ratification of any compact, which is to form a part of the supreme law of the land, should . . . depend upon the concurrent approbation of every branch of the congress, ..."

18. *Annals of Congress*, House, 16th Cong., 1st Sess., 963; *Annals of Congress*, Senate, 16th Cong., 1st Sess., 206.

19. *Annals of Congress*, Senate, 16th Cong., 1st Sess., 205–06, 216, 241, 284–85, 290.

20. *Annals of Congress*, Senate, 16th Cong., 1st Sess., 244, 285; *Annals of Congress*, House, 16th Cong., 1st Sess., 1030–31. Tallmadge argued that the residents of the Louisiana Territory already possessed guaranteed rights, privileges, and immunities as all other citizens of the United States. If an individual from Missouri chose to remove to Virginia, then he could take his slaves with him; but, if he removed to Indiana, or to any other states carved out of the Northwest Territory, he could not take slaves with him. If the Tallmadge Amendment prevailed, the inhabitants of Louisiana or the citizens of the United States could neither take slaves into the state of Missouri. Therefore, all enjoyed equal privileges. *Annals of Congress*, House, 15th Cong., 2d Sess., 1209.

21. *Annals of Congress*, House, 16th Cong., 1st Sess., 1040, 1422–23, 1424.

22. *Annals of Congress*, House, 16th Cong., 1st Sess., 962, 1422; *Annals of Congress*, Senate, 16th Cong., 1st Sess., 145–46.

23. *Annals of Congress*, House, 16th Cong., 1st Sess., 1146; *Annals of Congress*, Senate, 16th Cong., 1st Sess., 327–28.

24. *Annals of Congress*, House, 15th Cong., 2d Sess., 1173; *Annals of Congress*, House, 16th Cong., 1st Sess., 1444–45.

25. *Annals of Congress*, House, 15th Cong., 2d Sess., 1199, 1200; *Annals of Congress*, House, 16th Cong., 1st Sess., 1340, 1341, 1477, 1478.

26. *Annals of Congress*, Senate, 16th Cong., 1st Sess., 1038, 215–16; Jefferson to Madison, in Ford, ed., *Works*, 10: 91–92.

27. *Annals of Congress*, House, 16th Cong., 1st Sess., 1103–04, 1202, 1203, 1444–45.

28. *Annals of Congress*, House, 16th Cong., 1st Sess., 1445; *Annals of Congress*, Senate, 16th Cong., 1st Sess., 215–16, 240–42, 244–46.

29. *Annals of Congress*, Senate, 16th Cong., 1st Sess., 172–73, 327–28.

Index

Figure references indicate illustrations in the center section